BEYOND THE SYNAGOGUE

Beyond the Synagogue

Jewish Nostalgia as Religious Practice

Rachel B. Gross

NEW YORK UNIVERSITY PRESS

New York

NEW YORK UNIVERSITY PRESS
New York
www.nyupress.org

References to Internet websites (URLs) were accurate at the time of writing. Neither the author nor New York University Press is responsible for URLs that may have expired or changed since the manuscript was prepared.

Library of Congress Cataloging-in-Publication Data
Names: Gross, Rachel B., author.
Title: Beyond the synagogue : Jewish nostalgia as religious practice / Rachel B. Gross.
Description: New York : New York University Press, [2021] | Series: North American religions | Includes bibliographical references and index.
Identifiers: LCCN 2020015030 (print) | LCCN 2020015031 (ebook) |
ISBN 9781479803385 (cloth) | ISBN 9781479820511 (paperback) |
ISBN 9781479803361 (ebook) | ISBN 9781479803408 (ebook)
Subjects: LCSH: Jews—United States—Identity. | Jews—Cultural assimilation—United States. | Homesickness—Europe, Eastern. | Nostalgia. | Judaism—United States.
Classification: LCC E184.36.E84 G76 2021 (print) | LCC E184.36.E84 (ebook) |
DDC 305.800973—dc23
LC record available at https://lccn.loc.gov/2020015030
LC ebook record available at https://lccn.loc.gov/2020015031

New York University Press books are printed on acid-free paper, and their binding materials are chosen for strength and durability. We strive to use environmentally responsible suppliers and materials to the greatest extent possible in publishing our books.

Manufactured in the United States of America

10 9 8 7 6 5 4 3

Also available as an ebook

In memory of my grandparents, who had mixed feelings about nostalgia.

Ethel Scher Gross
Lawrence Samuel Gross
Harold Louis Wesley
Lois Birner Wesley

Build me a clock I can feel
Every minute is history.
[...]
I want an archaeology of the living.
Give me a calendar that can record
without reducing.
—Jennifer Margulies, "Timepiece"

CONTENTS

FIGURES

Introduction

Feeling Jewish

The visitors to the Museum at Eldridge Street sat in the pews of the restored 1887 Eldridge Street Synagogue. Looking upward, they admired the elaborate Moorish-style interior. A docent described Eastern European Jewish immigrants' lives and aspirations at the turn of the century, when they worshipped in the grand synagogue. The Eldridge Street Synagogue was the first synagogue building the immigrants constructed in the crowded Lower East Side neighborhood. But, over the years, the congregation dwindled and the building decayed. The cavernous sanctuary was shut up for four decades. Finally, after two decades of effort, preservationists restored it to its former glory. When the docent finished her story, she started to lead the group out of the sanctuary.

On her way out, the docent paused at the back of the room. She instructed her group to assemble in an open space where the Museum had removed pews. "Step into the indentations in the floorboards," she told them. Soon, people had arranged themselves into straight lines. Pointing to the pattern of indentations, she asked, "Why do you think these are here?" Slowly, the group realized that they stood in footprints of former male congregants. The indentations had been made by men shuckling, rocking back and forth in front of their pew as they prayed in a traditional Jewish fashion. Over the years, they had left their mark in the soft pine floorboards. The docent demonstrated the movement, and others copied her. A few tourists were familiar with the rocking motion from their own synagogue services. Most shuffled more awkwardly, if enthusiastically.[1]

Standing in the footprints of former congregants provides an immediate, sensory connection to the past, one that engages visitors' entire bodies. The experience is a highlight for many tourists. As one wrote on Yelp, "You literally feel the history at your feet."[2] Roberta Berken,

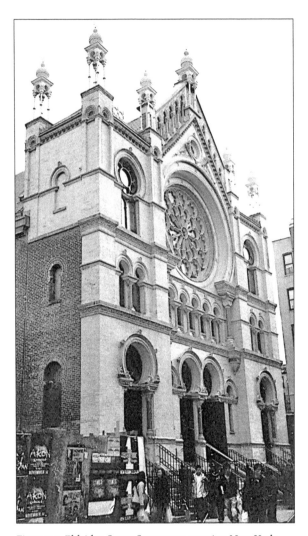

Figure 1.1. Eldridge Street Synagogue exterior, New York.
Photo by Viktor Korchenov, 2006. Licensed under CC
BY-SA 3.0.

who has served as a docent at the Museum at Eldridge Street for over a decade, relates as she shows people the floorboards:

> Perhaps the boots which made these grooves came from Minsk or from the shoe store on Essex Street. A prosperous man may have had new shoes. On the way to shul [synagogue] he may have stopped to have his shoes shined by Max the shoe shine boy, there with his shine box. A working man would have walked with his oft-mended shoes on his way to shul. Both walked through the snow in winter and the hot pavements in summer. The words and rhythm of Yiddish filled the [streets]. The Yiddish signs announced "Fresh fish!" "Fresh baked challah!" or "Pumpernickel and 3 pounds of potatoes for a penny."[3]

Berken fills in her story with imaginative details about the lives of early congregants. She uses the floorboards to help visitors picture a lost world of the early twentieth-century immigrant neighborhood and develop an emotional relationship to it.

Tourists did not just happen to arrive at this synagogue and place their feet in the grooves of long-ago congregants. The Lower East Side has long been seen as an authentic site of emotional connection to American Jewish pasts. American Jewish immigrants began to move their families out of the crowded neighborhood for more spacious parts of the city and suburbs in the early to mid-twentieth century. Still, they kept thinking about the neighborhood, and some kept coming back. In the early twentieth century, those Jews who left the Lower East Side were replaced by new arrivals, until Congress severely limited immigration in 1924. Beginning in the 1970s and 1980s, as a white ethnic revival developed and many Americans turned their attention to their ancestries, American Jews thought about their former urban ethnic neighborhoods with nostalgic longing.

As part of this movement to feel a connection to the places where their ancestors had lived, worked, and prayed, the Eldridge Street Project began to raise money to restore and preserve the Eldridge Street Synagogue in 1986, and the building formally opened to the public as the Museum at Eldridge Street in 2007. Preservationists made careful and strategic choices about the building's restoration, such as leaving intact the worn pine floorboards in order to foster a sense of physical connection with earlier generations. This book argues that the tourist activity of visiting the Museum at Eldridge Street—and the nostalgia it both inspires and is inspired by—should be understood as an American Jewish religious practice. Indeed, this book makes the case that American Jews participate in a broad array of ostensibly nonreligious activities—including visiting Jewish historic sites, conducting genealogical research, purchasing books and toys that teach Jewish nostalgia to children, and seeking out traditional Jewish foods—that are properly understood as religious. Understanding these practices as religious ones illuminates the ways many American Jews are finding and making meaning within American Judaism today.

The American Jewish Mitzvah

Although Jewish history in the Americas dates back to the earliest years of European contact with North America, the majority of American Jews are descendants of Central and Eastern Europeans who immigrated to the United States between the 1880s and 1924, often settling in urban ethnic enclaves like the Lower East Side. American Jews' attention to these communal origins has increased steadily since the 1970s. Stories about Eastern European Jewish immigrants have become increasingly standardized by organizations such as Jewish genealogy groups, museums, publishers, and restaurants—and an expected emotional response to such stories has become standardized, too. Engaging with the standardized nostalgia for Eastern European Jewish immigration history should, I argue, be understood as an American Jewish religious practice.

Jews in many times and places have used physical materials and spaces to create communities with present-day co-religionists. This is certainly the case in the United States, dating back to the seventeenth-century origins of Jewish communities in the Americas in networks of Sephardi merchants.[4] But items of Eastern European and immigrant Jewish nostalgia, such as the Eldridge Street Synagogue's floorboards, do more than connect American Jews to their contemporary co-religionists. They are religious materials, providing powerful sacred meaning that actively places individuals in relation to past, present, and future communities. American Jews' interactions with items and spaces invoke imagined communities that include both the living and the dead, providing meaning in the present by narrating the past. Through particularly American emphases on material culture and institutional organization, nostalgia—a wishful affection or sentimental longing for an irrevocable past—functions as religion for American Jews, complicating notions of a divide between Judaism, the religion, and Jewishness, the culture.

This book aims to shift where scholars and Jews identify American Jewish religion. Describing American Jewish nostalgia as an American Jewish religious practice matters, both because the term "religion" helps us to understand the practices and ideas that are meaningful to American Jews and because definitions of American Jewish religion have real-life implications. Religion is commonly understood by non-specialists to be a private set of beliefs and practices related to worship of a deity. In contrast, although belief in God is one aspect of Judaism, the existence of God may not be of primary importance to the religious identity and practice of many Jews.[5] Religion serves to provide existential meaning, answering questions about life's purpose. Jewish religion includes a broad variety of practices, both public and private, that connect Jews to present-day Jewish communities, inspire remembrance of ancestors, or involve traditional Jewish texts, rituals, or practices. Both explicitly and (more often) implicitly, such activities shape Jews' imagination of past, present, and future Jewish communities and provide existential meaning for Jews.[6]

Since the mid-twentieth century, American Jewish communal leaders have worried loudly that American Jews' religiosity is declining. These communal leaders define Jewish religiosity narrowly, in terms of practices that can be measured in sociological studies, such as attending synagogue, keeping kosher, or sending children to Jewish religious schools. In the decades since then, these fears have been seemingly confirmed in widely accepted social scientific studies that appear to demonstrate an American Jewish "continuity crisis" or a "marriage crisis," the latter emphasizing communal fears about marriages between Jews and non-Jews.[7] Dismay over intermarriage and its effects on Jewish religious continuity has been articulated in sociological language from the pulpit, by Jewish organizations, and in large-scale philanthropy. Proponents of the continuity crisis rely on divisions between activities seen as "good for the Jews"—largely those identified as religious Jewish practices, which these leaders want to encourage—and those activities seen as "bad for the Jews"—generally, cultural Jewish practices seen as encouraging secularism, assimilation, and intermarriage, which they want to discourage.[8] These studies have guided the determination of which American Jews count, literally and metaphorically, and they have influenced the funding and aims of local and national Jewish communal organizations.

This book argues that the premise of American Jewish religious decline and the studies supporting a continuity crisis incorrectly identify the ways that Jews think about and practice Judaism in the United States. When Jewish communal leaders and sociologists distinguish between Jewish culture and Jewish religion, many of the ways that American Jews create individual and communal meaning in their lives are flattened or even erased. Rather than turning to—or turning only to—the institutions that have previously guided American Jewish communal life, such as synagogues, religious schools, Jewish community centers, and Jewish Federations, many American Jews are increasingly communicating Jewish values and ideas to their children by engaging with the products of museums, gift shops, restaurants, publishing companies, toy manufacturers, philanthropies, and other ostensibly secular institutions. These products are often described as Jewish cultural materials, but they are better understood as Jewish religious ones.

Religion is best understood as meaningful relationships and the practices, narratives, and emotions that create and support these relationships. Religious studies scholar Robert Orsi defines religion as networks of relationships among the living, between the living and the dead, or between humans and the divine, each of which may be highlighted to varying degrees in different contexts.[9] While Orsi focuses on Catholics' relationship to sacred figures, American Jews tend to emphasize other forms of religious relationships, such as between the living and their ancestors. "Whatever else religion might be, it is a way of describing structures by which we are bound or connected to one another," explains religious studies scholar Kathryn Lofton.[10] Understanding religion as relationships and structures makes families, communities, and memory central to religious activity.

Using this framework, religion may be found both within and beyond traditional religious institutions and rituals. A conception of religion as constituted by individuals' relationships with families, communities, ancestors, and the divine allows us to see the significance of purportedly secular activities and organizations. It helps us consider how individuals who do not regard themselves "religious" make meaning in their lives, as well as how those who do see themselves as religious find meaning outside of traditional practices. The meaning-making work of religion helps people understand the world around them by construing or making sense of life events, relationships, and themselves. Jewish communal leaders and philanthropists bemoan the supposed decrease in American Jewish religious practice, but if we reorient where we look for American Jewish religion and reconsider how we define it, then we start to find a lot more of it.

In shifting where we look for American Jewish religion, I employ the lived religion approach of religious studies. The study of lived religion focuses our attention on the ways in which people enact their religious identities on a daily basis, through ordinary activities such as eating, cooking, shopping, reading, or entertaining.[11] Most people do not recognize the practices of lived religion as religious actions similar to celebrating a holiday or reciting prayers; they are rather seen as the mundane practices that provide the structure of our lives or the leisure activities that we engage in throughout the week. Commerce, in particular, is often dismissed as a profane activity. But what we spend our money on often illuminates our values more than our words do.[12] Certain commercial institutions and materials can inspire emotions, like nostalgia, that are commonly interpreted within established patterns. Using a lived religion approach, I contend that buying and selling certain items connects people to religious networks through affective norms. Buying a pastrami sandwich from a deli is an ordinary activity, but many American Jews understand the sandwich as a connection to other Jews past and present. It may remind them of other delis where they have eaten, perhaps with their families. They may think sentimentally of how Jews in the past have eaten, imagining that the sandwich links them to their ancestors. The nostalgia inspired by a pastrami sandwich, I argue, is part of American Jewish religion.

This book examines institutions and products that encourage the feeling of nostalgia for Eastern European immigrant pasts as an American Jewish religious activity, one that especially emphasizes the religious practices of remembering ancestors and creating community. For American Jews, nostalgia for Eastern European Jewish pasts functions as a mitzvah (literally, commandment). Mitzvot (plural of mitzvah) are the building blocks of Jewish religion. According to rabbinic tradition, there are not only ten commandments, but 613 divinely commanded mitzvot articulated throughout the Torah, forming the basis of halakha, Jewish law.[13] In American Jews' colloquial use, the term is even broader. Jews have long used the language of mitzvot to describe a variety of practices they consider sacred.[14] In everyday speech, a mitzvah is both a divinely mandated ordinance and, more loosely, a good deed. Expanding upon biblical commands to honor one's parents and to remember certain biblical stories, Jews have come to understand honoring their ancestors and remembering Jewish histories as mitzvot.[15] American Jewish nostalgia for Eastern Europe fulfills and expands upon both of these mitzvot. Like other mitzvot, Jewish nostalgia has become both praiseworthy and obligatory for American Jews.

Looking for Judaism in All the Wrong Places

Viewing nostalgic activities such as touring the Museum at Eldridge Street or buying a pastrami sandwich at a deli as religious practices helps us to refute the claims of sociologist Steven M. Cohen and religious studies scholar Arnold M. Eisen in *The Jew Within: Self, Family, and Community*, a book widely acclaimed by academics, Jewish communal professionals, and lay Jews. *The Jew Within* identifies a "profound individualism," an overwhelming focus on the "sovereign self," as the guiding force of many American Jews' lives.[16] Cohen and Eisen, leading proponents of the idea of the American Jewish continuity crisis, see in this increasing individualism a fearful problem that could "contribute to the dissolution of communal institutions and intergenerational commitment" and weaken Judaism itself. In large part, this manufactured crisis rests on the premise that American Jews, especially interfaith families, lack the religiosity of their parents and grandparents.[17] In the catastrophic imaginings of Cohen, Eisen, and their followers, the assimilation of individuals into a generic American culture could cause the disappearance of American Jews altogether. These fears about assimilation resist the idea that Judaism, like all human endeavors, has and always will change over time. They rely on the idea of a static Judaism and a static American culture, seeing the two as mutually exclusive rather than responsive to one another. By focusing on what they see as the waning religious practices of American Jews in institutions like synagogues, these scholars are looking for Judaism, especially public forms of American Judaism, in all the wrong places.

Bemoaning the decline of American Judaism as they recognize it, Cohen and Eisen argue that, for American Jews, "the importance of the public sphere . . . has severely diminished. The institutional arena is no longer the primary site where American Jews find and define the selves they are and the selves they want to be." Cohen and Eisen identify synagogues, Jewish community centers, and Jewish Federations as the primary sites of public and institutional Judaism and as spaces in which American Jews could be "most themselves."[18] Looking for the content of Jewish public life, they fixate on American Jews' public engagement with memorialization of the Holocaust and public support for Israel. They worry that American Jews' interpretation of "universal lessons" in the history of the Holocaust signifies reduced concern for Jewish particularity and that American Jews' criticism of Israeli governments and the Israeli Rabbinate (state-sanctioned Orthodox religious authority) implies lessened political engagement as Jews.

But where Cohen and Eisen fret about American Jews' decreasing attention to the Holocaust and Israel, more recent studies make it clear that American Jews remain preoccupied with both issues, though how they do so may have changed.[19] At the same time, American Jews do continue to define themselves through institutions, but not exclusively through the institutions or public conversations that Cohen and Eisen have in mind. American Jews have in no way "retreated from public Judaism," but they enact their Judaism in institutions and public settings that Cohen and Eisen fail to consider. Cohen and Eisen are right that personal identity and family are important to American Jews, as they are to other Americans. But many American Jews today understand themselves and their families through emotional and narrative frameworks provided by ostensibly non-religious institutions that—as this book argues—perform religious functions.

Definitions of religion are not only topics for academic theory. They matter in real life. Beyond internal Jewish concerns about "continuity," defining religion in the United States has been essential to issues of religious freedom. Discussions of religious freedom have long been used to strengthen white Protestants' claims to racial and religious supremacy, and historical and recent court cases have addressed the intersection between everyday activities and religion. Racial and religious minorities, including Jews, have deliberately defined certain practices and beliefs as religious in order to improve their status and situation in the United States.[20]

At the same time, scholars of lived religion help us see religion in ordinary activities generally considered "secular." These scholars identify religion and religious practices in baseball, Coca-Cola, Tupperware, celebrity worship, weight-loss culture, and the American office, to name just a few subjects. Broadening the category of religion in this way helps us to take seriously the structures, commitments, and activities that shape everyday life. Anything can become a religious object, depending on how it is used and understood. Expanding the conventional definitions of religion to include everyday practices and materials identifies the social value placed upon them and the communities developed around them. Eating a pastrami sandwich or fangirling Kim Kardashian can be a religious activity, not just because it is personally meaningful, but because of a shared cultural framework ascribing particular kinds of meaning to those activities.[21]

Just as religious studies scholars have long identified practices as "religious" that practitioners themselves might not label in this way, the people I study would not necessarily call their activities nostalgic. Indeed, I do not claim that all American Jews are nostalgic or that everyone who makes, buys, and sells the materials examined here is wholly nostalgic. Rather, this book makes the case that nostalgia has become a pervasive, normative mode of American Jewish religious thought and practice, particularly through commercial practices that have become increasingly common since the 1970s.

In this book, I use the term nostalgia as a way to engage and complicate conversations about Jewish memory, history, and heritage, popular accounts of the past that give it meaning in the present. Acclaimed Jewish historian Yosef Hayim Yerushalmi identifies Jewish memory and Jewish history as "radically different relations to the past."[22] Memory is the dynamic product of community, he says, while history is the product of scholars. Yerushalmi worries that a detached Jewish history has overtaken Jewish memory. Later theorists recognize a more complex relationship between history and memory, drawing attention to the ways that Jews and other peoples may use each in the service of the other.[23] For individuals and organizations, I argue, nostalgia bridges historical scholarship and social memory. It is both an individual feeling and a shared practice. Individual Jews' feelings about the past shape and are shaped by their families, communal institutions, academic scholarship, American capitalism, and other forces.

To examine nostalgia, we need to take seriously the feminist saying, "the personal is political." Scholars of affect theory emphasize that emotions are political, too. Individuals' emotions and their embodied experiences are closely connected to public life, communities, and civic bodies. Identifying American Jewish nostalgia as a "public feeling" and as a religious activity highlights the connections between how individuals make and find meaning in their own lives and how communal institutions guide the emotions that we share. Like others who study public feelings, I am not overly concerned with the distinctions between "emotion," "feeling," and "affect."[24] These terms are all usefully imprecise, retaining ambiguity about the origins of emotions as individual expressions or as inspired by public sentiment or corporate interest.

The institutions of nostalgia that promote and enable these feelings and practices, such as the Museum at Eldridge Street, are far from the first seemingly non-religious institutions to guide American Jews' shared emotions toward historical events. In the second half of the twentieth century, much of American Jewish communal identity rested on commemoration of the Holocaust and support for the State of Israel. Holocaust museums and memorials increased throughout the country, and organizations that raised money for Israeli groups served as major social and political outlets for American Jews. Though the institutions of Holocaust commemoration and American Zionism were ostensibly nonsectarian, they created and upheld guiding sacred narratives for American Jews. They were so closely tied up with American Jewish identity that visiting and supporting Holocaust commemorations and Israel could be considered a religious activity on a par with attending a Passover seder. In their American contexts, both Holocaust commemoration and Zionist advocacy have conveyed stories about Jewish pasts, presents, and futures, connecting American Jews to present-day Jewish communities and stories about ancestors—precisely the work of religion.[25] Recognizing Holocaust commemoration and Zionist advocacy as widespread Jewish religious activities counters Cohen and Eisen's claims about the dissolution of Jewish communal institutions and intergenerational commitment.

Alongside these trends, the focus on Eastern European Jewish history and Jewish immigration to the United States has grown steadily since the 1970s, providing an additional narrative of modern Jewish history. In the early twenty-first century, this narrative has come to fruition as another significant mode of being Jewish in the United States. Nostalgia for immigrant pasts emphasizes American Jews' journey toward success in the American middle class. The materials of American Jewish nostalgia are a sign of liberal American Jews' faith in progress—the past was bad, but things are better now, and they will continue to improve. In this, it provides early twenty-first century American Jews with a communal narrative that can be more cheerful than the remembrance of the Holocaust and less communally divisive than Israeli politics. It is also more comfortable for American Jews to welcome non-Jews' participation in Jewish nostalgia than in commemorations of the Holocaust or support for Israel, in which non-Jewish voices may be seen as secondary or even threatening. At the same time, just as many Jews have seen Holocaust commemoration and Zionist activism as supporting one another and not mutually exclusive, American Jewish nostalgia is not necessarily a replacement for the other two narratives but can also complement them. All three narratives provide stories of progress that structure an approach to Jewish pasts and presents.

Case Studies

This book examines four case studies of the institutions and materials of American Jewish nostalgia: researching and recording American Jews' genealogy; the use of historic synagogues as heritage sites, such as the Eldridge Street Synagogue; the informal pedagogical tools of children's books and dolls; and a Jewish culinary revival, including "artisanal" kosher-style restaurants. The following chapters trace the development of American Jewish nostalgia from the 1970s through the present day, each focusing on a specific case study as well as a certain decade, in chronological order. While each of these pursuits might be an interesting example of American Jewish culture in its own right, together they provide a window into the ways in which American Jews have created Jewish religious activities through supposedly secular institutions in which individuals can preserve, produce, and engage with materials that convey nostalgia for particular Jewish pasts. Each of these cases provides ways of emotionally engaging with Eastern European Jewish culture in America, building on a normative story about Central and Eastern European Jews who immigrated to the United States around the turn of the century.

Each case study highlights a different aspect of American Jewish nostalgia for Eastern European pasts and the integral ways in which material culture, institutional organization, and feelings construct American Jews' religious practices and identities. These are exceptionally useful examples of American Jewish nostalgia, but they are far from the only ones. This book does not present a comprehensive overview of American Jewish nostalgia but rather focuses on examples that ably demonstrate the connection between material culture, institutions, and religious practice for American Jews as individuals and communities. A surprisingly large number of American Jews practice the activities we will examine in the following chapter—including people of all ages, all genders, and all and no denominational affiliations and types of Jewish practice—though this number is not easily quantified. On the whole, the subjects of these case studies have not received considerable sustained attention from scholars of American Jews. Each of these activities takes place largely outside of traditional Jewish religious institutions, and they do not require or lend themselves to denominational affiliation, though they can be comfortable companions to traditional religious practices. Examined together, these activities demonstrate that engagement with nostalgic materials constitutes a religious experience for many American Jews, uniting them through shared feelings toward a particular past.

Each case study focuses on familial and communal concerns in different ways: Jewish genealogists focus on tracing their own ancestral lines but build local and digital organizations; historic synagogues are institutions that tell local, communal histories; children's books created and distributed by particular organizations use family histories to create generalized narratives that draw children and parents into a shared emotional response; and restaurants are sites of commerce that include patrons in the restaurateurs' family stories. At the same time, each case study examines the complementary relationships among familial, communal, and institutional Jewish histories. Nostalgia functions differently in each of the case studies, as alternately authoritative, intimate, playful, ironic, or elegiac ways of longing for the past and providing meaning in the present. American Jewish nostalgia is at once individualistic, familial, and communal, as well as commercial, cultural, and religious. In all four case studies, this nostalgia relies heavily on material culture, organizational structures, and transactional relations to teach and induce emotional connections to a purportedly authentic past.

Like Holocaust remembrance and Zionist advocacy, the other primary narratives of twentieth-century and twenty-first-century American Judaism, nostalgia for Eastern European Jewish immigrant pasts helps American Jews engage seriously and deeply with their place in Jewish history. As with Holocaust commemoration and support for the State of Israel, Jewish nostalgia can be a brief activity or a dedicated lifelong pursuit. While Holocaust commemoration focuses on Jewish suffering and support for Israel can tell an uplifting narrative of Jewish progress, nostalgia looks backward from the vantage point of an ostensible American Jewish success. The materials of American Jewish nostalgia express longing for an imagined period, before the Holocaust, when Jews suffered from poverty but were comforted by the warmth of strong familial and communal narratives.

To pursue this research on the commonplace practices and emotions of American Jewish nostalgia, I have conducted interviews, engaged in short-term ethnographic research, and analyzed material and digital culture. I observed participants in genealogical society meetings and staff and visitors at historic synagogues. I conducted interviews with over sixty people in fields related to American Jewish nostalgia, including genealogists, authors, and software designers working on family history research; staff members and volunteers at heritage sites; philanthropists; authors, illustrators, and editors of children's books; Jewish communal professionals; and restaurateurs, cookbook authors, journalists, and entrepreneurs in the food industry. When possible, I conducted interviews in person, in my interlocutors' places of business, their homes, or in coffee shops convenient to their home or work. The wide-ranging nature of my research also led me to conduct a number of telephone interviews in order to capture as many voices as possible. I conducted one group interview, a conversation with board members of the Jewish Genealogical Society in New York.

If particular types of American Jewish culture can serve as American Jewish religion, then the creators of these forms might be considered new kinds of Jewish communal leaders or religious experts. The following chapters focus most on the Jewish genealogists, museum staff members, children's book authors, and restaurateurs who create the nostalgic materials of American Jewish popular culture. They are Jews who have rarely been recognized as leaders or experts either in scholarship or in Jewish communal conversations, and they do not necessarily see themselves as Jewish leaders. Often, staff members at such organizations deliberately minimize their own impact, emphasizing the authority of their patrons. Acknowledging the leadership of these content creators points to the importance of the new types of Jewish communal organization. Examining them as Jewish communal and religious leaders reveals how they now guide American Jews at least as much as those whose Jewish communal leadership has been recognized throughout much of the twentieth century, such as rabbis and directors of Jewish Federations, American Zionist organizations, and certain other Jewish non-profits.

At the same time, following the approach of lived religion rather than the earlier scholarly model of popular religion—which focused scholarly attention on laypeople rather than clergy—I resist an overly rigid distinction between the practices of "leaders" and "everyday practitioners." Scholars of lived religion pay attention to the ways that both leaders and laypeople engage in the same patterns of behavior.[26] I complement my interviews with institutional organizers and content creators with ethnographic observations of casual visitors to Jewish genealogical society talks and meetings, tourists at historic synagogues, and patrons at restaurants. I also take seriously online reviews of the programs, institutions, and materials I examine. The activities examined in this book are typically thought of as leisure activities, and they can take up as much time and money as one allows. Interviewing those who devote the most time to these activities affords us the clearest perspective on strongly held ideas about these activities and on those who shape their development, but I repeatedly balance this perspective with attention to those who engage more passively with these activities. The fact that nostalgia may recede into the background of an American Jew's life, only to reappear repeatedly in different contexts, points to its role in structuring individual experiences into broader narratives of meaning—the very work of religion.

In addition to interviews and participant observation, my research draws upon my study of American Jewish material and digital culture, including family trees, memoirs, historic spaces, museum exhibits, illustrated children's books, dolls, menus, meals, websites, online reviews, and other iterations of the cultures of American Jews. This wide-ranging research into the commercial objects and digital sites of American Jews'

lived religion allows me to make claims about the broad national phenomenon of American Jewish nostalgia as well as examine how it functions within particular locales and communities of like-minded people.
While concepts such as religion, memory, and feeling are abstract and
intangible, we can see how they operate among people by looking at
the objects, images, and spaces they create and the conversations those
items inspire.[27] Nostalgic materials are often dismissed as kitschy, sentimental, and inconsequential, but they offer us a window into a central
aspect of lived religion within American Judaism, the ways American
Jews enact their religion on a daily basis.

The Breadth and Boundaries of Nostalgia

In providing a particular narrative of the past, American Jewish nostalgia, like all historical narratives, necessarily creates boundaries about what
does and does not count as authentic and representative Jewish history.
Twentieth- and twenty-first-century American Jews have continually
policed authenticity by using texts, objects, and practices to make claims
regarding what is and is not "really Jewish."[28] Within the practices of
American Jewish nostalgia, authentic history is evaluated by the emotions
it elicits.[29] The authentic objects of American Jewish nostalgia are those
that create an abiding emotional connection to a particular imagined past.

Standardization narrows the stories told about American Jews, but,
paradoxically, it also expands who can engage with them. The story of
American Jewish pasts has become expansive enough to encompass and
include those whose families do not match the narrative—one does not
have to be descended from New York Jews, or even be Jewish, to have a
meaningful emotional connection to the past by visiting the Museum at
Eldridge Street or reading a children's book about Eastern European Jewish immigration. At the same time, the standardization of nostalgia for
Eastern European Jewish heritage and its increased popularity necessarily marginalizes the communal and familial histories of Jews who do not
descend from Eastern European immigrants and of converts to Judaism.

The power of this narrative is so dominant that sites of public history
that do not fit the pattern of Jewish nostalgia for Eastern Europe are often
folded into it. As we will see, the Touro Synagogue in Newport, Rhode Island dates back to 1763, but it is presented to the public with the nostalgic

themes of longing for immigrant pasts that derive from the presentation of late nineteenth- and early twentieth-century synagogues. Likewise, some of the restaurateurs we will meet incorporate dishes from the cuisines of Sephardi and Mizrachi Jews (Jews of Spanish or Portuguese descent and Middle Eastern Jews) into their menus, but these are generally side dishes that do not distract from the Eastern European-focused nostalgia that propels their enterprises. American Jewish nostalgia, particularly nostalgic commerce, can incorporate stories that deviate from the standard narrative without losing the magnetic power of its central story.

Family histories that do not fit the story of Eastern European immigration rest more uneasily alongside the standard narrative. Those adopted into Jewish families are also encouraged to feel nostalgia for their biological and adoptive family histories. While genealogist Arthur Kurzweil told me that he prides himself on his work helping adoptees find their biological families, his Jewish genealogy manual also strongly suggests that adoptees research the family history of their adoptive parents. "Just as they adopted you as their child, you can adopt their history as your own," he optimistically advises.[30] This is a generous view of what family history means, but it may also narrow the possibilities of what ancestries of Jews may mean. This advice, too, does not help adult converts to Judaism find their way into the geographies of America Jewish nostalgia.

Those whose families do not fit traditional models in other ways run into difficulties, too. Rabbi Jo David found this when she taught Jewish genealogy to a religious school class in the early 1990s. When her students handed in their genealogy charts, one girl had only completed her matrilineal line. As David later told me, when she pressed her student on the incomplete assignment, her student said, "I don't have a father." David asked if her parents were divorced or if her father had passed away. "No," the student replied. "For you to be here, there had to be a man in your mother's life somewhere!" David said, exasperated. "No," the student said. "My mother went to a sperm bank."[31] Reflecting on this moment years later, David told me that the episode taught her not to make assumptions about people's family backgrounds. She had learned to be more attentive to children of single parents and those with gay and lesbian parents, and she would have handled the situation differently. As an adult in the twenty-first century, David's student might find her mother's sperm donor through DNA testing and genealogy websites, and she might make choices about the presence or absence of her biological father and other paternal relatives in her life. Still, the story points to how genealogy research, and American Jewish nostalgia more broadly, rests on assumptions about biological inheritance and normative family structures. Those whose family structures do not fit a normative pattern are often shoehorned into traditional models and must work hard to make these models accommodate their family histories.

But, on the whole, the mitzvah of nostalgia for Eastern European immigration history is flexible enough to accommodate the diverse religious needs of American Jews. It is suitable for those who only have time and interest to devote occasional moments to it and those who pursue extended engagements with it. Clinical psychologist Sallyann Amdur Sack, an early leader of Jewish genealogy, told me that her interest in genealogy began when her fifteen-year-old daughter, Kathy, came across Dan Rottenberg's newly published *Finding Our Fathers: A Guidebook to Jewish Genealogy* in a bookstore in the summer of 1977. Kathy handed the book to her mother, saying, "Here, I brought you a present. I want to learn all about my ancestors." Delighted to spend time with her teenage daughter, Sack followed Rottenberg's instructions to write to relatives, asking for permission to interview them. "And then," Sack told me, "because Kathy was fifteen, the inevitable happened. She got a boyfriend." Kathy lost interest in the project, but her mother was still receiving replies to their letters. "And it was so fascinating," Sack said. "People who do genealogy, or do Jewish genealogy, will tell you it's like a virus. It just sort of bites you. In any case, I started answering all the letters and corresponding. And before I knew it, it was just an obsession."[32]

As in Sack's experience, American Jewish nostalgia is practiced by Jews of all ages and Jews with varied schedules and attention spans. While retirees may have more time and financial resources to devote to protracted genealogical research or to work as a docent at a historic synagogue, one may get one's DNA tested, flip through a historic synagogue's Instagram account, read a picture book, or pick up a pastrami sandwich without a great deal of fuss. This is American Jewish religion—the commonplace personal practices and feelings that are mediated and standardized by certain materials and institutions. These are the everyday activities that connect Jews to past, present, and future Jewish communities. They are structures and feelings by which American Jews are bound together.

1

How Do You Solve a Problem like Nostalgia?

I do not want anything to happen in Jewish history without
it happening to me.
—Elie Wiesel, quoted in Arthur Kurzweil, *From Generation to Generation: How to Trace Your Jewish Genealogy and
Family History* (San Francisco: Jossey-Bass, 2004)

Tiny replicas of the façade of the Jewish Museum of Florida appear
throughout the museum. Located in Miami Beach's South Beach neighborhood, the institution is housed in two former synagogue buildings.
The museum's main entrance is the front of a 1936 synagogue building designed by the well-known Floridian Art Deco architect Henry
Hohauser.[1] In the museum's gift shop, located by the front entrance,
one may purchase Jewish ritual objects—tzedakah (charity) boxes and
mezuzah cases (ritual objects affixed to doorframes)—in the shape of the
Hohauser building with which to decorate one's home or give as a gift.[2]
In an amusingly self-referential gesture, mezuzahs with the Hohauser
façade hang on the internal doorways of the passageway between the
two buildings. As they pass between museum spaces, tourists can admire
the image of the building even as they stand within it. More traditionally
minded Jewish visitors might ritually touch a museum-shaped mezuzah
and kiss their fingers as they walk within the museum.

Such hollow, resin miniatures of synagogue buildings are ubiquitous
in Jewish gift shops and on websites of Judaica retailers. One can buy
replicas of the grand synagogues of Europe, the landmarks of ancient
Israel, and American synagogues. They are the kind of tchotchke that
might be easily dismissed as an inconsequential item of Jewish culture,
not significantly representative of Jews' beliefs, values, and practices.
Alternatively, they might be understood as religious because of their
traditional forms, as ritual objects fulfilling the religious mitzvot of giving charity and hanging mezuzahs. But these miniatures also should be

Figure 1.1. Mezuzah depicting the façade of the
Jewish Museum of Florida. Photo by author, 2012.

understood as religious objects for another reason: They encourage the
American Jewish mitzvah of longing for an imagined communal Eastern European Jewish immigration history.

"I would like others to believe as I do—that it is a mitzvah for each
of us, in our own unique way, to do what we can to honor our Jewish ancestors—to learn about, preserve, and perpetuate our memories
of them and the world in which they lived," Jewish genealogist Steven
Lasky wrote in a cover story for *Dorot: The Journal of the Jewish Genealogical Society* in 2007.[3] Drawing on the past for affective meaning in the
present, the mitzvah of nostalgia is both praiseworthy and something
American Jews must do. American Jewish nostalgia articulates shared
narratives of the past and honors ancestors, creating community in the

present and passing on certain sentiments, affections, and values to the next generation. Understanding nostalgia as a mitzvah complicates simplistic, if common, divisions between "religious" and "secular" Jews and between religious and secular Jewish activities. If nostalgia is a mitzvah, a reexamination of American Jewish religion is necessary.

Redefining American Jewish Religion

In 2013, the Pew Research Center released a sociological study of American Jews, *A Portrait of Jewish Americans*, which, like other sociological studies of American Jews, received a great deal of attention from Jewish organizations and communal leaders.[4] The Pew study identified 78 percent of the 6.7 million Americans as Jews as "Jews by religion." The remaining 22 percent comprised the category of "Jews of no religion."[5] American Jews' panicked public responses to the survey were ritualized and predictably alarmist. In newspapers, on blogs, and from the pulpit, American Jews repeatedly interpreted the results in ways that intensified their fears of secularism and assimilation. Jane Eisner, who had set the survey in motion when she was editor-in-chief of the prominent Jewish newspaper *The Forward*, told *The New York Times* that she found the results "devastating" because "I thought there would be more American Jews who cared about religion." She continued, "This should serve as a wake-up call for all of us as Jews to think about what kind of community we're going to be able to sustain if we have so much assimilation," assuming that readers shared her understanding of "assimilation" as a negative force in American Jewish communities.[6]

As with previous surveys of American Jews, the buzzwords of this survey—"Jews by religion" and "Jews of no religion"—will be repeated until another national survey of American Jews is published. The previous national telephone survey of American Jews, the 2000 National Jewish Population Survey (NJPS), differentiated between "highly involved" Jews and "people of Jewish background," seeing a wide gulf between these groups. Jewish institutions and philanthropists repeatedly employed these terms for a decade. In the 2013 survey, Pew presented American Jews with a distinction between Jews by religion and Jews of no religion, a Jewish version of the "nones," the current sociological term used to identify the religiously unaffiliated, and a label used by Pew as well.[7] As Pew researchers were quick to remind readers, Americans as a whole increasingly identify themselves as having no religion. The share of American Jews who say they have no religion (22 percent) is similar to the share of "nones" in the general public (20 percent). Still, commentators on American Jews—rabbis, sociologists, demographers, cultural critics, and others—remain concerned about what they see as an increasing number of "Jews of no religion."[8] These scholars and communal leaders see Judaism as threatened by American culture. In cultural commentaries and in sermons, they tell a widely believed story about American Jews that is one of increasing secularism, or, as American Jews say, "assimilation." These cultural commentators imagine American Jews transitioning from a more pure or essential religious Judaism toward watered-down Jewish identities. In more catastrophic visions, they predict the potential disappearance of American Jews altogether. According to this fearful worldview, secularism could complete the destruction of world Jewry begun in the Holocaust.

But American Jews' Jewish lives are richer and more complex than these studies and commentaries portray. Divisions between Judaism (the religion) and Jewishness (the culture) are no longer useful, if they ever were. This dichotomy assumes a distinction between beliefs and rituals, on the one hand, and the arts and lifestyle activities, such as foodways and humor, on the other hand. It ignores the overlap between ritual and lifestyle, and the influence each has on the other. In reality, activities understood as both religious and cultural provide existential meaning for American Jews and connect them to imagined transhistorical communities of Jews past, present, and future. Simplistic divisions between "religious" and "secular" Jews do not accurately describe the diversity of American Jewish practice.

At the same time, the declension narrative of assimilation and secularism, like many such narratives, is historically inaccurate. It plainly overlooks the dynamic developments in Jewish culture and ritual around the globe over the past two thousand years as well as changes and diversity in Jewish culture and religion in North America over the past three centuries. Narratives of assimilation are closely aligned with narratives of American Jewish economic success, which fail to take into account both wealthy Jews of the early twentieth century and impoverished Jews of the present day. Meanwhile, as the Pew researchers highlight at the beginning of their report, "Jews by religion" and "Jews of no religion" are both overwhelmingly proud to be Jewish and have a strong sense of belonging to the Jewish people.[9] Examining practices shared by religious and secular Jews that provide fundamental narrative meanings in their lives and connect them to imagined communities in the past, present, and future allows us to see different patterns in American Jewish religion. Nostalgic practices are part of the unrecognized religious practices of American Jews across and beyond denominational structures, divisions that have become increasingly fluid.[10]

Moreover, the concept of religion is a modern, Protestant creation, and Jewish practices have frequently fit uncomfortably in the category of religion, despite the best efforts of Jewish thinkers to separate religious and cultural aspects of Jewish practice. Though uses of the word date back to Roman and early Christian settings, the origins of how we understand the term today lie in Protestants' efforts to differentiate their religion from Catholicism and colonialists' efforts to distinguish Christianity from non-Christian religions, both efforts that emphasized personal faith or belief over practice and ritual.[11] The political emancipation of Jews, which allowed Jews to become citizens of modern Western nation-states over the course of the eighteenth through early twentieth centuries, required Jews to define Judaism as a voluntary religious association. Before emancipation, European Jewish communities had largely governed themselves. As newly minted citizens in modern nation-states, Jews gave up their communal autonomy and used the language of religion to articulate themselves as a group. But traditional understandings of "religion," emphasizing individual, private, and voluntary confessions of faith, have rested uneasily with Jewish realities, which have a greater focus on communities and practices.[12]

In the United States, Jews continued to characterize religion as an individual matter of belief and choice rather than one mandated by ethnicity and community. American Jews have created dynamic communal arrangements and rituals, but many of these activities are dismissed as mere cultural habits, insignificant activities without religious implications. In the multiculturalism of the late twentieth- and early twenty-first-century United States, religious habits are seen as distinctive to particular groups, while cultural habits are understood as analogous across different groups. Culture is seen as something can be shared with outsiders, while religious practices are limited to adherents. For American Jews—who rarely emphasize belief, often share religious practices with non-Jewish family members, and transmit communal identity through ostensibly secular activities—this divide between religion and culture is overdrawn.[13]

In the 1950s, a time of American church growth in general, American Jewish leaders worked to frame their shared endeavors as a religion. Throughout World War I, World War II, and the postwar years, the American government, the military, and religious leaders viewed democracy and religious faith as shared endeavors. In contrast to fascists who identified as "Christian" and anti-religious communists, they articulated American democracy as a "Judeo-Christian" endeavor, resting on the three pillars of Protestantism, Catholicism, and Judaism. Participating in these political conversations, Jewish leaders employed the language of religion in order to demonstrate Jews' Americanness.[14] This rhetoric also helped Jews of European ancestry identify as white by framing Judaism as a religious rather than a racial minority.[15]

In the postwar years, synagogue building and membership burgeoned as Jews, like other white Americans, reorganized themselves in the newly built suburbs. Mid-century sociologists of American Jews "noted the paradox of Jews defining themselves overwhelmingly by religion while at the same time showing indifference and apathy for actual religious practice."[16] Perhaps this is because what sociologists recognized as "actual religious practice" did not adequately capture the realities of American Judaism. In fact, the trends of the 1950s should be recognized as the exception and not the norm for American Jews. In the decades following World War II, American Jews organized themselves aggressively, but not necessarily through synagogue memberships. "To be a Jew is to belong to an organization," one observer noted. "To manifest Jewish culture is to carry out . . . the program of an organization."[17] Many of these manifestly Jewish organizations included apparently secular groups. A large number were devoted to supporting the State of Israel. Many groups focused on memorializing and publicizing the murder of European Jews and the destruction of Jewish communities in the Holocaust.[18] Other Jews organized around liberal social justice causes, including the Civil Rights Movement. By the 1960s and 1970s, Jews were participating in the broader counterculture movements as well as turning countercultural critiques towards Jewish communities.[19]

In the second half of the twentieth century, Jewish organizations were plentiful, but synagogue attendance was declining. However, even in the heyday of American synagogues, attendance at services was never particularly high: One 1945 survey found that only 24 percent of Jews claimed to attend religious services at least once a month, compared to 81 percent of Catholics and 62 percent of Protestants, and only nine percent of Jews claimed to attend at least once a week. By 1970, only eight percent of Jewish household heads attended religious services fifty times or more per year, and fifty-five percent attended fewer than four times per year.[20] However, this does not mean that Jewish communities were dissolving. Instead, it means that attending public religious services was not where most Jews found existential meaning. Rather, the sacred relationships of Jewish community extended beyond these conventional indicators of religion.

Mid-twentieth-century synagogues served the dual primary functions of providing a place for adults to associate with other Jews and to socialize and educate children as Jews.[21] By the end of the twentieth century, synagogues competed for these roles with a variety of other institutions. The organizations we will examine in the following chapters—Jewish genealogical societies, historic synagogues, publishers and distributors of children's books, and Jewish restaurants—are some of the many institutions that provide these functions. These organizations serve many of the same essential functions of the mid-twentieth-century synagogue: facilitating spending time with other Jews, socializing and educating children, and placing these activities within a historical narrative. Like synagogues, the institutions of American Jewish nostalgia create imagined communities, allowing participants to think of themselves in terms of sacred relationships with those around them as well as with Jews in other places and times, both past and present.

In the early twenty-first century, American Jews with a broad array of religious affiliations and no affiliation engage in the ostensibly nonreligious activities of Jewish genealogical research, attending Jewish historic sites, consuming markedly Jewish food, and purchasing books and toys that teach Jewish heritage to their children. These are mundane activities, yet engagement with them can provide a core emotional connection to a Jewish identity. When social scientists measure such practices, the way they phrase survey questions may mask respondents' views of their significance. When Pew asked respondents, "What's essential to being Jewish?" only fourteen percent of Jews found "eating traditional Jewish foods" to be essential to their Jewish identities. An additional 39 percent described the activity as important but not essential.[22] The very wording of the question, however, reflects the Pew Research Center's essentialist ideas about what counts as "religion" for American Jews. Eating traditional Jewish foods, particularly in a public setting such as a deli, may be a meaningful part of a Jew's life, but it may be too ordinary, too easily overlooked, to be described as essential or important. Moreover, the survey's essentialist phrasing makes it unclear whether the respondent is solely reporting on his or her own practice or pronouncing on the boundaries of Jewish identity and declaring the practice mandatory. Commonplace activities such as eating Jewish foods are often quietly fundamental to religious identities rather than explicitly identified as essential to them.

By claiming as religious those activities generally recognized as secular, I highlight the significance of shared meanings and practices for Jewish individuals, families, and communities. Like other Americans, American Jews are not necessarily very good at articulating and recognizing sacred practices, places, or narratives in their lives. Activities like eating Jewish foods may provide a connection to Jewish history through consuming traditional dishes. It often provides a community in the present, too, as one is surrounded by others doing the same thing—much like attending a synagogue, but with perhaps more immediate gratification.

In North America, both "religion" and "spirituality" have been identified with Christian notions of belief and theology to such an extent that both scholars and practitioners have failed to recognize the meaning-making practices of other traditions as religious.[23] The inadequacy of common uses of these terms is particularly evident for traditions and practices that place little or no focus on theistic beliefs, as is the case for much of American Judaism. Examining the material religion and consumption of American Jewish nostalgia expands the concept of religion and demonstrates that religious meaning is contingent upon practices and narratives as well as beliefs and occurs in a variety of supposedly non-religious settings.

Susan King, an early leader in Jewish genealogy who developed online platforms connecting Jewish genealogists, told me that, for her, "doing the research and finding the truth is a spiritual journey." She explained, "I am a Jew, I will always be a Jew, I just don't have to practice all the quote 'religious' beliefs to be spiritual. . . . In this lifetime I have followed my truth. I have done service to the community."[24] For King, the work of Jewish genealogy, including both family history research and building online communities of genealogists, is the pursuit of her "truth" and sacred work on behalf of Jews living and dead. Like many other American Jews, King shies away from the word "religious," which many American Jews associate with formal organizations and mandated activities, such as belonging to a synagogue and following dietary laws. Nonetheless, we can understand King's work as religious because it provides existential meaning for her and her clients by placing them in a meaningful relationship with individuals and communities in the past and the present. King's genealogical research is in line with an understanding of the religiosity of activities that provide social and existential meaning in Jews' lives, even when they do not define those activities as religious.

Understanding nostalgic practices as religious activities challenges assumptions about the limited role of religion among non-Orthodox Jews in modern America. Doing so highlights normative practices that American Jews hold in common across and beyond the standard spectrum of American Jewish movements. The American Jews in this book identify with all and no denominational structures. They are people of all genders and all ages. They live throughout the United States and have a variety of economic situations. Nostalgia is a standardized mode of American Judaism that fosters a particular, affective response to the past, cutting across the statistical categories of religious affiliation, gender, class, and age that delineate American Jews.

It is not incidental that when I asked Robert Friedman, the former director of the Genealogy Institute at the Center for Jewish History in New York, how he got started as a genealogist, he began by explaining, "I didn't have a particularly religious upbringing. I did have a bar mitzvah, but I didn't really identify with the process, particularly." Recalling this typical American Jewish experience, he laughed, and continued, "However, I was extremely close with my father's parents, who were Hungarian immigrants who came to this country in 1921. And as I was growing up, my grandfather used to tell me all kinds of stories about the old country."[25] For American Jews, emotional engagement with ancestral pasts is a religious activity, one that can take the place of or exist alongside traditional religious practices.

Thematic research on nostalgia moves beyond the scholarly distinctions between Judaism and Jewishness and beyond the simplistic divisions between "religious" and "secular" Jews; these oppositions obscure the diversity of American Jewish practice. American Jews of all types of religious affiliation, including no affiliation, engage in ostensibly nonreligious activities that provide personally meaningful engagements with American Jewish pasts. Attention to American Jewish nostalgia identifies robust forms of religious meaning in works of public and personal histories, emphasizing the centrality of emotional and commemorative norms in American and Jewish religious practices and consumer habits.[26] Studying the consumption of nostalgia reveals normative themes about historical periods, immigration, and religious practices often taken for granted in American Jews' relation to history. Emotional connections to narratives about familial and communal pasts, and engagement with materials representing those narratives, are not merely cultural activities but religious ones.

Histories of Nostalgia

Like religion, nostalgia is a term that is often taken for granted but that has a complicated history. Scholars and cultural critics have referred to nostalgia and the related concept of sentimentality with derision, dismissing both as inauthentic and overly feminine emotions. At their worst, they may be considered "dangerous, like any ready-made emotion." They have been dismissed as prefabricated feelings that allow the absence of individual, reflective thinking and subsequent abdication of personal responsibility.[27] Philosopher Michael Tanner condemns sentimentality as a "disease of the feelings" and an "excuse for indulgence." "The feelings which are worth having are those which it costs an effort to have," Tanner proclaims.[28] Recognizing nostalgia as a backward-facing sentimentality, historian Charles Maier calls nostalgia "coffee table longing" and a "stereotyped yearning."[29]

In contrast, I argue that nostalgia is not merely reductive; it can also be productive. It reduces complicated histories to an accessible narrative, certainly, but it also produces personal and communal meaning for people of all genders. Even as critics disdain it as an inauthentic emotion, nostalgia fulfills individuals' search for an authentic past, creating communal cohesion through shared religious affect and consumption. American Jewish nostalgia is "a structure of feeling," an emotional reaction to the past that is learned and taught.[30] While academics and others have disparaged nostalgia for its emphasis on exaggerated emotion, it is, in fact, a way of finding one's place in the world and of laying claim to the past. The institutions of American Jewish nostalgia encourage their patrons to claim ancestral heritages in ways that are meaningful beyond simplistic divisions among religion, spirituality, and culture.

Though we take nostalgia for granted today as an emotion, it is, like religion, a supremely modern concept. Initially a diagnosable and curable disease, nostalgia was first identified by Johannes Hofer in his 1688 dissertation in Basel. Hofer diagnosed young Swiss mercenaries longing for their native land with a term he coined from the Greek *nosos*, return home, and *algos*, sorrow. Subsequent scholars and medics built upon Hofer's "disorder of the imagination." The Enlightenment-era neurologist Philippe Pinel described the symptoms, beginning with "a sad, melancholy appearance . . . countenance at times lifeless," progressing to "a rather constant torpor" broken by fits of weeping while asleep. The worst cases refused to leave their beds, remaining obstinately silent and refusing food and drink, leading to malnutrition and eventual death. Unlike the more philosophical ailment of melancholia, which befell elite intellectuals such as monks and philosophers, nostalgia was a lowbrow disease, afflicting soldiers, sailors, and country people who had moved to the cities. Political and military leaders were particularly worried about the unstable and contagious nature of nostalgia, as the infirmity of longing for distant homelands both enforced and challenged the emerging concepts of nationalism and patriotism.[31] Treatments included leeches, purges, "hypnotic emulsions," opium, and blood-letting. A Russian general in 1733 found terror successfully restorative—he only had to bury alive two or three incapacitated nostalgic soldiers before the outbreak subsided. But the only certain cure remained a return home.[32]

Americans have often had an ambivalent and contested relationship with nostalgia as a condition of acute homesickness. Seventeenth- and eighteenth-century Americans of European descent considered homesickness for Europe a mark of a refined character. By the time of the market revolution in the nineteenth century, however, white American men idealized the self-made man, who conquered his homesickness and whose rugged individualism supported capitalist activity.[33] Nostalgia's medical associations proved surprisingly resilient, too. As late as World War II, the U.S. Surgeon General included nostalgia on a list of contagious disorders that might "spread with the speed of an epidemic" through induction centers.[34]

But even as some Americans—especially male intellectuals—have eschewed nostalgia in favor of personal histories emphasizing rugged individualism, sentimentality and nostalgia have long been an essential part of American Protestant piety. Sentimental materials are those that "appeal to tender feelings" to solicit an ethical or political response.[35] Sentimentality blurs the boundaries between recognized categories of spirituality, religion, literary culture, and popular culture. In the nineteenth century, this was particularly evident in Christian writings by and for middle-class women that aimed to reshape American morality. The broadly popular materials of sentimental novels, poems, and hymns established Protestant women as religious leaders by presenting them as moral authorities. Harriet Beecher's Stowe's *Uncle Tom's Cabin* is only the most famous example of this genre.[36] Sentimentality and nostalgia would remain essential to American evangelicalism through the present day. For American Protestants, sentimentality and nostalgia strengthen emotional connections to leaders' religious messages, identify the family as a sacred but fragile nucleus of Christianity, and fuel political efforts to influence national mores.[37] American Jewish nostalgia would draw on this American Protestant legacy by making similar connections between emotion and morality, emphasizing the sanctity of family, and linking religious nostalgia to American patriotism.

In addition to its American Protestant roots, American Jewish nostalgia has deep roots in nineteenth-century European Judaism. Nostalgia for imagined Eastern European shtetls (Yiddish for "town"; used to refer to small, predominately Jewish towns) can be traced to nineteenth-century Europe, when Jews entered mainstream European society as recently emancipated citizens.[38] Where nineteenth-century American Protestant sentimentality was largely the work of nineteenth-century female writers, men generally created nineteenth-century European Jewish nostalgia. Male writers and artists who had left small, predominantly

Jewish towns for cosmopolitan Western European cities and had shed traditional Jewish religious practices repeatedly reminisced about the religious practices of their youth and their immediate and distant ancestors. As these enlightened Jewish men de-emphasized traditional ritual observance, they awarded nostalgia "a centrality that it likely never before possessed" in Jewish practice.[39] Memories of pious forebears were essential for Jews forging new, modern Jewish identities.[40]

In the United States, Jewish nostalgic materials began to appear with increasing frequency after World War II. In the wake of the destruction of European Jewry, the term "shtetl" began to appear untranslated in non-Jewish languages, including English, much more frequently.[41] For most American Jews, like nineteenth-century European Jewish writers and artists, shtetl nostalgia has been a means of yearning for a time and place that they have not personally experienced. "Shtetl" came to stand in for an increasingly nostalgic vision of European, particularly Eastern European Jewish life, generally imagined as a lost world that had been backward, pre-modern, and impoverished but warm in community spirit. Nostalgia for nineteenth-century European shtetls—itself originating in the nineteenth century—blended neatly with American Jews' mourning for communities destroyed in the Holocaust. Images of shtetls and urban ethnic neighborhoods, writes historian Hasia Diner, "could be found almost anywhere. Their images ran through the imaginative world of American Jews as instant mnemonics of places that everyone knew, but, ultimately, few had lived in."[42] By 1955, one writer observed, "the wave of nostalgia was overwhelming. Memory of the shtetl, which for decades had been relegated to the back of the mind . . . now came into its own in the thinking of American Jews. It was recalled vividly and with love."[43]

By the 1960s, American Jewish nostalgia blossomed. As American studies scholar Matthew Frye Jacobson documents, since the 1960s a white ethnic revival has recast mythological American origins from Plymouth Rock to Ellis Island, emphasizing Central and Eastern European immigrants who came to the United States between 1880 and 1924. White Americans increasingly identified themselves with ethnic minority statuses based on ancestral national origins, as in Polish Americans, Italian Americans, and Irish Americans.[44] Ashkenazi Jews, those of Central and Eastern European origins, enthusiastically embraced this

idea, substituting Jewishness for European nationalism. The white ethnic revival helped American Jews to frame Jewishness as an ethnic difference while they benefited from the gains of increased recognition of
Ashkenazi Jews as white.[45]

That is not to say that earlier generations of American Jews were
not nostalgic. Americans have a persistent popular belief in "Hansen's
Law," historian Marcus Lee Hansen's 1930 assertion that what the second
generation wishes to forget the third wishes to remember. In fact, the
second generation forgot considerably less than later generations pre-
sumed they did. Examining newspaper accounts, public monuments,
pageants, parades, and children's books of the early and mid-twentieth
century, Jacobson finds that, "whatever death or slumber ethnicity was
supposedly 'revived' *from* in the ethnic revival, the hiatus could not have
been very long."[46] What is different since the 1970s is not that American
Jewish nostalgia exists, but how it has been organized and standardized and how it has become a central way of being Jewish. At the same
time, a belief in Hansen's Law shaped Americans' understanding of the
ethnic revival of the 1960s and their continued "rediscovery" of communal pasts in the subsequent decades. For Ashkenazi Jews and other
ethnic Americans, these rediscovered histories are frequently stories of
the hardship and deprivation of earlier generations and their subsequent
economic success in the United States. The nostalgic longing for recovery of a European and immigrant American past is coupled with a narrative of progress, underscoring a fervent if unstated hope that perceived
upward economic trends of American Jews will continue in the future.

American Jews' nostalgia for Eastern European origins is not totally
distinct from another major focal point of American Jewish communities since the mid-twentieth century: support for Israel. In traditional
Jewish models of longing for the biblical Land of Israel, those living outside of the region were living in the diaspora or, in Hebrew, galut (golus,
in the Ashkenazi Yiddish pronunciation), an inherently negative term
suggesting spiritual diminishment and exile. In traditional liturgies and
mystical texts, Jews have expressed a yearning to return to Zion under
the guidance of the Messiah. At the same time, Jews have been far more
at home in the diaspora than this trope would suggest, creating vibrant
communities around the world that influenced and were influenced by
the cultures surrounding them.[47] Following the establishment of the

State of Israel, American Jews and others reorganized their communities to make support for Israel into a civil religion—in which nationalism functions as a religion—around which they could build Jewish identity within and beyond religious institutions. Mainstream American Jewish organizations have encouraged Jews to connect to Israel through philanthropy, education, tourism, lobbying, and business ventures.

American Zionism provided a model of a religiously inflected attachment to place that Jews practiced through consumption, one that mitigated the traditional understanding of galut as spiritual exile. From the 1950s and 1960s onward, American Jews purchased "Israeli patina menorahs and mezuzot, olivewood ashtrays, letter openers, and coins fashioned into keys chains and jewelry."[48] American Jews used Israeli objects as tools used to build American Jewish communities, providing shared physical and emotional connections to a distant place. (Some American synagogues are literally built out of "Jerusalem stone" imported from Israel.) Israeli goods provided a shared affection and longing for a distant past while creating distinctive Jewish communities in the United States, just as materials evoking nostalgia for Eastern European Jewish immigration histories would.[49]

To some extent, American Jews' nostalgia reframed Ashkenazi Jews' diaspora as an exile from Eastern Europe and urban American neighborhoods rather than from the Land of Israel. Echoing their Zionist consumer habits, American Jews purchased tchotchkes like synagogue tzedakah boxes and *Fiddler on the Roof* snow globes. But nostalgia for European origins also existed comfortably alongside Zionism. American Jewish nostalgia for immigrant homelands does not necessarily replace a connection to Israel, and the Jews in this study have a range of opinions about Zionism, representative of the current range of American Jewish opinions about the State of Israel.[50] Nonetheless, as debates about Israel's policies have increasingly divided American Jews, a turn toward nostalgic consumption of immigration history has provided a seemingly more unifying practice for members of this diverse community.

Popular Culture and Public History

As American Jews have grown increasingly distant from the objects of communal longing—urban immigrant neighborhoods and imagined

Eastern European shtetl origins—popular culture and public history have played an increasingly essential role in American Jews' lives. Despite American Jews' general fears about a lack of Jewish differentiation, Jews have rarely feared engagement with the materials of American popular culture. Popular culture on its own did not threaten Jewish continuity; failing to complement it with a firm grounding in Jewish religion, culture, and traditions did. Ostensibly non-religious institutions of public history and popular cultural materials now instruct Jews and other Americans on how to feel Jewish, including how to long for particular Jewish pasts. Institutions such as museums and restaurants make nostalgia a consumable product as well as an emotion and a religious practice, while popular culture and public history function as religious objects and sites.

This is not altogether new. Jews have long identified forms of engagement with material culture as religious and spiritual practices. As religious studies scholar Vanessa Ochs explains, "in Judaism, the spiritual is material."[51] When they recall mythic ancestors who were freed from slavery in Egypt at the Passover seder or display family photographs of grandparents, American Jews engage in the mitzvah of remembering forebears, creating a transhistorical sense of community as Jews pass on to their children the sensibilities they believe were held by past generations. American Jews' practices reveal them engaging with popular culture and public history in ways that are not merely entertaining but point to the sacred values by which they organize their lives.[52]

In the nineteenth- and the twentieth-century United States, the popular heritage narratives of American Jews, like those of other American ethnic and religious groups, focused on Jewish patriotic participation in the American Revolution and the Civil War. Through these stories, they claimed essential roles in the major events of American history to underscore the nation's acceptance of Judaism.[53] While this Jewish heritage work focusing on the formation of the United States persists—it is notably present in the Smithsonian-affiliated National Museum of American Jewish History, which reopened on Philadelphia's Independence Mall in 2005—it has been largely overshadowed by the emphasis on European heritage in the white ethnic revival that began in the 1960s and 1970s.

American public history changed in both form and content in the 1970s. Public histories of the American Revolution and the Civil War had used material culture such as relics, replicas, and monuments to represent the past as both distant and different from the present. But starting in the 1970s, Americans increasingly and explicitly wanted to feel something about the past as well as remember it. They were eager for personal, emotional connections to the past in a variety of popular cultural forms—not just in museums, but also in film, television, novels, fashion, music, games, and toys. Public history increasingly became an emotional enterprise, and it could be found everywhere.[54] The creators, staff, and participants at the institutions examined in this book encourage patrons to use their materials to form emotional connections to Jewish pasts that are inaccessible by other means. As the Jewish Museum of Florida told its prospective members, "This Museum is about you—and for you."[55]

As this new nostalgia for white ethnic pasts got underway, American Jewish nostalgia found its cultural lodestone in *Fiddler on the Roof*, the 1964 Broadway musical and 1971 film based on short stories written in Yiddish by Sholem Aleichem between 1894 and 1914. While Sholem Aleichem's original tales of Tevye the Dairyman were funny and bitingly sarcastic critiques of European Jews trying—and often failing—to respond to social changes at the turn of the twentieth century, late-twentieth-century American Jews approached the stories with a serious sentimentality. Jewish and non-Jewish audiences used *Fiddler's* story of Eastern European shtetl life to respond to the turbulent social changes of the 1960s, including women's liberation, the Civil Rights Movement, and representations of the United States as a nation of immigrants. *Fiddler* itself became part of American Jewish heritage. Attending the musical, listening to the cast album, and watching the film became important means of expressing American Jewishness.[56] American Jews brought *Fiddler* and its safely nostalgic longing into their lives through countless references, and recognized its sanctity by singing its songs—or even enacting its "bottle dance"—at weddings and bar and bat mitzvahs.[57] The *Fiddler* song "Sunrise, Sunset," explains religious studies scholar Ronald L. Grimes, "is Jewishly nondenominational in the way that commencement prayers are Christianly nondenominational."[58] Here, nondenominational in no way means "non-religious," but rather Jewishly religious *and* broadly accessible to those both within and beyond religious boundaries.

As I researched American Jewish nostalgia, *Fiddler* was ever-present in conversations and materials. In the *Avotaynu Guide to Jewish Genealogy*, Harold Rhode advises Jewish genealogists to think critically about the recorded and unrecorded pasts of Eastern European Jews. "Registration with the authorities in Eastern Europe invariably meant trouble," he explains. He continues,

> One way to understand this is to remember what Tevye, the main character in "Fiddler on the Roof," asked the shtetl rabbi: "Is there a blessing for the czar?" The rabbi answers: "A blessing for the czar? Of course. May G-d keep the czar far, far away from us!" This short exchange sums up how our ancestors viewed government.[59]

More than most American Jews, Rhode knows how to do archival and scholarly research to trace his genealogy and place his ancestors in their historical contexts. Nonetheless, Rhode, like many others, employs *Fiddler on the Roof* as a nostalgic referent, a shorthand way to gesture toward a bygone world that contemporary Jews know primarily through popular culture.[60]

New forms of American Jewish public history and popular culture followed suit. In the mid-1970s, inspired by the "roots movement" that was born of the popularity of Alex Haley's 1976 book *Roots: The Saga of an American Family* and the ABC mini-series the following year, American Jewish genealogists began to organize and educate themselves, writing manuals and creating Jewish genealogical societies. A decade later, historians and preservationists started paying attention in earnest to the role historic synagogues might play in Jewish public life. In the 1990s, mainstream publishing houses started publishing increasing numbers of children's books depicting stories of Jewish immigration as part of the American story of multiculturalism. And in the early twenty-first century, the Eastern European Jewish culinary revival began in earnest.

These new forms of American Jewish public history encourage a more active longing for Eastern European Jewish immigration history. American Jews could connect to this past, and other Jewish histories, through a variety of older types of Jewish institutions and media, such as passively watching a movie or performance. The materials of the new Jewish public history lead American Jews to practice a more active longing for this Jewish past, beyond expressing a desire to connect to it. Longing activates their agency in this religious practice beyond a passive connection. Jewish genealogists actively research their family histories; visitors at historic synagogues step into the footprints of past congregants; parents read illustrated books aloud and children are encouraged to play with dolls; and restaurant patrons literally consume their longing for Eastern European Jewish immigration history.

While some forms of nostalgic popular culture are accessible for audiences of all ages—like the catchy tunes, memorable dances, and iconic images of *Fiddler on the Roof*, which one can view as a film or high school play or Broadway performance—other forms of nostalgic pop culture are specifically designed for children of certain ages and their parents. The institutions that create and distribute children's books and dolls help parents to prime children to understand American Jewish values, including nostalgia. As Dianne Hess, executive editor at Scholastic Press, which has published many Jewish children's books, told me, "Most kids don't have any Jewish background now and don't have that nostalgia for the immigrant grandparents. And for me, it's like you can't lose that, because that's sort of the glue that's been holding the culture together."[61] Some of the books Hess publishes, particularly the work of acclaimed children's book author Eric Kimmel, address this perceived disconnect. The commercial exchange of certain Jewish children's books reconstitutes nostalgic longing, passing it from one generation to the next.[62]

Restaurants, too, can be institutions of public history, and food is an essential but ephemeral form of popular culture. The immediate intimacy of eating encourages asking and answering questions about one's self, identity, and community, and Jewish restaurants encourage patrons to relate family stories.[63] "A lot of people come in and they want to tell us their experiences they've had with this food growing up," said Ilyse Lerner, owner of On Rye, a deli in Washington, D.C.[64] The restaurateurs and purveyors of Jewish food examined in this book relate stories of their family histories and of Jewish communal histories through their food, décor, and presentation. Like all sites of public history, these eateries have a particular point of view. For Karen Adelman, co-owner of Saul's Deli in Berkeley, California, "the principal story" told in Saul's Deli is that of "Ashkenazi Jews from the Old World and then New York, and then they continue going west" until they reach California, making Saul's Deli—and its patrons—the apotheosis of Jewish history.

Looking beyond traditional religious institutions and practices to ostensibly secular sites of popular culture and public history reveals that nostalgic institutions and practices are an alternate, as yet under-appreciated, way of being Jewish and of maintaining Jewish continuity. These institutions and practices help Jews establish and sustain an emotional connection to an imagined transhistorical Jewish community. Nostalgia helps us to expand the concept of religion, demonstrating that religious meaning is contingent upon practices and narratives, not only on beliefs, attendance at religious services, and participation in established institutions. Once we think to look for it, we can see Jewish religious meaning and experience in a variety of seemingly non-religious settings.

Beyond the door of the synagogue or Jewish community center, American Jews' religious lives are rich, complex, and hard to pin down. American Jews with a broad array of religious affiliations and those with no affiliation engage in the ostensibly non-religious activities of Jewish genealogical research, visiting Jewish historic sites, consuming markedly Jewish food, and purchasing books and toys that teach the mitzvah of Jewish nostalgia to their children. These activities can provide personally meaningful, emotionally driven engagement with American Jewish pasts that inspire longing for Jewish communities across time and space. Attention to American Jewish nostalgia helps us to look for American Judaism in new places, identifying robust forms of religious meaning in works of public and private history and emphasizing the centrality of emotional norms in American Jewish religion.

2

Give Us Our Name

Creating Jewish Genealogy

Arthur Kurzweil—Talmudist, magician, and author of the popular manual *From Generation to Generation*—is a popular speaker at Jewish genealogy conferences.[1] With his long white beard, wire-frame glasses, and kippah, Kurzweil looks like the Orthodox educator that he is. But rather than telling his audience simply to trust in his authority and expertise, he tells them to trust themselves and their emotions. In his trademark calm but impassioned tone, he directly connects genealogy to familiar Jewish practices. Kurzweil reminds audiences of the biblical command quoted in the haggadah, the text read at the Passover seder: "In every generation, each individual is bound to regard himself as if he had gone personally forth from Egypt; as it is said, 'And you shall relate to your son that day, saying, "This is on account of what the Lord did for me, when I went forth from Egypt."'"[2] Speaking to Jewish genealogists—often crowds of mostly non-Orthodox Jews—Kurzweil extends this obligation to place oneself within the biblical narrative in order to encourage his listeners to place themselves within the more recent past. In his talks and writings Kurzweil traces his identity to an Eastern European shtetl. As he writes in his manual, "I am a Dobromiler," identifying as a resident of his ancestral town in Poland. "I was born in New York but came out of a shtetl."[3] Without ever having laid foot in Dobromil, Kurzweil claims it as his own, in a move he finds as obligatory as the biblical command to remember the Exodus. For Kurzweil, and for the many Jewish genealogists heartened by his talks, family history research is not only a matter of historical research of one's ancestries, but also the meaning-making process of claiming foreign pasts as one's own through an intimate and authoritative nostalgia. The story of Central and Eastern European ancestors becomes the central religious narrative of many Jewish genealogists.

American Jewish genealogists were among the first to collectively develop and standardize narratives of nostalgic longing for Eastern European Jewish history and turn-of-the-century American Jewish immigration history. Since the 1970s, Jewish genealogists have developed a nostalgia that functions as American Jewish religion, one that asks and answers weighty, existential questions. Genealogists, Jewish and otherwise, regularly ask questions that emotionally connect them to imagined communities that include the living, the dead, and future generations: Who am I? Where did I come from? What sacrifices did my ancestors make, and what values do I want to pass on to my children? The ordinariness of these identity questions should make them no less remarkable. The act of asking and answering these everyday questions through family history research is the work of "holy leisure," seemingly mundane activities that can be understood as sacred within particular contexts.[4]

Because this holy leisure occurs in a variety of contexts, my research took a range of forms. I conducted interviews with genealogists throughout the United States (and one American based in Europe), women and men ranging in age from their mid-twenties to their eighties. Although some outsiders assume that family history is primarily a women's domain, people of all genders pursue Jewish genealogy. Some of my informants identify as religious, including both Orthodox and religiously liberal Jews, and others are avowedly secular. I spoke with both amateur and professional genealogists, terms that refer respectively to those who research their own family histories and those who research others' histories for pay. I pursued ethnographic participant observation, attending meetings of the Jewish Genealogical Society meetings in New York City, the oldest and one of the largest branches of Jewish genealogical societies in the United States. I also examined the written materials of Jewish genealogy, in print and online, including how-to manuals, trade journals, memoirs, family history books, institutional websites, and personal blogs. I balance findings from interviews and ethnographic research with analyses of national Jewish genealogical publications in order to make claims about larger trends.

The genealogists I spoke with learned how to find their authoritative voices and how to understand their work as deeply meaningful by forming in-person and online institutions and communities. While genealogy research could, in theory, be the solitary activity of a lone researcher,

Jewish genealogists share information with one another over formal and informal networks, write and purchase how-to books, participate in Jewish Genealogy Societies, and draw upon resources and tips from other genealogists through databases, online services such as JewishGen and Ancestry.com, and social media platforms, especially Facebook. These ostensibly secular organizations and networks become sites of lived religion as they help Jewish genealogists see themselves in terms of sacred relationships with those around them in the present and with Jews in other places and other times.[5]

American Jewish genealogists are often inspired to begin their research after hearing stories from grandparents or considering family lore passed down the generations. They move on to engage with the immediacy of primary sources, including family photographs, heirlooms, or documents that evoke an intimacy with ancestors. Genealogy can be an occasional hobby or an all-encompassing full-time occupation. The most dedicated Jewish genealogists spend hours poring over birth, marriage, and death records, immigration and naturalization records, and census records in online databases and on-site archives. They visit cemeteries to get ancestors' Jewish names from tombstones.[6] They spend time determining the present-day names of ancestral towns and learning whether local records have survived and where they are located. They may develop language skills to acquire and interpret this information. As journalist Bill Gladstone writes in the Jewish genealogy journal *Avotaynu*, Jewish genealogists pursue their research for "the emotional payoff that comes from rooting through antiquated records in musty archives, entering the forbidding precincts of old cemeteries, and traveling vast distances to ancestral villages in search of an authentic connection to our family's past."[7] These days, researchers also utilize DNA testing to discover near and distant relations. As they pursue this research, genealogists find themselves drawing closer to ancestors' lives and, in turn, longing to know more.

Many Jewish genealogists are disciplined researchers who draw conclusions from evidence and make determinations about where to find new evidence to answer the research questions that arise, like other historical researchers.[8] As they sift through historical materials, genealogists learn to trust or distrust family stories and historical records, appraising sources' authority and, in the process, becoming authorities in their own right. Genealogy is not free of power relations: There are archival issues of who decided to record what about whom, how information has been preserved, and in what manner the public may access it. Senior relatives become gatekeepers, deciding what stories to share with their descendants. Genealogists decide which branches to pursue and how to do so, and they go on to make decisions about what to share and through what medium.[9] Establishing their own authority as researchers and narrators is essential to the work of genealogists.

A number of historical factors set Jewish genealogy apart from family history research of other ethnic groups, including but not limited to the Holocaust. Some Jews are drawn to genealogy because they want to learn more about branches of their families destroyed by the Holocaust. The Holocaust differentiates Ashkenazi Jewish genealogy both in terms of research methods—searching Nazi documents and tracing communities destroyed in the Holocaust—and in conceptions of some kinds of Jewish genealogy as a form of Holocaust memorialization. In this, as in other aspects of Jewish genealogy, nostalgic longing for lost worlds— and the innovative practices and rituals that longing inspires—allow American Jews to actively place themselves and their families within larger narratives of Jewish history.

The authoritative genealogist may be either a "professional" or an "amateur" genealogist. In general, someone who solely researches his or her own genealogy is an amateur genealogist, while someone who researches another person's genealogy for pay is a professional genealogist. Amateur and professional genealogists generally do the same research with the same tools, and most genealogists, amateur or professional, are not formally trained in historical research, but have learned research skills informally, through practice and from other genealogists.[10] In fact, while much of the leadership of non-Jewish genealogy organizations has genealogy certifications, this is not the case for Jewish genealogy leadership, in which authority is primarily "earned from within the community by doing work others deem legitimate and substantive," rather than from outside organizations, according to Pittsburgh-based Jewish genealogist Tammy Hepps.[11]

Since professionalization is not a measure of authority, genealogists' authority is measured in other terms. Authoritative Jewish genealogists are those who uphold communal standards while honoring their family histories by researching and memorializing them. While Jewish gene-alogists make their own decisions about what honoring their family his-tory looks like, the researcher does not make these decisions in isolation. Rather, Jewish genealogists participate in a shared religious framework of intimate and authoritative nostalgia in interpreting these materials. Many Jewish genealogists describe their work as being in line with Jew-ish memorial activities, literary forms, and historical accounts, in order to find language appropriate to their lived religious experience. Others view their longing for the past and their recovery of it as a "spiritual journey" that would provide them their own authoritative place in Jew-ish history.

Hobby, Commitment, or Mitzvah

In contrast to the explicitly theological purpose of the Latter-day Saints' genealogical research, the goal of which is to baptize the deceased by proxy and reunify family members in the afterlife, Jewish genea-logical research is not an officially recognized religious practice with implications for salvation. Yet, like other American spiritual pursuits, genealogical research, while appearing to be individualistic, connects practitioners to a broader imagined community that includes deceased ancestors, living relatives, and fellow genealogists. While the origins of American spirituality are traditionally found in Protestant traditions, science, and philosophy, the spirituality of Jewish genealogists provides an alternate genealogy for American spirituality itself, one that draws upon older Jewish practices, literary forms, and historical accounts.[12] While popular American conceptions of spirituality depict it as a uni-versal and individualistic quality related to belief, awe, or ineffable metaphysical experiences, many American Jews understand spiritual-ity as a quality of personally meaningful religious *practices*, including markedly Jewish practices.[13] In identifying their work as a "spiritual practice" with origins in Jewish traditions, Jewish genealogists argue that American spirituality is not just a variation of Protestant practices—as is commonly assumed—but can be authentically Jewish, too.

In the 1970s, Jewish genealogists took cues from their Latter-day Saints counterparts while simultaneously distancing themselves from what was seen as the Saints' outlandish theology regarding conversion of the dead. Journalist Dan Rottenberg explains in his 1977 *Finding Our Fathers: A Guidebook to Jewish Genealogy*, the first American Jewish genealogy manual, "Each time I have uncovered the name of one of my long-forgotten ancestors I have been filled with the mystical feeling that I was indeed rescuing that ancestor—not from hellfire, perhaps, but from oblivion."[14] Here Rottenberg builds on traditional Jewish ideas that saying kaddish, the mourner's prayer, and otherwise memorializing the dead provide salvation for the deceased, even elevating the soul of the deceased in heavenly realms. As Jewish genealogists have searched for their own language to articulate the meaning of genealogy, the fact that it is not a traditional religious rite allows them a greater freedom of interpretation of their practices as a form of lived religion, including references to biblical genealogies, traditional mitzvot, and spiritual journeys.

Jewish genealogy manuals routinely reference the genealogies in Genesis—long lists of who "begat" whom—to legitimize the Jewishness of the practice of genealogy. As Arthur Kurzweil, the Orthodox educator, declares, "Genealogy has always been an important topic within Jewish tradition. . . . We find genealogy in the very first chapters of the Bible itself, and genealogy can be seen as playing a part in the lives of Jews from ancient times to the present."[15] Jo David, a rabbi ordained by the transdenominational Academy for Jewish Religion, goes so far as to describe the list of the descendants of Adam and Eve as "a blueprint for modern genealogists."[16] While Jewish genealogists perform a very different kind of genealogy than the genealogical lists in Genesis, references to biblical models identify genealogy as a traditional religious activity.[17]

The contemporary practice of Jewish genealogy also builds on traditional Jewish understandings of honorable lineages. Yikhus, the Ashkenazi term for pedigree, primarily referred to one's descent from well-known rabbis or from an illustrious family and served as a measure of one's worth on the marriage market.[18] (In some Orthodox circles, yikhus continues to operate in this way.) While some genealogists see themselves continuing the traditions of recording rabbinic lineage, since the late 1970s, many Jewish genealogists have responded to the rise of social history and a growing interest in the history of less illustrious figures by valorizing more humble family histories.[19] In the context of Eastern European nostalgia, American Jewish genealogists find yikhus in proletarian origins more often than traditional lineages do, including reveling in stories of "tough Jews," ancestors who participated in organized crime or performed other misdeeds.

While Jewish traditions provide legitimacy for genealogy as a Jewish practice, contemporary Jewish genealogy is a modern religious activity, best understood in the language of contemporary American religious life. For some genealogists, the hobby is "a spiritual pilgrimage," a religiously meaningful act of self-discovery and connection to tradition. Kurzweil explicitly describes Jewish genealogy as both a spiritual journey and as a mitzvah. He explains,

> The act of looking back on our heritage is a spiritual deed in itself. I am not saying that anyone who does Jewish genealogical research is going to become a traditional, religion-focused Jew. Nevertheless, I do maintain that each person who is doing Jewish genealogical research, whether or not he or she acknowledges it, is responding to an inner yearning for a connection to our heritage.[20]

In Kurzweil's usage, genealogy fits the dual ways that American Jews understand mitzvot, as both obligations and good deeds. It benefits the researcher, but it is also something he must do. Like other activities Americans describe as "spiritual," Jewish genealogy is a leisure activity typically understood as secular and individualistic, but one that provides religious meaning and connects participants to broader communities.

As an Orthodox educator, Kurzweil eagerly points to a specific traditional mitzvot performed by genealogists, connecting genealogical research to specific biblical and rabbinic values: Genealogists honor the elderly and demonstrate respect for others by listening to their stories. They honor the dead by visiting cemeteries. They ask historical questions, emulating the questions of Talmudic rabbis and, according to Kurzweil, inspiring humility. Genealogists engage in "perfecting the art of remembering, which, of course, is a mitzvah in itself," says Kurzweil. Kurzweil sees their attention to the diversity of Jews as inspiring "ahavat Yisrael" (love of the People of Israel), which he explains as toleration of difference among Jews. He likens placing oneself in a family tree to the Jewish liturgical style of invoking the biblical patriarchs Abraham, Isaac, and Jacob. Finally, sometimes, as in Kurzweil's own experience, genealogical research inspires a more traditionally observant lifestyle.[21]

Kurzweil's affirmation of genealogical research as inherently good, in line with Jewish values more broadly and enacting specific biblical and rabbinic obligations, resonates with many Jewish genealogists. He articulates how they instinctively envision their work as a particularly Jewish activity, even when, to outsiders, it may seem parallel to the work of non-Jewish genealogists. A number of Jewish genealogists told me that they "wouldn't think in those words" and might feel more comfortable speaking of "passion" rather than "spirituality," but they affirm that Kurzweil provides language for how some Jewish genealogists feel about their research. American Jewish religion often appears in places that practitioners recognize as deeply meaningful but do not recognize as religious. Kurzweil provides some genealogists with the language to articulate both how genealogy is meaningful for them as individuals and the value they see it contributing to their families, communities, and the Jewish people.

Kurzweil is not the only genealogist to use the language of mitzvot. Chicago attorney Leonard Kofkin reflected on decades of family history research by asking, "Was the construction of the Kofkin Family Tree a hobby, a commitment or a mitzvah? Given such a choice, the answer is, 'yes.'" Kofkin identifies his family history work as a mitzvah because it preserves family information as a "gift" for future generations. It also encourages living relatives to feel a "renewed appreciation of 'family,'" even bringing together cousins who had not seen each other for forty years. "Is that not also a mitzvah?" he asks rhetorically.[22] For Kofkin, a mitzvah is a good deed that makes one feel good about one's family, one's history, and the future, as well as being an obligation to family and a broader Jewish community. Here, mitzvot are identified by emotional intimacy, inculcating longing for relationships with the living and the dead. Additional ritual practices, such as saying kaddish for the dead, are not required for genealogy to be the performance of a mitzvah.

Both Jewish and non-Jewish genealogists commonly create relationships with deceased ancestors and living relatives they "discover" by identifying recurrent family traits.[23] Learning about one's family becomes a window into learning about oneself. This emphasis on personal meaning and self-exploration is characteristic of the "seeker religion" that came to the fore in the late twentieth century, focusing on self-discovery as a path to a richer, more meaningful life. Articulating family traits serves as a way to shed light on the genealogist's own identity, a journey of self-discovery that parallels the focus on personal growth in other forms of seeker religion.[24] In *Avotaynu*, Rabbi Ben-Zion Saydman explains that genealogy serves as "a spiritual journey into the lives of those who made us what we are today." Saydman discovered that his great-great-grandfather had been president of Congregation Kesher Israel in Philadelphia, and he draws a direct connection between that ancestor and his parents' involvement in founding a synagogue in Orange County, California. His research culminated in the "spiritual experience" of leading morning services at the Philadelphia synagogue. "Imagine standing in the same spot, in the same shul, saying the same prayers as had your ancestor more than 100 years ago!"[25] Delighting in finding familial connections, Saydman proclaims, "This is *Yiddishe Nakhes* (Jewish joy), and it transcends time and space."[26] While "nakhes" is generally used to refer to the pride elders take in their descendants, Saydman uses it both to invoke his ancestors' imagined pride in their descendants and inverts it to express his own pride in his ancestors' accomplishments. Like other practitioners of seeker religion, Saydman sees historical similarities as spiritual resources.[27] His interrogation of his ancestors' past is an exploration of his own identity, and his spiritual journey is both emotional and imaginative.

In the foreword to his memoir *An Orphan in History: Retrieving a Jewish Legacy*, journalist Paul Cowan writes:

> Many people who might have once explored the nation's physical or economic frontiers are journeying inward: they are the Kit Carsons of the soul. Some adopt creeds that are new to them—Eastern religions, or an all-embracing born-again Christianity. But many, like me, seek to synthesize their Old World heritage with the America that has shaped their consciousness.[28]

For Cowan, family historians are the frontiersmen of the soul, searching for a spiritually meaningful present in the records of their family's past.[29] He explicitly equates a search for one's family history with traditional religious practices. Grounding spiritual exploration—which might be seen as having Protestant rather than Jewish origins—in "Old World" Jewish heritage presents this form of spirituality as both audaciously bold and authentically Jewish. Like the work of American frontiersmen who expanded the borders of the United States by claiming land, the spiritual journey of family history research involves a search for ownership. Like Kit Carson, the nineteenth-century American frontiersman, Jewish genealogists fight to gain a form of possession over their territory, the authentic "Old World heritage" they seek.

The Lineage of American Jewish Genealogy

Genealogy in the United States began as a recording of lineages, in which genealogists traced a few lines of descent with class implications. Over the course of American history, genealogy shifted from white Americans' efforts to assert their racial and national pedigree to a broader effort of many people to assert their ethnic identity in a multicultural national milieu. In the early years of the republic, middle-class Americans created family trees in order to reinforce the significance of the family as a moral, civic, and social unit. Hereditary societies that formed after the Civil War, such as the Daughters of the American Revolution, used family history research to support their ideas of nativism, classism, and racial purity, and to assert their members' unequivocal status as Americans in the face of unprecedented immigration from Eastern and Southern Europe.[30] These nativist and nationalist impulses would continue to motivate some American genealogists though the mid-twentieth century.

At the same time, in the late nineteenth and early twentieth centuries, members of the Church of Jesus Christ of Latter-day Saints came to believe that their missionary work could be continued in the spirit world. Collecting the names of deceased relatives through genealogical research became an essential part of this otherworldly missionary work, in order to identify ancestors who were not Church members and baptize them by proxy, to seal families together in the afterlife.[31] The Genealogical Society of Utah, now officially known as the Family History Department of the Church, was founded in 1894.[32] Latter-day Saints quickly became the premier researchers and collectors of their own and others' genealogy. They have gained the respect and gratitude of other American genealogists, though the purpose of their genealogical research, the sacred ordinances they perform on behalf of the dead, is not without controversy, as many genealogists outside the Church object to the posthumous baptism of their ancestors.[33] Many Jewish genealogists will use Church records for their research but will not upload their own family trees to FamilySearch.org, the Church's genealogy website, out of concern that their ancestors will be baptized.[34]

As general American interest in genealogy increased in the 1920s and 1930s, some American Jews began independently constructing family trees based on living memories.[35] A few decades later, the rise of academic social history expanded scholarly and popular interests in family and local histories, including among Jews. In this context, while serving as a congregational rabbi at a Reform temple in Norfolk Virginia, Malcolm H. Stern completed a doctoral dissertation on early American Jews at Hebrew Union College. Stern began serving as the genealogist for the American Jewish Archives in Cincinnati in 1949 and published *Americans of Jewish Descent*, documenting the earliest American Jewish families, in 1960.[36] While Stern would later be recognized as the "father of American Jewish genealogy," in the 1960s and early 1970s, interest in Jewish genealogy was largely an academic enterprise.

Americans' widespread interest in family history burgeoned with the ethnic heritage revival of the 1970s. In 1976, Alex Haley published his wildly popular book, *Roots: The Saga of an American Family*. An eight-episode, twelve-hour television miniseries based on Haley's story appeared on ABC in January 1977 to much fanfare. Both the book and the miniseries tell the history of Haley's family over six generations, beginning with the story of an enslaved African man. While *Roots* later came under attack for factual inaccuracy, at the time, it led Americans to believe that radical breakthroughs in family history research were possible.[37] Published in the same year that state and local celebrations of the nation's bicentennial across the country offered a multiplicity of American histories, *Roots* encouraged a genealogical fervor and ethnic pride that challenged the master narrative of American history. *Roots* has been credited with a great deal: inspiring African Americans' renewed interested in Africa, furthering interest in "hyphenated American" identities inclusive of a variety of ethnicities, enabling both blacks and whites to see African American history in a sympathetic light, and igniting Americans' interest in genealogy.[38] *Roots* was a symptom as much as a cause of many of these cultural shifts, but it certainly marked a turning point.

Among many others, Warren Blatt, the managing director and former president of JewishGen, credits *Roots* for first inspiring him, at the age of fourteen, to puzzle out relationships in his large extended family.[39]

In the midst of what became known as Americans' "roots craze," as African Americans, white ethnic groups, and others began to think about the particularities of researching their family histories, American Jewish genealogy began in earnest. As an activity that helped Jews think about themselves as an ethnicity, Jewish genealogy was one of a number of activities that helped middle-class Jews deal with their discomfort with whiteness in the late twentieth century. Though early American Jews were often referred to as the Hebrew race (alongside Celtic, Slavic, and Mediterranean "races"), Jewish immigrants entered the country as "free white persons" under American naturalization law. In the mid-twentieth century, upwardly mobile Jews were able to purchase homes in some whites-only suburban neighborhoods, benefitting from redlining that discriminated against African Americans. At the same time, the Civil Rights Movement made Jews more conscious of the privileges of whiteness, while black nationalism and the emergence of multiculturalism provided models of ethnic difference that appealed to American Jews. By the late twentieth century, statements like "I'm not white; I'm Jewish" became "badges of pride, not shame."[40] Jewish genealogy helped Jews—especially white Ashkenazi Jews—think about themselves as a discrete biological unit in terms of ethnicity and heritage, while papering over discomfort with the privileges of whiteness. For many American Jews, whiteness is unsatisfying on its own terms, and genealogy provides a means of articulating Jewish distinctiveness.

A year after the premier of *Roots*, in April 1978, NBC broadcast the four-part, 9.5-hour miniseries *Holocaust: The Story of the Family Weiss*. *Holocaust* was clearly intended to be a Jewish parallel to *Roots*, drawing comparisons between enslavement of African Americans and the destruction of European Jewry in the Holocaust in the two family dramas.[41] Some Jewish genealogists would go on to liken the challenges of tracing the fate of family members during the Holocaust to African Americans' search for the history of enslaved ancestors, the origin of the roots movement. The Holocaust, like the trans-Atlantic slave trade, "created voids in Jewish family histories that are difficult to fill because certain practices separated or eradicated families," writes comparative literature scholar Rachel Leah Jablon.[42] The comparison between Holocaust genealogy and African American genealogy places Jewish genealogy within the context of a distinctively American practice, identifying both African Americans and Ashkenazi Jews as American minorities who have suffered trauma.

In 1977, the same year as the *Roots* miniseries, Rottenberg published the first American Jewish genealogy manual. *Finding Our Fathers* did much to establish Jewish genealogy as a distinct category, beginning to identify the ways that Ashkenazi genealogy required particular research methods, language skills, and historical and religious background. Explaining the need for a manual specifically devoted to Jewish genealogy, Rottenberg described the genealogists' exploration of Jewish history in lurid terms:

> We are now ready . . . to plunge deeper into the past, and this excursion will inevitably take us into that dark, strange, confusing and very exciting land known as the Diaspora. Just as a tourist is likely to be left behind on a safari if he shows up wearing a fedora and loafers instead of a pith helmet and swamp boots, so you are likely to get lost in the Diaspora if you're unprepared.[43]

Caught up in the roots craze, Rottenberg's excitement was palpable. An implicit allusion to Haley's saga of African American history and identity-making, published the year before, might be found in Rottenberg's description of genealogy as a safari in a "dark" land, referencing a romantic vision of colonial Africa. The European diaspora would be to Jews what Africa was to Haley. Claiming Europe as an exotic, pre-modern past allowed American Jews to assert that they were other-than-white. Along with providing practical tips on Jewish genealogy research—the "pith helmet and swamp boots"—Rottenberg's book and later manuals introduced would-be genealogists to the prevailing sentiments that guide this research, helping both authors and readers establish themselves as experts on family and Jewish history.

Around the country, Jews who read Rottenberg's manual were "bitten by the genealogy bug," as genealogists say. Jews interested in genealogy began to assemble—physically, in literary publications, and on the developing Internet. They helped each other learn how to research their family histories, systematizing the activity by developing organizations and publications through which they could share knowledge about what techniques to use, what information was available, and how to access and use it. The popular excitement about ancestry sparked by *Roots* was "an opportunity not to be missed," an early Jewish genealogist later explained. In 1977—the same year the *Roots* miniseries and Rottenberg's manual appeared—surgeon Neil Rosenstein and archivist and LGBT community organizer Stephen Siegel founded the first Jewish Genealogical Society (JGS) in New York, and Siegel and Kurzweil published the first issue of *Toledot*, the first Jewish genealogical journal, named for the biblical Hebrew word for "generations" or "descendants." Both the organization and publication served to legitimize and professionalize Jewish genealogical research by institutionalizing and standardizing what had been an individual practice.[44]

As Jewish genealogists organized themselves, they held their first conference in 1981.[45] Conference-goers encouraged each other to create local JGSs when they returned to their hometowns, and by 1987 thirty such groups existed throughout the United States. Meanwhile, Sallyann Amdur Sack, a clinical psychologist, and Gary Mokotoff, a software engineer, founded *Avotaynu: The International Review of Jewish Genealogy* in 1985. The journal, Sack told me, helped Jewish genealogists feel that they had that central piece of American religion, "a community . . . that they could participate in."[46] These organizational efforts heartened Jewish genealogists, who found others who shared their interests and encountered similar challenges, guiding those "lost in the Diaspora," in Rottenberg's words. They shared their frustrations with the difficulties of acquiring information in ancestral homelands, now communist countries, and compared techniques for acquiring information from beyond the Iron Curtain.

At the same time, genealogy in general began to develop its digital presence, as the field grew alongside the Internet. JewishGen, today Jewish genealogy's primary online presence, began with a dial-up bulletin board that Susan King created in 1987, initially drawing about 150 participants.[47] King had a degree in communications, and as she later told me, she had been firmly inculcated with Marshall McLuhan's dictum that "the medium is the message." She was one of the first to realize the Internet's potential to shape genealogical research and create like-minded communities of genealogists. In 1989 through the early 1990s, King created a bulletin board, electronic mailing list, and newsgroup for JewishGen, making the forum accessible to individuals all over the world through a variety of electronic media. Interest in Jewish genealogy paralleled technological advances, allowing genealogists to create far-flung communities. At the forefront of these developments, King was drawn to building JewishGen because it drew on her background in broadcast communications and marketing and her personal interest in her family history. "The Internet was new, and nobody knew what was going to happen," King told me. "The Internet kind of guided us. . . . We just kind of rode right on the wave," she said.[48] The JewishGen website was created in 1995, and the first online databases were accessible a year later.[49]

As they connected online with others who shared their interest, Jewish genealogists began to feel like a community. "When I was growing up, I felt like the last person on the block to join in" any trend or activity, King told a journalist, and she worked to unite the disparate group. Sack told me that King helped Jewish genealogists "feel that they were part of a team," a community with an important shared purpose.[50] King called JewishGen the "first bringing together of the Jewish people since we left Egypt."[51] King may be alluding to the Jewish tradition that the souls of all future Jews were present at the revelation at Sinai.[52] Her use of this story connects Jewish genealogy to the concept of an eternal Jewish people and suggests the existential and theological significance of Jewish genealogy.

In the 1990s and early 2000s, Americans' interest in genealogy grew rapidly. The Internet allowed genealogists to share their findings, and the digitization of records made research easier. In 1995, four in ten American adults were at least somewhat interested in genealogy, and seven percent of Americans said that they were involved a great deal in tracing their lineage. According to that study, conducted by Maritz Marketing Research for the journal *American Demographics*, adults across all age and wealth brackets were interested in researching their genealogies, though the middle-aged and those with more disposable income showed the most interest—not surprisingly, as genealogy is a leisure activity that can take up as much time and money as one allows.[53]

Jewish genealogy burgeoned in the 1990s, aided by advances in technology and the fall of the Soviet Union, which opened up access to records. Genealogical archival research paralleled and often overlapped with the growth of heritage travel, as American Jews began to travel increasingly to their family homelands in Central and Eastern Europe with the opening of international borders.[54] As digitization technologies improved, researchers who remained at home could benefit from the work of those who went abroad, increasing communication and cooperation among researchers.

Connecting Jewish genealogists in the United States and around the world, JewishGen became the most important Jewish genealogical institution in the early twenty-first century. JewishGen includes a series of websites and databases, and it is the digital home for "special interest groups" connecting genealogists focused on particular geographic regions. JewishGen's web pages and databases were primarily created by volunteers working for free. Some researchers, photographers, and transcribers are paid using money raised by Jewish genealogists on the understanding that the resulting work product will remain freely available. JewishGen became a not-for-profit 501(c)(3) organization in 2001. Two years later, it became affiliated with New York's Museum of Jewish Heritage—A Living Memorial to the Holocaust (MJH). The affiliation provided greater financial stability and professionalization for JewishGen. Located in lower Manhattan, the MJH overlooks Ellis Island and the Statue of Liberty, "the symbolic point of entry of the personal research of most American Jews," as well as the literal point of entry for many of their ancestors. At the time, King described the "marriage" of the two organizations as "bashert" (Yiddish for fated, as in a couple meant to be together).[55] Together, these two organizations shape and reflect U.S. Jews' perspective on their ancestors' immigration histories. Like many JewishGen users, MJH draws a connection between the ruptures of early twentieth-century European Jewish immigration to the United States and the destruction of Jewish communities in the mid-twentieth century in the Holocaust. The two organizations complement one another, both focused on interpreting the meaning of the past for the present.

Despite the ideological coherence of the two organizations, the museum lacked the funds, staff members, and technology to keep up with demands on the JewishGen database as it served "a growing and demanding public."[56] In 2008, JewishGen entered into an agreement with Ancestry.com, the dominant for-profit genealogy search website, allowing JewishGen to post some of its databases on Ancestry's site.[57] The resulting uproar was painful for many JewishGen leaders. A number of JewishGen users saw the affiliation with Ancestry as JewishGen "selling out," turning over materials and hard-won knowledge that volunteers had contributed for free to a for-profit organization that requires a paid subscription to access its databases. JewishGen also appeared to be "selling out" to non-Jews—Ancestry is owned by Latter-day Saints—and seemingly de-Judaizing the project of Jewish genealogy.

Irate genealogists sent the director of the Museum of Jewish Heritage "nearly incoherent, even threatening messages" before it was made clear that JewishGen's databases would remain free to its members.[58] But more than money was at stake in Jewish genealogists' objections to JewishGen's partnership with Ancestry, though that was certainly important. As a Jewish heritage institution, JewishGen represents a Jewish community, and Jewish communities demand that their members be Jewish. The relationship with Ancestry seemed to threaten the boundaries and self-definition of this religious community. Defending the partnership in *Avotaynu*, Sallyann Sack carefully explained that the merger was "one of those delightful win/win situations."[59] With access to Ancestry's databases, Jewish genealogists would have the potential to discover more family connections, and Ancestry users would have some reciprocal access to JewishGen's resources, but the JewishGen website would maintain its pre-partnership appearance, with only the addition of a small Ancestry logo. Broadening access to resources, Sack asserted, would not destroy the singular tone of this broad but distinctive community.

As American Jewish genealogy has continued to develop, it has continued to grow alongside the Internet and other technologies. As genealogy becomes increasingly popular and seemingly more accessible—as home DNA kits become cheaper, more people input family trees on genealogy websites, and an increasing number of records become available online—newcomers to Jewish genealogy often think they can pursue Jewish genealogy on their own. But many people find themselves turning to Jewish genealogy communities for help interpreting the data they collect or advice on pursuing further leads. As it has since its beginnings, rather than simply encouraging atomization as one might expect, the Internet continues to enable collaboration and community-building among Jewish genealogists. In supporting the work of Jewish genealogists, the Internet and other technologies become tools of religion, supporting sacred relationships and enabling the acquisition of existential meaning.

Write Your Family History *Now*!

As genealogists seek authentic and meaningful family histories, they make choices at every turn—what lines to follow, how to acquire information, how to record it, how to interpret it, and how to share that interpretation with others. Sociologist Eviatar Zerubavel explains, "relatedness is not a biological given but a social construct," and the assembly of that construct is revealed by the work of genealogists.[60] In researching and compiling their family histories, genealogists become arbiters of history, constructing Jewish history even as they uncover it. As spiritual seekers, they frame their research in terms of narratives that hold personal meaning.[61] Genealogy functions as American Jewish religion because it invests authority in individual researchers, not in spite of it. Like other spiritual seekers, Jewish genealogists engage in the religious activities of relating individual stories to group experiences, arriving at "their own understandings of truth in a supportive and negotiated context."[62] The tension between individual and communal authority in Jewish genealogy parallels such tensions in other forms of American religious activity.[63]

To some extent, authors of genealogy manuals must establish themselves as experts to be trusted by their readers. Yet even as they guide novice family historians, authors of Jewish genealogy manuals often express their own lack of credentials, placing authority back in the hands of the reader. In the first American Jewish genealogy manual, Dan Rottenberg explains his book's origins: "I found myself wishing someone would write a guidebook for Jewish genealogists. I thought about that some more and wondered, 'Why shouldn't I write it?'" But Rottenberg brings himself up short:

> There was, in fact, a good reason why I shouldn't. Ideally, a book on Jewish genealogy should be written by a scholar or a professional genealogist or an expert on Judaica, and I am none of these. I am simply a journalist

who happens to be Jewish and who enjoys tracing his ancestors in his spare time.[64]

Rottenberg's self-deprecation aligns him with the novice reader, establishing the intimacy of shared ignorance. Likewise, decades after Jewish genealogy had become an established field, Jo David describes her manual, *How to Trace Your Jewish Roots*, as "different from all other Jewish genealogy books" because it is "written for someone like me—a real beginner."[65] While this actually makes David's book typical of the genre, her claim is still necessary. Authors' self-deprecation helps readers understand that the authoritative genealogist is one who both upholds communal research standards and who feels a connection with his or her family history, not necessarily someone with particular credentials.

In searching for narratives that "feel right," Jewish genealogists often select a particular lineage of immigration stories. Genealogists engage in "social norms (and therefore parts of particular social traditions) of remembering and forgetting."[66] While American Jewish genealogical organizations may include members of various backgrounds, they are dominated by Ashkenazi Jews who focus on Eastern European origins. For instance, Schelly Dardashti, creator and moderator of the popular Facebook group "Tracing the Tribe," began her genealogy research by searching for her husband's Persian Jewish family, but members' posts in her Facebook group are overwhelmingly about Ashkenazi history. Moreover, Ashkenazi Jews are drawn to family histories of Eastern Europe rather than Western Europe. Jo David writes that she identifies strongly as the granddaughter of Eastern European immigrants, as she is on her mother's side, even though her great-grandparents on her father's side were German Jews who immigrated earlier than the Eastern Europeans. "For some reason," she writes, "the German part of my heritage has no emotional pull on me. I identify completely through my maternal grandparents' immigrant experience and cherish that link to the past."[67] David explains this identification by way of her closer relationship with her mother's parents, their greater Jewish observance, and their "exotic" Old World ways. That is, these are ancestors who represented "real Judaism." They also align more closely with common depictions of American Jewish ancestry. Through privileging some lineages over others—including some forms of Ashkenazi heritage over others—tracing one's ancestors becomes a means of finding oneself within a larger group narrative and making the narrative one's own.

Perhaps because they are people who claim authority for themselves even as they renounce it—and often do so without professional training—Jewish genealogists have their share of detractors, particularly academic historians. Writing in *Commentary* in 1980, a young professor named Jonathan Sarna provided a scathing review of Arthur Kurzweil's *From Generation to Generation*.[68] Sarna would go on to become one of the most prominent historians of American Jews, widely acclaimed by laypeople—not least Jewish genealogists—as well as academics. But in *Commentary*, he calls into question the entire genealogical project. He baldly labels American Jews' search for their ancestral pasts "narcissism projected backward in time."[69] In response to a reader's defense of Jewish genealogy, Sarna continued, "The theory that narcissistic interest in personal roots will magically stimulate interest in Jewish history . . . remains to be proved."[70] His critique of Jewish genealogists is in line with critiques of other forms of seeker religion in the 1980s. In their 1985 book *Habits of the Heart*, sociologist Robert Bellah and his coauthors made young nurse Sheila Larson an infamous example of religious vacuity and self-absorption for, in a moment of whimsy, naming her religious beliefs "Sheilaism" after herself.[71]

In his censure of Jewish genealogists, Sarna, like Bellah and his coauthors, overlook the ways that family histories and spiritual journeys connect individuals to a larger imagined community. Today Sarna regularly speaks at Jewish genealogy conferences and has appeared as a Jewish history consultant on Henry Louis Gates's genealogy television show, *Finding Your Roots*. Nonetheless, Sarna told me that he largely maintains the views of his 1980 review.[72] Four decades after his review, however, Jewish genealogists have repeatedly made the case that they use family history research to explore broader themes in Jewish history, including the structure of Jewish families and communities, Jewish migration and settlement patterns, and the study of Jewish surnames. Linda Cantor, a retired teacher who served as president of the Jewish Genealogical Society in New York, explained:

> It's not just that we're looking for names on a family tree. . . . As you get
> involved you get interested in reading about the history of what was going

on in Europe. What were their lives like? Most of us don't have pictures of the people, but we can look at the towns. We are in contact with other people whose families come from there [and] some of them have photographs. It just becomes this quest to really know our history beyond our own family.[73]

Cantor recognizes that family histories are made meaningful by being placed within larger narratives of Jewish history. As Tammy Hepps told me, "the larger narrative of Jewish history is also enriched by having our individual family narratives as examples."[74] "The work of historians isn't wrong—it is merely incomplete," Hepps writes.[75]

Moreover, after the fall of the Soviet Union, Jewish genealogists did much to open up archives that contained material on Jewish history. Jewish genealogists routinely ask academic Jewish historians—including Sarna—to speak at their meetings and conferences. They are often an enthusiastic non-academic audience for Jewish historians' books. Nonetheless, academic historians' bias against genealogy persists, even as postmodern academics question the futility of aspiring for objectivity and as much of genealogical work has become more thoroughly researched and better documented.[76] Genealogy provokes the ire of academic historians in a way that other pastimes do not, because it raises the central questions of who is authorized to interpret history and who determines what is worthy of interpretation. The defensiveness of specialists, who instinctively bristle in the face of apparent amateurs encroaching upon their intellectual territory and raising uncomfortable questions about the value of their training, plays a large part. Genealogists guided by a sentimental or experiential approach are not bad academic historians, failing to actualize an objective history; they have different goals. While academics generally seek a broader view, placing primary sources in an expansive historical context, genealogists generally focus on the personal, familial, and communal meanings of their primary sources.[77]

Some Jewish genealogists are working to make genealogy more appealing to academics. The International Institute for Jewish Genealogy (IIJG), located at the National Library of Israel at the Hebrew University of Jerusalem, aims to transform Jewish genealogy into "a recognized field of academic investigation, within the realm of Jewish Studies." Its efforts to remake public perception of Jewish genealogy, including encouraging genealogy courses at the university level, have, to date, been an uphill battle.[78] (In contrast, Brigham Young University's History Department offers both family history courses and offers the only bachelor's degree in Family History/Genealogy in North America.[79]) But academic recognition is not the goal of all—or even most—genealogists. Jewish genealogists encourage each other to publish and present their material in a variety of ways, both formally and informally. They remind each other to consolidate their findings in a binder, on a website, or in a self-published book to share with their families, other genealogists, and any other interested parties (say, a researcher studying Jewish genealogists; I thank the many genealogists who generously shared their books with me). When family members ask to see the material that genealogists have gathered, says Massachusetts-based professional genealogist Eileen Polakoff, "Sometimes we answered, 'When I'm finished,' but in our heart of hearts, we know that the work will never really be finished."[80] Genealogists remind themselves to compile and share their work because doing so transforms the work from an individual hobby to participation in a familial and communal narrative. This transformative moment, connecting individual interests to communal values, is the work of religion.

New York-based professional Jewish genealogist Avrum Geller explains that Jewish genealogists owe it to their ancestors to publish their material: "Publishing brings your relatives back to life, gives them immortality, and is a gift that will last a lifetime and beyond."[81] The language of bringing relatives back to life and giving them immortality is not incidental. This is sacred work that has an effect on the dead as well as the living and the yet-to-be-born. Compiling their research material allows genealogists with a wide variety of religious and non-religious identities and practices to place themselves within communities consisting of past, present, and future relatives and other Jews.

Genealogists remind each other that they must resign themselves to sharing necessarily incomplete research. Mike Karsen, a professional genealogist and past president of the JGS of Illinois, drives this point home with the emphatically urgent title of his public talks: "Write Your Family History NOW!"[82] The flexibility of online publication suits the ongoing nature of genealogy. "With genealogy we are dealing with something that may never be *done* in the same way that a needlepoint pillow is done," says Polakoff, and a website provides the flexibility to reflect new information gleaned about family history as genealogists discover new facts about living family members. "A family history website is a living thing," she explains. "You are only limited by your imagination."[83] This "living thing" is the ongoing work of religious experience, a continual recreation of family history narratives fueled by longing for the past.

Building upon the similarities between the work of curators and genealogists, each shaping a narrative, Steven Lasky created the online Museum of Family History, which includes virtual "exhibits" on family stories, genealogy research, and Jewish history created by Lasky and other contributors. The website includes floor plans in which he lays out the exhibits as if they existed in a physical museum. As Lasky explained to me, "A museum is an institution that displays the best a culture has to offer." Placing a family history in a museum "elevates an object, a material object to a certain status. . . . By creating this museum as a museum, I'm saying that each person who wants to participate has a way of honoring their own family."[84] For Lasky, engaging in the traditional mitzvah of honoring one's ancestors means to put them on a virtual pedestal, an act that gives honor and authority to both ancestors and descendant.

The work of digital media developer and Jewish genealogist Tammy Hepps also underscores the importance of curation as a central feature in genealogy. Hepps is the creator of Treelines, family history software that shifts the focus of display from family trees—lines of ascent, descent, and relation—to the family stories and material artifacts that inspire genealogists.[85] As one enthusiastic user of Treelines said, Hepps is "showing us something new: how to take the 'dry' documents that we are researching and reveal the vibrant, living people they represent."[86] Like Lansky, Hepps describes the genealogist's work as a deliberate act of arranging and presenting the past in ways that provide meaning in the present. In a blog post, Hepps draws together themes from Lin-Manuel Miranda's acclaimed musical *Hamilton* and his first musical, *In the Heights*—"Who lives, who dies, who tells your story" and "If not me, who keeps our legacies?" Hepps views these lines as a "call to arms." She asks, "Who will write our ancestral communities back into the narrative? Everyday people like Usnavi [the protagonist of *In the Heights*].

Figure 2.1. Image from Treelines family history story, "How the Yorkers Immigrated to Philadelphia" by Tammy Hepps. Used with permission of Tammy Hepps.

People like us."[87] For Hepps, genealogy is a personal obligation and an act with political consequences, allowing her to write her ancestors into mainstream historical narratives.

Searching for a meaningful emotional connection to the past, some Jewish feminists understand genealogy as a way to elevate female ancestors. Samantha Katz Seal, who is both a genealogist and a scholar of English literature, explained to me that her work is "a way of trying to write women back into the record." Unlike other types of historical records, in which women may not appear, the family tree is "one record that women can't be taken out of and can't be rendered unimportant in."[88] This view is in line with Esther Broner and Naomi Nimrod's classic Jewish feminist text, *The Women's Haggadah*, based on a 1976 women's seder and first published in *Ms.* magazine. *The Women's Haggadah* exhorts readers: "Who are our mothers? / Who are our ancestors? / What is our history? / Give us our name. Name our genealogy."[89] For feminist genealogists, as for Lasky, the authority of the genealogist as researcher has the power to validate the subject of study as well—which in turn provides meaning and shared authority to the researcher.

Like other genealogists, Jewish feminists find a narrative that resonates for them, focusing on strong female ancestors who in some ways resisted the patriarchal confines of their times. Marla Raucher Osborn, a former California lawyer who now lives in Europe and researches her family history full-time, focuses her research on Rohatyn (now Rogatin), Ukraine, the birthplace of her last living grandmother. She told me:

> She was quite a strong woman, a feminist, a traveler, a Communist her whole life. . . . Even though I had the least amount of information on that part of the family, that was the part of the family I identified with the most. The women were all very well educated—they were European-born and educated.[90]

Osborn focuses on a particular grandmother's line because these bold, educated women are ancestors she can make part of her own self-narrative. Likewise, Ann Goodsell, a professional editor, writes about her affection for Clara, a distant relative who helped Goodsell's grandfather establish himself in the United States. Goodsell's reflection on Clara echoes the feminist haggadah:

> Clara, my first cousin three times removed, has become part of the private cosmology I share with my sisters. We've adopted her as a point of entry into the past, a means of claiming our share of the profound commonplace. She reassures us that forgetting isn't obliteration, that the past still exists and is recoverable from a card catalogue or microfilm carousel or website somewhere.[91]

Goodsell continues, "Women probably vanish from memory a little bit faster . . . because their lives are rarely simple tales. Embedded, intricate, they lack that crucial and compelling narrative line."[92] Feminist-oriented genealogy aims to transform traditional narratives of Jewish longing for the past. It recognizes the power of the researcher to shift the traditional male-oriented narrative. But feminist genealogies can be less overtly subversive than one might think, especially if they simply insert women into pre-existing historical narratives. Rather, feminism and Jewish genealogy can fit neatly together, highlighting the researcher's emotional connection to her ancestry. The radical change may happen within individual and familial memories.

A Permanent Memorial to Them

As Jewish genealogists build their emotional connections to their family histories, many see their work as Holocaust memorials, fulfilling the traditional Jewish mitzvah of memorializing deceased ancestors. Incorporating genealogy into the framework of memorials challenges our conceptions of both "public" and "memorial" and highlights the emotional and religious functions of memorials. In contrast to the well-funded, highly visible Holocaust museums and public monuments that dot the American landscape and have attracted much critical attention, the memorial work of genealogists consists of private, small-scale affairs, sometimes shared with a select group of family and friends online or through self-published books.[93] Nonetheless, many Jewish genealogists understand their research into family lines decimated by the Holocaust as concrete and significant markers of family histories, even when they exist solely in private records. Holocaust-related genealogy may encompass not only the research of Holocaust victims, but also the research of older relatives whose communities would later be destroyed by the Holocaust, as well as connections forged with living relatives related by branches of one's family tree cut off by the events of World War II and only rediscovered by genealogical research. Many Jewish genealogists consider the archival memorialization of Holocaust victims and their family lines, and the connections these lines lead to among living relatives, to be a religious obligation.

In *Getting Started in Jewish Genealogy*, Gary Mokotoff and Warren Blatt explain that every Jewish family with roots in Central and Eastern Europe—that is, the majority of American Jews—has relatives, however distant, who were murdered in the Holocaust. They elaborate: "Most of your family members murdered in the Holocaust died without a tombstone or gravesite to mark their passing. . . . Placing them in your family tree documents that they once lived; it is a permanent memorial to them."[94] For Mokotoff and Blatt, a genealogist's notes on paper or in a digital record are a "public monument," akin to a physical structure that can withstand the test of time. Likewise, Arthur Kurzweil writes of collecting the names and details of more than a hundred relatives killed in the Holocaust: "There are no graves for these cousins of mine, no memorials. My family tree was their memorial. I wanted the family to know them and to remember them."[95] For Kurzweil, as for Mokotoff and Blatt, contextualizing victims' family trees fulfills the religious obligation to memorialize ancestors, as does sharing this information with living family members, even if other family members do not appreciate this information. It is the *feeling* of memorializing that largely serves as the memorial itself, along with the acts and small markers that follow from it. In contrast to physical memorials, genealogical records express a "public feeling," not so much by presenting an emotion to the public, but by expressing a shared participation in nostalgic longing for Jewish pasts.[96]

Sometimes the religious memorial of emotion is made tangible in published works. Helen Epstein's memoir *Where She Came From: A Daughter's Search for Her Mother's History* is a literary memorial for her mother's female ancestors in Central Europe, acculturated Jewish women in Czech and German lands whose history was eliminated by the Holocaust. After her mother's death, Epstein wrote:

> There are no Fruchts nor other Jews left and, apart from tombstones in the cemetery, no artifacts. . . . This dearth of a tangible past—people, objects, physical context—with which I had grown up and to which I had become accustomed was made suddenly intolerable by my mother's death. 'To be able to give, one has to possess,' wrote Simone Weil and, as I went about my daily routines, those words gave the twelve-page chronicle that had been lying in my desk a sudden and urgent importance.[97]

Epstein's travels to Central Europe and, even more so, the literary account she produces detailing her female ancestors' pasts and her journey to find them, serve to replace the absence of "a tangible past." Following Simone Weil, Epstein goes on to "possess" not material goods but the feelings evoked by her heritage travel, the nostalgic longing evoked by her physical journey to her ancestral homeland. Epstein's very longing for the inaccessible past makes it her own. Her memoir is the tangible memorial to her ancestors she seeks and an account of her spiritual journey.

While Epstein's memoir is a largely solitary memorial, individuals' emotional memorialization of genealogy need not be disconnected from large institutions or from ritual practices. Some Jewish genealogists submit "Pages of Testimony," records of Holocaust victims' names and biographical data, to Yad Vashem, Israel's Holocaust memorial museum, to be physically housed in the museum's Hall of Names and documented online in the Central Database of Shoah Victims' Names.[98] Some say kaddish on the anniversaries of the deaths of people they "discovered," distant relatives who were victims of the Holocaust and have no one else to say it for them, an act seen as virtuous on the part of the genealogist and of metaphysical benefit to the deceased. Rabbi Norbert Weinberg created an exhibit in the virtual Museum of Family History describing his mother's experience of surviving the Holocaust disguised as a non-Jewish woman under Nazi-controlled Lviv and Warsaw.[99] On his mother's yahrzeit (anniversary of her death), Weinberg posted a link to his Museum of Family History "exhibit" on Facebook.[100] These actions and creations act as memorials of feeling, whether they are physical, digital, or verbal markers of remembrance.

These genealogically driven memorials of feeling are most effective for practitioners when they can include a broader community in their ritual work. In his homemade haggadah used as part of his family's Passover seder ritual, David Mink, a Jewish genealogist in Philadelphia, creatively weaves together his genealogical research and traditional Jewish rituals of memory by including the names of relatives he had traced who died in the Holocaust. Mink highlights the fruits of his research, naming the relatives he has discovered and articulating their connections to the family members gathered at the seder table, as well as where they perished and how old they were. His memorial ritual fits seamlessly into the American seder, which is both endlessly flexible and rich with symbols that can be appropriated for new uses, because the memorial act is already a religious one for Jewish genealogists.[101]

Mink's act of remembrance becomes tangible as he converts the act of drinking the fourth cup of wine, an integral part of the traditional seder, into a genealogical ritual. While the fourth cup of wine normally references Jews' covenant with God and anticipates a messianic redemption, Mink's haggadah reminds participants of their obligations to remember the past. Family members recite, "We will drink the fourth cup of wine to the memory of our family and all of those who perished because their only fault was that they were born Jewish. May their souls be elevated and rise to greater heights, through our actions."[102] Jewish traditions hold that acts done in memory of deceased relatives—saying kaddish, doing mitzvot, and engaging in Jewish text study—elevate the souls of the deceased in the afterlife. While Mink references future actions, it is primarily the act of memory here that elevates relatives' souls.

Finally, some Jewish genealogists also work to remove the names of Holocaust victims from what are seen as inappropriate memorials. Some Latter-day Saints' desire to offer salvation to the dead and to conduct the Church work of proxy baptisms have led them to gather names of the dead indiscriminately from other vital records, including records of Holocaust victims, which are easily acquired in government records.[103] In 1994, Jewish genealogists learned that the names of Holocaust victims and other deceased Jews were listed as baptized and sealed in the Church's International Genealogical Index (IGI). In an exchange of letters with Church Elder J. Richard Clark, Gary Mokotoff writes, "Baptism is a Christian ceremony that is particularly repugnant to Jews. It reminds us of the centuries of persecution against Jews where our ancestors were given a choice; be baptized or suffer death."[104] Mokotoff and likeminded Jews see the posthumous baptism of Holocaust victims as a desecration, a further indignity imposed upon them in death.

Following Clark's and Mokotoff's correspondence, Mokotoff and other Jewish leaders worked to persuade Latter-day Saints to change their policies regarding baptisms. In May 1995, representatives of the Church signed an agreement to remove all Holocaust victims' names from the IGI and to discontinue baptisms of deceased Jews who were not direct ancestors of Church members by requiring permission for posthumous baptism from the closest living relatives of any deceased individual who died within the last 95 years.[105] In 2012, this rule was changed to 110 years.[106] Nonetheless, the issue remains "the controversy that won't go away," as Mokotoff says. Jewish genealogists continue to discover names of Jews added to the IGI before the 1995 agreement, and individual Latter-day Saints and local churches continue to add Jewish names in defiance of the official Church position.[107] In early 2012, it was revealed that the parents of Simon Wiesenthal, the late Holocaust survivor and Nazi-hunter, had been baptized. Leaders of the Church apologized and announced that the person who had entered the names into the database had been disciplined.[108] Not long after, the Church admitted that Anne Frank, the most recognizable Holocaust victim worldwide, had been baptized by Latter-day Saints in a church in the Dominican Republic.[109] The Church now employs four full-time staffers who watch the database for additions of names of Holocaust victims and others that should not be added, using lists of Holocaust victims provided by the Simon Wiesenthal Center in Los Angeles. But individual Saints continue to baptize Holocaust victims, and Jewish leaders debate whether the Church is doing enough to police proxy baptisms.[110]

Jews do not believe that the Latter-day Saints' proxy baptisms actually convert the dead. So why are they upset by the baptisms? Some Jews are not bothered by them. As journalist Jeff Jacoby writes in the *Boston Globe*, he finds proxy baptism of his relatives killed in Auschwitz "eccentric, not offensive." In fact, he writes, "I was grateful for any gesture that might help preserve some remembrance of these family members whose lives had been so cruelly cut short."[111] But Jacoby is in the minority. His tolerance and gratitude are drowned out by denunciations by prominent Jews, including famed Holocaust survivor and Nobel Laureate Elie Wiesel, whose own name was entered into the Church registry while he was still alive.[112] Arthur Kurzweil's emphasis on the particular significance of the names of Holocaust victims to Jewish genealogists helps explain their outrage:

> Most people in the world don't know what to do with the Holocaust. But I think we genealogists have found out what to do with the Holocaust. We remember names. When the Nazis rounded up our relatives, they took away their names and gave them numbers. What we genealogists are involved with is taking away the numbers and giving them back their names.[113]

Some Jews criticize the proxy baptisms because they appear to be taking away the Holocaust victims' membership in the Jewish community, just as the Nazis did by replacing the victims' names with numbers. To memorialize is, in many ways, to possess, as Epstein's quote from Simone Weil suggests. Jews object to Latter-day Saints' ritual conversion of the victims because it is an act of ownership over them. In collecting the names of Holocaust victims, building memorials of emotion, Jewish genealogists see themselves as reclaiming the victims, taking them back into the narrative fold of their people. Jewish genealogical memorialization, no less than Latter-day Saints' baptism by proxy, is a religious act that claims an intangible and emotional ownership over the past.

Grandpa Didn't Tell the Truth

As genealogists search for authentic pasts and memorialize their relatives, they, like other historical researchers, must evaluate the truth claims of their sources. In many cases, genealogists find the truth of family stories and archival documents of dubious origins not only in their factual accuracy but also in the feelings of familial connection and longing for the past that they elicit. Just as many religious liberals, including many Jews, find that religious texts and myths may still hold a truth even if they are not factually accurate, some genealogists maintain that inaccurate stories and records have a deeper meaning. Sometimes, genealogy is Jewish religion because family stories are found to be true in some sense, even though they are not factual.[114]

Articles in *Avotaynu* frequently advise readers to bring a healthy skepticism and a critical eye to both historical documents and relatives' oral histories.[115] In the *Avotaynu Guide to Jewish Genealogy*, Harold Rhode, an Orthodox Jew and a retired Pentagon analyst on the Islamic world, advises Jewish genealogists to be skeptical of Jews' recorded past in Eastern European governmental documents. "Registration with the authorities in Eastern Europe invariably meant trouble," he explains. "People, therefore, developed methods to evade taxes and military service."[116] For Rhode, even when records are incorrect or missing, they point to a more enduring truth—an abiding shared nostalgia for imagined Eastern European Jewish history. As a source of truth, this nostalgia functions as a religious ethos.

Similarly, Sallyann Amdur Sack found that her research required her to discard long-held beliefs about family members' characters and assimilate new facts into her conception of her family history. In an article entitled, "Grandpa Didn't Tell the Truth," Sack recounts that she found that her grandfather, who emigrated from Poland to North America, recorded his birthplace as Łódź on Canadian legal records but as Plotsk on his subsequent citizen application in the United States. Though he insisted he came from Plotsk, his ailing brother told Sack that they were from a town he called "Vishkovo." On top of this, though Sack knew her grandfather's surname as Steinsnider, he revealed to her that it had originally been Dubner, explaining that he had "bought papers from a guy named Steinsnider" to escape the Czar's army, as many Russian Jews did to avoid the horrors of conscription into the front lines of the Russo-Japanese War. "Certain that he would not lie to his eldest grandchild," Sack contacted the Polish state archivist to research this newly revealed family name, but the archivist found no evidence that anyone with that name ever lived in Plotsk. Years later, via the Jewish genealogical network, Sack learned of a Dubner family in the Polish town of Pultusk, not far from the town of Wyszków, providing an elegant solution in line with both her grandfather's and his brother's stories. "Old habits die hard," Sack explained, understanding her grandfather's shifting origin story as a continual effort to evade the Russian government, even deliberately misleading his family many decades later.[117] For Sack, the search for her grandfather's true origin involved a re-evaluation of family members' characters and their relationships to her. Every stage involved careful historical research, reevaluations of family stories, and emotional responses to the revised history.

Some Jewish genealogists respond to revising inherited narratives by employing a postmodern evaluation of "truth" that balances ethical obligations to family traditions and factual accuracy, much as postmodern professional historians affirm the value of communal myths and narratives. Manny Hillman, a retired research chemist based in Brooklyn, recounts that he had always been told that his father was born in Graz, Austria, even though the rest of his family came to the Americas from Jerusalem. When he found documentation that his father had emigrated from Jerusalem, he assumed that the documents were wrong—following the guidelines Rhode laid out—but an Israeli cousin affirmed their veracity. Hillman's father had been born in Jerusalem four months after his own father died. He had grown up in an orphanage, visiting his impoverished, widowed mother on weekends. When confronted with the evidence, Hillman's father admitted that he had been born in Jerusalem, not Graz. He had chosen to disguise a traumatic childhood by inventing an alternative personal history, perhaps providing a way to avoid uncomfortable questions. Nonetheless, Hillman recounts, "When my father died, I listed his birthplace as Graz on his death certificate as a tribute to that part of his life that obviously had troubled him."[118] While

Hillman maintains that the "moral" of his story is to approach family legends as well as documents with suspicion, he also offers an ethical model of honoring the stories that have shaped others' lives, regardless of their factual accuracy. Here, to be virtuous is not only to proclaim the truth of uncovered facts but also to honor what has held emotional significance for others and what continues to hold sentimental meaning for the genealogist.

Along similar lines, Arthur Kurzweil advises Jewish genealogists to exercise caution in accepting all family legends as factually accurate without dismissing those that seem incredible. Kurzweil recounts advice he received from Elie Wiesel: "This is very important. You should collect as many stories as you can. Write them down. Save them. You should have a file. Label the folders by name and save the stories. This is very important." Kurzweil responded to the famed Holocaust survivor and author that he did not accept all of the stories as truth. "'What does it matter if they are true?' Wiesel replied, a glimmer in his eyes. 'They're stories!'" That is, genealogists can still find family stories meaningful, even if they are not factually accurate. Eli Wiesel's name lends a hefty weight of authority to this instructional narrative. "Whoever listens to a witness becomes a witness," Wiesel famously said of listening to Holocaust survivors' testimonies, underscoring how seriously he took storytelling.[119] Though the seriousness with which he approached Holocaust testimony and his lighthearted response regarding family stories might seem irreconcilable, Wiesel maintains his belief in the importance of personal narratives and his respect for the storyteller in both contexts.

Elaborating on Wiesel's comment, Kurzweil explains to his readers that while he believes that "claiming things that are false is the worst family history 'sin' possible," the family historian should "record the story, remember it, and even pass it along to the next generation. It is our job to learn the stories, enjoy them, check them out if we can, and perhaps speculate as to how or why the story originated."[120] While Kurzweil advises genealogists to be wary of common Ashkenazi Jewish family legends—such as claiming descent from the biblical King David or Spanish Jews who fled the Inquisition (and thus Sephardi heritage), or relation to prominent figures such as the Baal Shem Tov, the Vilna Gaon, or the Rothschild family—he does not dismiss the significance they can have for the storyteller and the audience. These stories serve to

connect the particular family to the themes of Jewish history and mythology more broadly and to make Jewish history personal. As in the
biblical command to feel as if one had personally left Egypt, making the
Jewish history one's own through family legend is a religious activity. In
this way, family legends function as religious myths; their "truth" is in
the meaning they hold for individuals and families rather than in their
historical accuracy.

In line with his view of genealogy as a "spiritual pilgrimage," Kurzweil, like Hillman, looks for moral lessons in family stories. A family
story has it that Kurzweil's great-great-grandfather once offered a plate
of food to a hungry man who happened to be Emperor Franz Joseph
of the Austro-Hungarian empire, who in turn made his great-great-
grandfather his personal guard. While Kurzweil doubts that the story
is factually accurate—Franz Joseph had policies friendly to Jewish residents and became a Jewish folk hero—Kurzweil maintains that the story
holds meaning for him and his family. It also passes on the lesson of
charity offered without thought of reward. Kurzweil advises genealogists
not simply to dismiss such stories but to "record the story, remember
it, and even pass it along to the next generation," while placing it in
its proper historical context.[121] Once again, genealogists are arbiters of
history, but they can be inclusive ones, interpreting why stories have
been meaningful for their family as well as determining their historical
accuracy.

In recent years, advances in genetics and the increasing ease of genetic testing have also contributed to and challenged Jewish genealogical
research. As religious studies scholars Sarah Imhoff and Hillary Kaell
observe, "gene talk" is "a religiously inflected practice" for Jews, one that
allows them to reflect and expand on traditional Jewish ideas of people-
hood and chosenness.[122] Among other genetic studies concerning the
origins of Jewish populations, several studies have examined the Cohen
Modal Haplotype (CMH), a set of markers found on the Y-chromosome
of many Ashkenazi and Sephardi men who identify as cohanim (plural
of cohen), descendants of the ancient Israelite priestly class. According
to Jewish tradition, cohanim are descended from the biblical Aaron,
brother of Moses. Studies of the CMH have provided evidence for the
genetic relationship of Sephardim and Ashkenazim despite centuries of
separation between these communities. As Imhoff and Kaell explain, for

most Jews, the scientific particulars rarely matter. Instead, such studies are used in the service of "a racialist logic of Jewish identity," emphasizing heritable characteristics and racial identity.[123] Scientific findings are used to uphold beliefs that Jews already maintained, affirming the "reality" of family identification as cohanim and ideas of Jews as a race. Imagined connections between distant relatives, once intangible or inferred through historical primary sources, are now seen upheld through the intimacy of bodily evidence.

In 2001, Jewish genealogist Bennett Greenspan founded Family Tree DNA, the first company to develop the commercial application of DNA testing for genealogical purposes. Previously, such tests had been available only for academic and scientific research.[124] The company originated from Greenspan's own frustration with dead-end paper trails in his family history research. As he told me, he had been interested in family history since he was a boy and began researching his genealogy in the 1970s.[125] In the 1990s, when he reached the end of paper resources, Greenspan contacted University of Arizona Professor Michael Hammer, one of the coauthors of a 1997 Y-chromosome study of cohanim. Hammer agreed to analyze Greenspan's DNA and that of a Buenos Aires genealogist who shared a family name, and he confirmed their genetic relationship.[126] At that point, Greenspan told me, he convinced Hammer to go into business with him, commercializing the DNA research for use by genealogists.[127]

Family Tree DNA and its parent company, Gene by Gene, owned by Greenspan and Max Blankfeld, have grown tremendously, forming partnerships with other genomics research institutions that allowed them access to larger databases and markets.[128] Other companies have followed suit, and individual genetic testing is a rapidly increasing activity, drawing more people to genealogy. Family Tree DNA now offers not only Y-chromosome (Y-DNA) and mitochondrial DNA tests, which test genetic relationships through straight paternal or maternal lines, but also a "Family Finder" test that uses autosomal DNA to trace genetic lines across gender lines.[129] (Greenspan advertised the Family Finder product with the tongue-in-cheek slogan, "Sex doesn't matter anymore."[130]) Family Tree DNA holds the world's largest DNA database for matching Ashkenazi Jewish male Y-DNA samples and, through *Avotaynu*, Mokotoff and Sack have urged Jewish genealogists to register their DNA with

Family Tree DNA in order to consolidate the database of Jewish genetics. "When even a single, unique Jewish male Y-DNA sample goes into a database other than the 'Jewish DNA Central' database, this is a loss for the entire community," they wrote.[131]

Jewish genealogists who are studious researchers often find genetic testing to be a useful tool that complements archival research. Genetic testing is being used to examine family legends, such as a relation to King David or Rashi, the twelfth-century French rabbi. As Mokotoff and Sack recount, DNA testing can confirm—or, more often, refute—family stories that "all persons with my surname are related."[132] Through online connections at MyFamily.com, a site owned by the same parent company as Ancestry.com, Elise Friedman, president of the Jewish Genealogy Society of Maryland, found thirty families with her family name, Palevsky, and she was able to convince four of the families to take DNA tests. "We matched," Friedman told reporter Barbara Pash. "I still have to do the research on how we're related. But the DNA tests put us on the track."[133] Genetic testing is powerful because of its affective quality—users without scientific backgrounds are convinced that the science is true because it provides an emotional moment and, in cases like Friedman's, confirms what they want to hear. Pash relates the emotional moment when Richard Goldman, a former president of the JGS of Maryland, received the results of his genetic test:

> "I said, 'Oh, my God,'" Mr. Goldman says of the results, a surprise to him. They showed that he was of Semitic origin and that, thousands of years ago, his male ancestors lived in the Middle East, roughly the area that is now Israel, Palestine and Jordan, and then migrated. "So my male line is not a Cossack, not Spanish nobility or a Roman general," says Mr. Goldman. "I might have a genetic link to Abraham. I have a connection all the way back to biblical times."[134]

Goldman's reaction demonstrates that genetic studies are convincing and powerful when the authority of science is used to affirm pre-existing narratives, such as the narrative of shared Jewish ancestry and distinctiveness.

Both genetic testing and digitization have allowed more people into the big tent of Jewish genealogy and nostalgia, complicating notions of who is a Jew. The Tracing the Tribe group on Facebook is filled with comments from first-time users who learned from DNA tests that they had some Ashkenazi ancestry—including adoptees and people whose families kept secrets—and asking what to do next. In a 2017 episode of the genealogy TV show *Who Do You Think You Are?* (co-created by Ancestry.com, which features prominently on the show), actress Jessica Biel, coached through digitized records, learns that she has Russian Jewish ancestry. "That's kind of a big deal to not know about!" she exclaims, camera-ready. "That sort of changes everything."[135] As Imhoff writes, these views of Jewish ancestry highlight how Jews and others continue to think of Jewishness in biological terms. While this broadens who is included as a Jew, it also establishes boundaries, narrowing the terms of self-definition for converts to Judaism or those adopted by Jewish families. Biological understandings of Jewishness often serve to support traditional religious and nostalgic understandings of who is a Jew, placing individuals within or beyond the boundaries of established narratives.

In many ways, the history of Jewish genealogy research from the 1970s to the present is a story of increasing institutionalization of an individualistic research experience and of personal meaning-making, a story of shared narratives. But in the early twenty-first century, while more people are drawn to genealogy due to its increasing ease in the era of digitized archives and genetic testing, many new family historians are not joining genealogy groups or even online forums to learn from other researchers. As Dardashti told a reporter, genealogy "has become so much more popular just because there are so many more resources accessible. You can sit at home in your jammies and bunny slippers and connect."[136] Longtime Jewish genealogists committed to communal efforts continue to insist that newcomers who think they can navigate these documents on their own are ignorant of the complexity of Jewish genealogical research.[137] Still, even as technological advances seem to have spurred a return to a more individualistic model, Jewish genealogy continues to be interpreted within the communal frameworks of Jewish nostalgia for the era of immigration.

Since its organizational beginnings in the 1970s, Jewish genealogy has offered an emotional and spiritual experience of Jewish history. Like the haggadah's command for each Jew "to regard himself as if he had gone personally forth from Egypt," Jewish genealogy is both broadly expansive and narrowly personal, as genealogists find their own ancestral legacies through which to lay claim to the past. As in Kurzweil's declaration, "I was born in New York but came out of a shtetl," Jewish genealogists merge ancestral past and individual present through nostalgic longing. Through their research, genealogists create new forms of Jewish lived religion. As they respond to *The Women's Haggadah*'s command to give ancestors their names, they establish their own authoritative place in Jewish history. The emotion connecting them to familial and communal histories is a means to claim ownership over the past and make it one's own.

3

Ghosts in the Gallery

Historic Synagogues as Heritage Sites

In December 1982, journalist and urban critic Roberta Brandes Gratz walked into the dilapidated sanctuary of the Eldridge Street Synagogue on New York's Lower East Side neighborhood for the first time. Years later, she would recall the impact of that first glimpse of the ravages of time on the Moorish Revival interior:

> Pigeons roosted in the attic and flew in and out of missing windows. Dust was so thick on the pews that you could carve your initials in it. Water was pouring through one corner of the roof. Prayer books were left strewn about. Little objects that worshippers long ago had left behind, including crystal drinking glasses, were randomly scattered. Pieces of stained glass from broken windows were everywhere.[1]

Gratz went on to found the Eldridge Street Project, which would restore the 1887 building. Today, docents at the Museum at Eldridge Street—the Project's name since 2007—like to show visitors pictures from around the time of Gratz's first encounter. They hold up large photographs that contrast with the restored synagogue visitors now see around them. The Project left a wall of the synagogue unrestored, so that visitors can not only see but also touch the contrasts between the building's disrepair and its restoration. Museum materials often use Gratz's words to describe that period: "It was as though the synagogue was held up by strings from heaven."[2] That is, it was nothing less than a miracle—divine providence— that the synagogue building survived, that it was found by preservationists, and that it was successfully restored so that visitors can stand in it today. This elegiac narrative of loss and salvation physically includes visitors in the story of the dramatic transformation of the space. The story is a founding myth of lived religion at the Eldridge Street Synagogue. At this site and other historic synagogues throughout the United States, nostalgia for American Jewish immigrant heritage forms the basis of a broad and ever-changing community's emotional connections to the past.

Interest in preserving historic synagogues, the primary architectural sites of Jewishness, began gradually in the 1980s, gained momentum in the 1990s, and continues unabated. These conservation efforts followed—and to some extent grew out of—American Jews' interest in genealogy, which began in the late 1970s. Ashkenazi Jews of Central and Eastern European origin, inspired by the white ethnic heritage movement of the 1970s, turned first to their own family histories in the United States and Europe, then looked outward around them toward the cityscapes where their immigrant ancestors had settled.[3] As these Jews articulated their longing for a particular immigrant heritage, they put their time and money into preserving certain historic synagogues and telling their stories in ways that held meaning for them in the present.[4] From the 1980s to the present, narratives about historic synagogues have become increasingly standardized. Preservationists present nostalgia for Eastern European immigrant histories as a fulfilment of a mitzvah of longing for the past in order to create relationships with Jews past, present, and future. Historic synagogues provide another clear example of the ways in which the fulfillment of the mitzvah of nostalgia is a central aspect of American Jewish religion.

In 2012 and 2013, I conducted short-term ethnographic studies of four historic synagogues, each located in an urban Jewish tourist destination. On the Lower East Side, the Museum at Eldridge Street has used the 1887 synagogue building as a site of public history since 1986, though a small congregation continues to hold Sabbath services there. At the 1763 Touro Synagogue in Newport, Rhode Island, a full-time congregation competes for control of the space with a number of historical institutions. The 1919 Vilna Shul in Boston is preserved by a cultural center and hosts Havurah on the Hill, a prayer group consisting mainly of participants in their twenties and thirties.[5] Finally, the Jewish Museum of Florida in Miami Beach uses the space of two abandoned synagogue buildings constructed in 1929 and 1936. At each site, I shadowed docents giving tours of the buildings, attended public events, and spent time observing, interviewing, and speaking informally with staff members, visitors, congregants, and philanthropists.

The four sites I examine demonstrate a range of possible uses and public faces of historic synagogue buildings employing nostalgia for immigrant pasts. Three of the sites were created by Ashkenazi Jews in the late nineteenth or twentieth century. The fourth, the colonial-era Touro Synagogue, was built by eighteenth-century Sephardi Jews of Spanish and Portuguese origin, though its primary occupants throughout its 250-year history have been Ashkenazi. I include Touro Synagogue in this study to demonstrate that the narrative of Eastern European immigrant nostalgia is so strong that it can be applied retroactively to other kinds of sites and other kinds of Jewish histories.

Each of these buildings once served a thriving urban Jewish community, and each congregation shrank as Jews moved elsewhere, generally for economic reasons. A large number of synagogue buildings throughout the United States have been abandoned by their congregations without being preserved for posterity; some are repurposed as churches for new immigrant groups in urban settings. These four synagogues, like others presented as heritage sites, generally owe their historic preservation more to circumstance and geographic convenience for later American Jews than particular historical significance. Some of these historic synagogues also continue to serve as meeting places for small congregations while others do not. There is no apparent pattern that determines continued congregational use. Small Orthodox congregations continue to use spaces at the Museum at Eldridge Street in New York and the Touro Synagogue in Newport, though they are better known as sites of heritage tourism; a small independent minyan (prayer group) borrows the space of the Vilna Shul in Boston; and synagogues of the Jewish Museum of Florida, in Miami Beach is no longer used by a congregation.

Nonetheless, while there is not a pattern to which synagogue buildings are preserved or whether they continue to be used for worship, there is a pattern to how they are presented to the public. Building on the work of anthropologist Talal Asad, who interrogates the "authorizing process by which 'religion' is created," historian Riv Ellen Prell observes that "Judaism is made authoritative through specific sets of relationships and processes."[6] At historic synagogues, the authorizing process of religion is a "shared" rather than "collective" nostalgia. Rather than longing for precisely the same collective image of the past, the multiple constituencies of historic synagogues long for variations on the same thing.[7] Staff members, visitors, congregants, and philanthropists often imagine different variations of synagogues' histories—emphasizing certain immigration narratives or ideas about American religious freedom, for instance—and have different goals for the present. Each constituency participates and competes in the authorizing processes of shared nostalgia that shapes the lived religion at historic synagogues. At synagogues used as heritage sites throughout the United States and around the world, visitors include American Jews of all and no religious affiliations and non-Jewish tourists from throughout the United States and around the world. All of these participants share in creating the dynamic religion of American Jewish nostalgia.

Through the rituals of heritage tourism, organizations instruct visitors in a certain kind of shared nostalgia—not a wish to return to the past, nor even necessarily a desire to revive the past within the present, but an elegiac nostalgia, one that recognizes that changes and improvements have come at a cost, mourns that which has been lost, and retrieves select stories and values as useful for the present. Neither visitors nor staff members at the Museum at Eldridge Street have any real desire to return to the Lower East Side of the early twentieth century—in fact, stories about the neighborhood often emphasize its filth and the grinding poverty of its residents—but they do want to engage in a productive longing for the past. This elegiac nostalgia is a religious practice—an obligatory and praiseworthy mitzvah. Like other forms of religion, this kind of nostalgia for Eastern European Jewish immigrant histories builds on and creates relationships among the living, between the living and the dead, and between humans and the divine. Emotional engagement with the materials of nostalgia provides the basis for sacred relationships that cross spatial and temporal boundaries.

Salvation Stories

Museums make excellent religious sites, or maybe religious sites make excellent museums. Both are places in which stories have the power to "change what people may know or think or feel, to affect what attitudes they may adopt or display, to influence what values they form," as scholar Stephen Weil writes about museums.[8] Religious sites, like museums and memorials, are "archives of public affect, 'repositories of feelings and emotions.'"[9] Growing numbers of contemporary American Jews, in particular, have come to utilize their local Jewish museums as community centers. Jewish museums are "a place to assemble with other Jews, to affirm one's identity, to define one's values, to take stock of the present, and to contemplate the past."[10] With increasing frequency, Jews employ museums as Jewish spaces appropriate for the celebration of weddings, bar mitzvahs, and other life cycle events.

When organizations tell the histories of synagogue buildings, they often employ a narrative like Roberta Gratz's description of her first sight of the crumbling sanctuary of the Eldridge Street Synagogue, a kind of narrative that I call a salvation story. Stakeholders in historic sites—including preservationists, philanthropists, congregants, and visitors—often experience sites as most sacred when they are seen to be in danger of desecration or when they have been saved from desecration.[11] Since nostalgia is a longing for a particular time and place, the renovated and restored historic synagogue, saved from ruin, presents a problem. The ostensibly authentic space of the past is both absent and present. Salvation stories solve the problem by tying together the simultaneous longing to have the site in its original glory, in the nadir of its ruin, and in its restored splendor. Telling salvation stories makes nostalgic longing an active religious force in the present. For American Jews, salvage is a form of salvation.

I describe these narratives as *salvation* stories deliberately. Like traditionally religious notions of salvation, narratives about the preservation of historic synagogues are stories of revival, wholeness, and reclaimed authenticity in the building's second life as heritage.[12] While Jews today tend to use the term *redemption* more often than the term *salvation*, both are longstanding concepts in Jewish theology; salvation suggests a recovery from a deterioration, but redemption does not. As in evangelical Christian narratives of being born again, the story of a historic synagogue's salvation must be told and retold in public settings. Salvation stories rely on allegories, narratives that both affirm and erase the symbol's original meaning.[13] Historic synagogues tell their particular stories, but they stand in for the broader narrative of American Jewish immigration history. Allegories of salvation encourage visitors to feel an emotional connection to the particular synagogue but also, more broadly, to particular American Jewish pasts. Salvation stories of historical synagogues suggest the role of divine providence in the revival of these buildings, which provide religious meaning for American Jews.

Though urban American synagogues were largely abandoned when Jews moved away from immigrant enclaves to the suburbs, in the post-Holocaust era any dilapidated synagogue provides a visual allusion to European synagogues that stand empty, their congregations murdered or displaced by the Holocaust. Since the collapse of the Soviet Union in 1989, interest in European Jewish life has increased exponentially. Jewish heritage tourism has become big business, and audiences who visit U.S. synagogues have become accustomed to associating abandoned synagogue buildings with tragedy.[14] Public historian Ruth Ellen Gruber explains, "The mere fact that a synagogue stands empty of Jews, used as an exhibit or housing an exhibit, may end up being the principal means of conveying a sense of loss: palpable absence may be the most important 'exhibit' on the Holocaust and post-Holocaust period."[15] Even though they have no direct connection to the Holocaust, abandoned American synagogues echo the melancholy of their European cousins. When synagogue buildings acquire a second life as heritage sites in the United States, staff members employ the sorrowful qualities of their salvation stories in the service of nostalgia, which not only mourns but also celebrates the past. The ghosts of the past include Holocaust victims as well as American immigrants.

These salvation stories have political consequences. Since the mid-twentieth century, suburban American Jews have practiced what historian Lila Corwin Berman calls "remote urbanism." When many American Jews left cities for the suburbs, their emotional and political investment in urban spaces "was intensified, not diminished, by urban flight and upheaval."[16] Jewish leaders, including would-be preservationists, asserted that one did not have to live in the city to have a stake in it. Emotional attachment to a neighborhood's history and subsequent preservation efforts were sufficient proof that particular cities, or at least particular neighborhoods, belonged to Jews. All four historic synagogues that I examine are located in neighborhoods that once hosted flourishing Jewish communities. Today, long after Jews have moved out of those neighborhoods—and in most cases, out of the cities altogether—the preservation of these historic synagogues announces that this is still a Jewish space, despite few local Jewish residents.

Figure 3.1. The Jewish Museum of Florida, Miami Beach. Photo by Alexf, 2008. Licensed under CC BY-SA 3.0.

Historic synagogues' salvation stories are political statements not only about legal ownership of a building, but emotional ownership of a neighborhood. The Jewish Museum of Florida is housed in two adjacent synagogue buildings once owned by a single congregation in the South Beach neighborhood of Miami Beach. As Jewish residents aged, "the neighborhood rapidly declined" in the 1980s, the museum's website explains. Crime soared in the wake the 1980 Mariel boatlift, the mass emigration of Cubans, including those released from jails and mental health facilities.[17] As Jews left South Beach, the synagogue was "abandoned and fell into disrepair," and the roof was ripped off by Hurricane Andrew in 1992: "The resulting torrents of water destroyed the ceilings, walls, foundation, decorative plaster moldings and oak floors. The stained-glass windows became the target of vandalism."[18] The building was slated for demolition, to be replaced by an apartment building. Luckily, so the story goes, at just that moment Marcia Jo Zerivitz was looking for a permanent home for her exhibit about the Jewish history of Florida. In 1993, "a wonderful marriage was made" between the vacant synagogue and Zerivitz's collection.[19] This ostensibly fated union affirmed South Beach as a Jewish place just as the neighborhood was attaining prominence as an international tourist destination. The museum both benefited from and hastened the neighborhood's gentrification as an act of religious reclamation.

The salvation story of the 1919 Vilna Shul in Boston also derives from a familiar history of Jews leaving the once-thriving immigrant Jewish neighborhood of Beacon Hill for the suburbs. But the case of the Vilna Shul has an unexpected twist. Rival Jewish institutions nearly succeeded in *preventing* the restoration of the synagogue and its adaptation to a heritage site and Jewish community center. The Vilna Shul's congregation had dwindled to three members by 1985, when its 87-year-old president, Mendel Miller, was mugged while setting up for holiday services. The attack cemented Miller's decision to disband the congregation, sell the building, and give the proceeds to the Israeli charities of his choice.[20]

But when Boston's Jewish community leaders learned of his plans, they rushed to stop him from selling the last remaining Jewish presence on Beacon Hill. "This has always been a Jewish institution and should remain so," would-be preservationists argued. Miller, the president, resentfully told Jewish community leaders that they had no authority over his space. They had never helped him to maintain the building or attract service participants. He griped, "I took care of the shul twenty-three years and no one in the Jewish community helped or was interested. Why should they be interested now?"[21] While Miller believed that the tiny congregation had dominion over the synagogue, preservationists saw the synagogue as the inheritance of a broader, loosely defined local Jewish community.

The battle heated up when it was revealed that a Massachusetts law on proceeds from dissolved charities would direct some of the assets from the sale of the Vilna Shul to the other struggling Orthodox synagogue in Boston, the Charles River Park Synagogue. "The proceeds should go to the living faith," said the lawyer for Charles River Park. Allan Green, the president of the Charles River Park Synagogue, said of the Vilna Shul, "We feel that designating this shell of a building" as a historical landmark has "no fruitful purpose."[22] "Judaism is considered a living religion, for the living," he argued, and turning the Vilna Shul into a museum would only commemorate the dead.[23]

Miller intended to sell the property to a real estate developer who, it was reported, would tear it down and build a parking garage in the now-gentrified neighborhood where parking is always at a premium. While the onetime threat of knocking down the synagogue to build a parking lot is mentioned to visitors who visit the Vilna Shul today, the reason it

Figure 3.2. The Vilna Shul, Boston. Photo by John Phelan, 2012. Licensed under CC BY-SA 3.0.

avoided this fate is rarely mentioned. In fact, the real estate developer sold an ounce of cocaine to an undercover agent. Narcotics agents seized two ounces of cocaine and an unlicensed, loaded semiautomatic pistol from his desk, and his plans to buy the synagogue fell through.[24] Invigorated by the sale's failure, preservationists turned Jewish communal debates into a matter of city politics, and they persuaded Boston's mayor to designate the synagogue's interior as a historical landmark. Opponents spent the better part of a year forcefully lobbying city councilors to veto the mayor's decision. Ultimately, preservationists won the battle.[25]

Today the Vilna Shul is run by Boston's Center for Jewish Culture and is open to visitors and used for community events. It hosts Havurah on the Hill (HOH), an independent group of twenty- and thirty-somethings who meet there for monthly services.[26] Aaron Mandell, a founder of the Havurah (fellowship) explained the appeal of meeting at the Vilna Shul: "When you come in here, you immediately feel like you're a part of Jewish history. I think it's a way to connect to Judaism that's very tangible."[27] In Mandell's view, just entering the historic synagogue allows Jewish visitors to feel a personal connection to Jewish history, echoing other "spiritual seekers" who use history in the service of personal growth.[28] A member of the center's board said, "It's the ghosts of people past, the ghosts of their great-grandparents or great-great-grandparents that really excite these young adults."[29] Ghosts are the symbol of an emotional connection to the past, but they have the power to frighten or command, too; one must listen to them. To heed their call—to perform the mitzvah of nostalgia—is, again, both compulsory and admirable. Still, this space belongs not to the ghosts but to the HOH participants. They are emboldened, not humbled, by engaging with this story of communal ancestors.

At a moment when the Jewish communal establishment worries loudly about the continuation of Jewish communal practices among post-college adults—driven primarily by fears about intermarriage—Havurah on the Hill has received a great deal of praise and financial support from Jewish foundations, particularly Boston's Combined Jewish Philanthropies (CJP). In a *Boston Globe* article that begins, "There are ghosts here," journalist Doug Most explicitly depicts HOH as a response to concerns about intermarriage.[30] Participants and supporters view Havurah on the Hill as the successful outcome of the Vilna Shul's salvation

story, assuaging Jewish communal concerns about young adults' participation in Jewish institutions.[31] The relationship between the Havurah
and the Vilna Shul allows Havurah participants and their financial supporters to comfortably enact longing for the past, mediated and authorized by layers of institutional support. The story of Havurah on the Hill
not only complements but is the culmination of the Vilna Shul's history.

The battle over the fate of the Vilna Shul was a *religious* clash between
the last president of the congregation, Mendel Miller, and other Jewish
communal leaders. The preservationists did not want full-time congregational use of the building, as Miller did. To Miller, the preservationists
demonstrated a personal longing for the past that only came to the fore
when the space was threatened and when it had unquestionably passed
its prime, when they could engage in activist efforts to "save" the building from the evils of real estate development. Miller correctly recognized
that preservationists and their funders did not prioritize congregational
use of this space. For them, elegiac nostalgia, culminating in the work
of Havurah on the Hill, was more poignant and, in some ways, possibly more important than traditional synagogue uses. Jonathan Kraft,
president of the New England Patriots, whose grandfather once led
services at the Vilna Shul, contributed $10,000 to the center's preserva-
tion efforts, saying, "To instill an energy back into a building like this is
unique. . . . It takes on a life of its own."[32] The Vilna Shul has a new but
no less religious role as a historic site where visitors can find personal
and communal meaning through a physical and emotional connection
to a specific Jewish past.

A Synagogue by Any Other Name

Once a historic synagogue is "saved" from destruction, a not-for-profit's
executive director or board of directors chooses how to present the
building to the public. "The 'biography' of memorials—the debates
and controversies around them—might be as important as their form,"
writes literature scholar Svetlana Boym, drawing attention to the shifting ways that memorials are used and understood after their creation.[33]
Throughout my research, I encountered a sizable number of visitors
who appeared to be confused about how a synagogue building could
function as a heritage site. Anticipating this confusion, organizations

overseeing historic synagogue buildings attempt to be as clear as possible about their purposes through their institutional names. In order to do so, some heritage organizations emphasize the term "synagogue" over "museum," which they use to emphasize that theirs is a religious space and a site of meaning for individuals and communities. A sizable contingent of both staff members and visitors perceive a contrast between a "living" synagogue, with a congregation led by a rabbi, and a "dead" museum, a reliquary for ghosts of the past, and staff members want to emphasize that their site falls into the former category. This choice demonstrates that preservationists perceive the site as a religious one and that communicating this is an important part of their efforts.

But while impressions of museums as tombs and reliquaries persist among the general public, museum professionals and museum studies scholars have long argued that museums are not only just as "alive" as any other site of public interaction, but that they are special and even sacred communal sites.[34] "To control a museum," art historian Carol Duncan explains, "means precisely to control the representation of a community and its highest values and truths."[35] Articulating communal truths and values is a religious process, which is why historic synagogues, in combining the symbolic power of both synagogue and museum, function as such powerful sites of communal and religious meaning-making for modern Jews, whether or not they currently house a congregation. Like Mendel Miller's fight with Boston's Jewish communal leaders over whether to preserve the Vilna Shul, debates about what to call historic synagogues are religious disagreements, debates about which of two religious modes will take precedence. Debates about what to call historic synagogues force their multiple constituencies to articulate *how* their histories make these spaces sacred, not *whether* they are sacred.

After preservationists won the rights to the Vilna Shul, they opened it to the public as "The Vilna Shul—Boston's Center for Jewish Culture." Jessica Antoline, the Vilna Shul's program manager, told me, "We don't have objects that we've brought in and we've decontextualized. We're the opposite. All of our objects have always been here. . . . We're not really a museum. We function a little bit differently."[36] In fact, since it lacks a full-time congregation and functions primarily as a historic heritage site, one might easily identify the Vilna Shul as a museum. In order to emphasize the ongoing communal activity at the Vilna Shul, Antoline relies on a narrow definition of a museum as an institution displaying artifacts out of context. She identifies the Vilna Shul, in contrast, as a more authentic space, displaying the building itself. The semantic distinction aids institutions in articulating how they actively engage Jewish communal life rather than simply mourning past glories, helping them include visitors in their vision of a community and persuade potential donors to contribute to preservation efforts.

Organizations located at the Touro Synagogue in Newport, Rhode Island, the oldest synagogue building in the United States, also debate the terms of their institutional conflicts. While day-tripping visitors to the historic synagogue rarely realize the complicated institutional relationships negotiated behind the scenes, Touro Synagogue is overseen by an abundance of organizations—five, by one count—each with their own historical agenda and relation to the labels of synagogue and museum.[37] None of them are officially "the Touro Synagogue," but popular references to "the Touro Synagogue" gently smooth over a complex history of competing organizations. Nostalgia emphasizes a seamless trajectory from the past to the present, not only smoothing over conflicting narratives and competing institutional claims but declaring a historical winner in the master narrative.

Unlike the other synagogues discussed in this chapter, institutions at Touro Synagogue tend to downplay the rift of a salvation story in order to emphasize continuity between its present uses and the site's original colonial congregation. Touro Synagogue traces its origins to fifteen Jewish families of Spanish and Portuguese origin who immigrated to Newport in 1658. They founded Congregation Jeshuat Israel (Salvation of Israel) not long after their arrival, but they did not construct a synagogue building until 1763.[38] The original congregation used the site only until 1776, when residents of Newport fled the British forces. In 1790, George Washington visited Newport to promote the Bill of Rights, and Moses Seixas, the warden of the empty synagogue, presented Washington with a letter. Washington's response echoes Seixas's wording, promising that the U.S. government "gives to bigotry no sanction, to persecution no assistance."[39] This famous letter became essential to the historical presentation of the synagogue, and the synagogue is inextricably tied to ideas of individual liberty and religious freedom in American and Jewish social memories.

Figure 3.3. Touro Synagogue, Newport, Rhode Island. Photo by Swampyank, 2009. Licensed under CC BY-SA 3.0.

Figure 3.4. Touro Synagogue interior, Newport, Rhode Island. Photo by S.d.tour, 2015. Licensed under CC BY-SA 4.0.

In 1805, the last remaining Jew in Newport handed the keys and the deed to the building to the Sephardi Congregation Shearith Israel in New York, the oldest synagogue congregation in the United States, to which Jeshuat Israel had long had closes ties. Throughout the nineteenth century, the building served as a state house, courthouse, town hall, and occasional tourist attraction for both Jews and Christians. But by the end of the century, Ashkenazi immigration revived Jewish life in Newport, and two rival congregations vied for use of the building. Shearith Israel gave its blessing to Congregation Jeshuat Israel, which is named for but has no connection to the original congregation. The new Jeshuat Israel congregation continues to use the building today. With the threatening spread of Reform Judaism on its mind, Shearith Israel insisted that Jeshuat Israel retain traditional Sephardi rites, though members of the congregation were Ashkenazi. Initially, Jeshuat Israel had a Sephardi rabbi, but the congregation hired its first Ashkenazi rabbi by 1902.[40] The congregation professes to follow the Sephardi rite to some degree, though they use Ashkenazi prayer books.[41] Today, tour guides at the historic synagogue, who work for the non-profit Touro Synagogue Foundation created by congregants, emphasize building's seventeenth- and eighteenth-century history along with the present day and generally gloss over the nineteenth century. Nostalgia for the colonial past helps tour guides create narrative continuity between the present congregation and the original, colonial congregants, smoothing over any discrepancies between the Sephardi designation and Ashkenazi realities.

Touro Synagogue has a constant stream of tourists to the resort city in the summer, but Jeshuat Israel has serious financial issues, which have sometimes threatened its rabbi's salary. Even though the site is far better known for its historical import—perhaps especially for that reason—the congregation's co-president, Bea Ross, told a reporter, "The minute it doesn't have a full-time rabbi, then it doesn't function as a synagogue anymore." She added, "If it isn't open as a house of worship, then it just becomes a museum, and the world doesn't need another museum."[42] Like Antoline at the Vilna Shul, Ross distinguishes "synagogue" from "museum" in order emphasize that the building houses a living Jewish community and therefore holds a particular meaning for visitors. Ross is well aware that the building has a particular importance because of its history, too. But even as the congregation and the preservationist organizations on the site provide complementary functions, they also compete for financial resources. Debates about which of the organizations at the Touro Synagogue take precedence are arguments about which mode best enacts the religious obligation of emotionally connecting to the past. These are religious debates with financial repercussions.

While the Foundation's docents at the Touro Synagogue building emphasize the site's ongoing Jewish history, docents at the Visitors Center next door present the site's past as a historic case study of American religious freedom. In the late 1990s and early 2000s, businessman and philanthropist John L. Loeb, Jr. purchased property next to the synagogue and built the Ambassador John L. Loeb Jr. Visitors Center. Loeb, a descendant of one of the synagogue's original congregants, gave the land to the congregation but maintained control of the Visitors Center's exhibits under the auspices of a newly created George Washington Institute for Religious Freedom (GWIRF). While the Foundation oversees docents at the historic building, docents at the Loeb Center work for GWIRF.[43] Nonetheless, even as they tell competing narratives, both sets of docents encourage visitors' emotional engagement with the site, and both groups present Touro Synagogue's history as providing obligatory and praiseworthy lessons in tolerance and religious freedom for all American visitors. This is an American Jewish mitzvah in which all Americans can participate, even as it retains its Jewish religious particularity as a synagogue and site of American Jewish heritage.

The final, ongoing competition over religious modes at the Touro Synagogue has been adjudicated in the courts. In December 2012, New York's Shearith Israel sued Touro Synagogue's Jeshuat Israel. Most immediately, the fight was over a pair of eighteenth-century silver Torah finials (rimonim, bells adorning the top of a Torah scroll), but it raised broader issues of which institutions should control Touro Synagogue. The Newport congregation planned to sell the finials to the Museum of Fine Arts in Boston for more than $7 million to raise funds the congregation could desperately use. In doing so, Jeshuat Israel would downplay the historic building's museum function in order to serve the present congregation's needs. But because of the relationship between the New York congregation and the congregation that had built Touro Synagogue in the late eighteenth and early nineteenth centuries, Shearith Israel claimed it owns the building and its artifacts, and it sued Jeshuat Israel to stop the sale. Shearith Israel's congregational president argued that selling the rimonim would "would profane the sanctity of these ritual objects."[44] The case has wound its way through the courts. In 2018, the First U.S. Circuit Court of Appeals let stand a decision in Shearith Israel's favor. Jeshuat Israel has announced it will seek review by the U.S. Supreme Court.[45] Both congregations see themselves as the guardians of Touro Synagogue's historical legacy and present-day religious significance. This legal case underlines the stakes of institutional contestation for control of heritage sites, especially those concerning the rights and obligations of congregations in these spaces.

For this reason, when Roberta Gratz's non-profit Eldridge Street Project raised funds to renovate the site and displayed it to the public between 1986 and 2007, staff members kept congregants' and donors' preferences in mind as they carefully avoided calling the building a museum. After all, a small congregation still owns the building and holds Sabbath services there. In the years when the sanctuary was closed off due to lack of funds for heating and preservation, the congregation continued to meet for services in the beit midrash (study hall) in the basement. But as Gratz and her fellow preservationists sought funding to restore the building, they struggled with how to present their preservationist effort and fulfill their obligation to the congregation at the same time. "We were like a fish out of water," Gratz said. "We fell into nobody's real category so people would say we don't have a category for you."[46] Even after the Project joined the American Association of Museums in 1991, its designation as a museum remained a "delicate point," said Amy Waterman, then the executive director of the Project. "Some of our board members would say, 'Don't call it a museum. It sounds like it's over, like it has ossified,'" she said in 2005.[47] Nonetheless, only two years later, upon the completion of the renovation in 2007, the Project became the Museum at Eldridge Street. Historian Jenna Weissman Joselit reflected popular sentiment about the change when she wrote in *The Forward*, "There's something about a synagogue-turned-museum that saddens, even disturbs. . . . It carries the whiff of disappointment, the sting of failure about itself."[48] The idea of museumification as a kind of death is hard to overcome.

Perhaps because of such reactions, Bonnie Dimun, executive director of the Museum at Eldridge Street, remains hesitant about the term.

She wonders if the Project rushed into the name change too fast. The new name causes confusion because many visitors expect a museum to have temporary and permanent object-based exhibits and imagine a museum site as a dead space, devoid of the ongoing community that this museum works hard to maintain through events, tours, and social media. As Dimun told me,

> The good news is it's alive and well. Call it whatever you want—a museum, a landmark, a heritage—whatever name works, the place is alive again. It is not alive again the way it was as a house of worship only, but it is alive again with music and events and history and the opportunity to tell the stories of the past and make it present.[49]

Dimun's understanding of the "life" of the Museum at Eldridge Street stands in sharp contrast to the opponents of the Vilna Shul restoration, who argued that turning the Boston synagogue into a heritage site would only serve the dead. These arguments about definition and authority are a common feature of religious discourse. Explanations about the "life" of the synagogue demonstrate that, to many Jews, these historic sites are important religious sites, regardless of whether they maintain active congregations.

In fact, the strength of these historic synagogues lies in the emotional reaction they provoke by sitting in the intersection between religious site and museum. In December 2012, the organization Pro Musica Hebraica hosted a concert at the Eldridge Street Synagogue in which fourteenth-generation cantor Netanel Hershtik sang classical hazzanut, the near-operatic form of Jewish cantorial performance, generally of liturgical pieces.[50] Hershtik's performance demonstrates that religious, cultural, and spiritual aspects of Eldridge Street remain intertwined. Hershtik, the cantor at the Hampton Synagogue in Westhampton, New York, has said that he views his work as a cantor as a religious obligation, even when he is performing a concert rather than during a service: "Standing in that synagogue [at Eldridge Street], it's a mission for me. I have a job to do in this world, to bring [classical hazzanut] to the world." Despite the concert setting, Hershtik said, "I'm not performing, I'm praying."[51] While not all visitors would recognize the performance as a prayerful one, Pro Musica Hebraica and Hershtik designed the event as a powerful experience of music recognized as authentically Jewish, deliberately held within a space noted for its authentic representation of the past. Through the combined sensory experiences of music and historical space, alluding to the long history of religious services there, Hershtik's performance encouraged patrons to long for a particular image of Jewish communal pasts while also celebrating the synagogue building's current use as a heritage site. The performance deliberately blurred the lines between synagogue and museum, highlighting their shared religious functions.[52]

You Probably Think This Museum Is about You

Once synagogues open to the public as heritage sites, their meanings continue to be made and remade by a number of actors, including staff members, volunteers, philanthropists, and visitors. The Jewish Museum of Florida encourages visitors' and donors' sense of authority over their space through its advertising slogan, "Whether your family came here 100 years ago or today, this Museum is about you—and for you."[53] It is not entirely clear which "you" is being addressed here. Do you need to be Jewish or Floridian or American? What happens when visitors' ideas of the past differ from staff members' visions? The museum intentionally leaves these questions unasked, allowing visitors to formulate their own answers in that void. The slogan's appeal is that you, whoever you are, have a stake in the museum's mission, regardless of your personal history and your view of the past. Shared nostalgia helps smooth over the differences between visitors' and heritage institutions' constructions of the past.[54]

Visitors arrive at historic synagogues seeking a purported authenticity—that certain events really happened there and that they can be demonstrated using historical artifacts—and museum staff members or congregational volunteers are on hand to provide evidence of authenticity by directing visitors' emotions. Explaining why the Vilna Shul deserves attention, the president of its board writes, "Even though we are not the oldest synagogue building [in Boston], we are the only one that still survives in its authentic form."[55] A feeling that they have proof of historical authenticity is the emotional exchange visitors expect in return for their time and, sometimes, their money. As Prell recognizes, in the twentieth century, individuals' emotions became one of the many authorizing processes of American Judaism. That is, things are Jewish because people have Jewish reactions to them.[56] Objects, institutions, and experiences are recognized as authentically Jewish because Jews *feel* they are Jewish. A search for authenticity is a hallmark of American religion, and historic synagogues promise visitors that they will find it within their walls.

As I observed in my ethnographic research at the Touro Synagogue in the summer of 2012, visitors to the Touro Synagogue in Newport, Rhode Island routinely object to paying an admission fee to view what they call "America's oldest synagogue"—that is, the oldest synagogue building within the United States—which they view as a heritage treasure that belongs to them as American Jews and should, therefore, be freely available to them. They balk when tour guides nudge them out the door at the half-hour mark in order to make room for the next group. Despite signs directing them to buy tickets at the Visitors Center next door, tourists routinely head straight for the synagogue building. Standing at the gate by the entrance to the synagogue, they promise docents that they will pay for the tour on their way out. Though they sometimes relent, docents told me that they are generally unmoved by pleas like "My nephew came all the way from Israel to see this synagogue!"—a claim I witnessed. Docents hear this kind of thing every day, and they are frustrated by visitors' inability to read signs or look up visiting hours before traveling. "It sometimes becomes a very unpleasant confrontation," one staff member told me. In extreme cases, visitors objecting to the admissions fee have "become very upset, to the point where they will slam doors, they will throw things at us." They are only pacified when staff members explain that the synagogue receives no funding from federal, state, or local governments and that the admissions fee is essential to the maintenance of the synagogue building. "Then some people realize, 'Okay, so my money is going to help the synagogue.' And then it's okay," a staff member recounted.[57] Explaining to visitors how historic synagogues use their entrance fees elevates the payment from a quotidian consumer exchange to a religious activity, akin to a charitable offering or a synagogue membership, if a temporary one.

While visitors arrive with their own sense of authority over the space, explicitly or implicitly, staff members provide visitors to historic synagogues with institutional rules of behavior. They often explain that the synagogue is operating as a museum, and hence behavior appropriate to museums is required; at other hours, as is the case at the Museum at Eldridge Street, the Vilna Shul, and the Touro Synagogue, a congregation may use the space, instituting a different set of behavioral expectations. Staff members delineate when one can enter the building, how much visitors must pay if there is a charge, in what order visitors should view the space, whether photographs are permitted, and whether men are required to cover their heads with kippot—a sartorial requirement that often blurs the boundaries between synagogue and museum functions and between ostensibly religious and non-religious uses of such spaces. Museum rules of "dos and don'ts" can themselves serve as ritual activities and expectations of comportment that set the space apart from other spaces, as sacred spaces and sites of community-building.[58]

But perhaps more than other heritage sites, visitors to historic synagogues routinely challenge staff members' authority. In the high tourist season in the summer, Newport has become a popular vacation spot for Orthodox Jews. They come to see the colonial Touro Synagogue and take tours, but they also expect to be able to use the synagogue space for their required thrice-daily prayers. While the congregation offers morning and evening prayer services before and after the tours run by the Visitors Center, Orthodox Jewish men are often shocked to learn that they cannot use the space for afternoon prayers, as the half-hour tours run continuously throughout the day, without breaking for services.[59] The institutions at play overseeing the Touro Synagogue simply cannot live up to visitors' demanding, conflicting expectations. Staff members encourage visitors to feel a sense of authority over the space, but many visitors arrive with a sense of entitlement to these places. Conflicts between visitors' agency and docents' control reveal the cracks in smoothly nostalgic narratives.[60]

Still, even as visitors and heritage institutions clash, they each contribute to enacting an overarching narrative together. Throughout my ethnographic research, I continually observed repeat visitors attempting to usurp the role of their tour guide, particularly if they felt greater attachment to another version of the building's history and thought the docent was not highlighting the most interesting parts. One repeat visitor to the Vilna Shul in Boston continually interrupted the docent to explain to her friends how the first time she entered the building, the synagogue's murals had not been uncovered and repainted, as they are now. She was not interested in the docent's practiced speech about the history of the synagogue; her retelling of the synagogue's history was *her* story. Preservationist institutions try to direct visitors' experiences toward a shared nostalgia, but the mitzvah of nostalgia is ultimately a personal one, guided by individuals' own emotions.

During my ethnographic research at the Jewish Museum of Florida in Miami Beach, I met a husband and wife who had responded to the museum's call for loans of materials for an exhibit of Florida Jewish family connections to Lithuania. When they had attended the opening of the exhibit a few weeks earlier, the couple had been dismayed to find that an item they had loaned the museum was not being used in the exhibit. The day I met them, they had returned solely to make sure that curators had now put it on display. They were possessive of the display, enacting the stated policy that the museum was about them and for them. Focused on their own lineage, they participated in a shared nostalgia rather than collective nostalgia, their nostalgic longing and their aims overlapping but not identical with those of the museum staff.

Public historian Sara Lowenburg, who began working at the Museum at Eldridge Street on the Lower East Side as a college intern in 2012 and later served as the Education and Programs Associate, told me that Orthodox visitors who correctly identify her as a non-Orthodox Jew often question her historical knowledge and challenge her authority as a tour guide. Such visitors frequently believe that they, as Orthodox Jews, have a greater claim to the religious space. In the summer of 2014, Lowenburg gave a tour to a challenging group of Orthodox high school girls, who tested her knowledge of Jewish history, "trying to ask me questions to throw me off." But by the end of the tour, she said, "I won them over and almost was deemed a suitable guide to the space." Lowenburg was not offended. Instead, she told me, "I think it's one of the reasons that Eldridge Street exists as a museum, that people can come in and relate to it" and claim it as their own.[61] Both the authority of the tour guide and the emotional authority visitors feel over the space are essential to the functioning of a historic synagogue as a heritage site. It is no wonder that the two occasionally clash. If the tour guide handles the tension between the two gracefully, the heritage site emerges a more stable site of public history and shared religious meaning.

Some institutions make a point of valuing public opinion, seeking visitors' suggestions and making certain decisions transparent. For many years, the Eldridge Street Project had held an ongoing conversation about historic preservation in which the public had been, and continues to be, included. Though the restoration of the Lower East Side synagogue was officially completed in 2007, preservationists had no available records of the original east window. The original rose window had been destroyed in a storm in 1944, at which point the congregation opted to pay off its mortgage rather than restoring the window, and glass blocks were put in as a placeholder to fill the space. As docents remind visitors, this decision preserved the building, if not the window, for future generations. Preservationists debated what to do about the window for years. The Project consulted experts in historical restoration and surveyed visitors: Should the glass blocks be kept in place? Should the Project create a new window, or should it imitate the intact west rose window? Some said the glass blocks were a part of the synagogue's history, a reminder of hard times, and the blocks were left in place for the rededication of the building when the Project became the Museum at Eldridge Street. After much debate, the museum's board decided to replace the window and held a competition for a new design that would make a contemporary work of stained glass a permanent part of the building. Dimun, the executive director, explained to me, "We decided not to try to recreate something when we did not know what that something really looked like."[62] Another staff member added that since the original plans for window were unknown, "This was the only place in the building where we could extend the story."[63] Following a suggestion by a visitor, the glass blocks were moved downstairs, to the synagogue's study space and offices, exhibiting them as part of the synagogue's material history.[64]

In 2009, the museum selected its contest winners, artist Kiki Smith and architect Deborah Gans. (The public was not consulted in this selection.) In the new window by Smith and Gans, yellow five-pointed stars are scattered throughout a blue green field, continuing the design of the synagogue's painted walls. The celestial field is broken up by six curved spokes of a steel frame, which radiate outward from the six points of a yellow cast glass star within a steel frame at the center of the window. As docents inform visitors, the artist, Smith, interpreted the five-pointed stars as a reference to the stars on the American flag; juxtaposed with the

Figure 3.5. Eldridge Street Synagogue interior, view from the women's balcony. The east window contains glass blocks put in place in 1944. Photo by Elliot Kaufman, 2000. Used with permission of Hana Iverson and Elliott Kaufman.

central six-pointed Star of David, they make a visual statement about American Jewish identity and the freedom to practice Judaism within the United States. Within the steel frame, the design team adhered the panels of colored glass together with modern silicone rather than the traditional method of using lead came to assemble stained glass. "What would have been lines of lead are lines of light," said Gans, the architect.[65] The window is thus presented to visitors as a visual symbol of the museum's role as a heritage institution, representing a reinterpretation of an older space in light of new demands upon it. It provides a visual narrative of elegy and restoration, culminating in emotional uplift and celebration of the present.

The installation of the new window provided the museum with a great deal of favorable publicity. Today, after the fact, the museum continues to ask visitors whether they would have made the choice to keep the glass blocks in place, create a new window, or imitate the west rose window. Visitors, particularly American Jews, feel free to voice their opinions, whether or not they are in line with the museum's decision. Some critique the museum for its lapse in a strict restoration. Others, swayed by the beauty of the new window, agree with the decision. One reviewer saw the window, designed by women, as emblematic of feminist empowerment against traditional Orthodox patriarchy, writing, "There's something touching to me about the fact that while once upon a time, women had no role in the ritual life of this building, now they've helped to create it."[66] The window now serves as another way for visitors

Figure 3.6. Eldridge Street Synagogue interior, view from the women's balcony with east window by Kiki Smith and Deborah Gans, installed in 2010. Photo by Rhododendrites, October 14, 2018. Licensed under CC BY-SA 4.0.

to make their own meanings out of their reactions to the space, demonstrating the dynamic and often conflicted process by which the shared elegiac nostalgia of historic synagogues is created.

View from the Balcony

Clashes between visitors' sense of authority over historic spaces and staff members' narratives frequently occur in the women's galleries of historic synagogues. Historic synagogues often present Orthodox spaces, in which men and women are separated for prayer, to a largely non-Orthodox public, including many American Jews who feel antagonistic toward the gender segregation of Orthodox rituals.[67] (Grand spaces of liberal denominations from the early twentieth century or earlier are much rarer than Orthodox ones.) Despite the danger of outbursts from visitors, docents at the Museum at Eldridge Street make a point of bringing visitors up to the women's gallery. When I conducted fieldwork at the museum in 2012 and 2013, I frequently heard docents explain to visitors, "If the women were in a separate place, they were also in the best place," in that they had the best view of the sanctuary.[68] In a space where non-Orthodox visitors, particularly liberal Jews, might feel antagonistic toward what they see as the oppression of Orthodox women, docents are trained to represent the early female congregants as historical actors. They emphasize women's active roles in the congregation, often in opposition to male leaders. They draw visitors' attention to a crystal chandelier above the women's space that contrasts sharply with the brass light fixtures throughout the rest of the sanctuary. Docents explain that they imagine the women complained that they did not have enough light and that they suspect a wealthy congregant who had an extra chandelier donated the fixture, a narrative that simultaneously emphasizes women's agency and reinforces ideas about women's secondary position in Orthodox Judaism.[69]

Another story utilizes the view from the women's gallery as an illustration of early female congregants' active roles in the synagogue and the neighborhood. Docents and staff members recount female congregants' participation in the kosher meat boycotts of 1902, when New York's kosher butchers raised the price of meat to a price that immigrant women, their primary customers, could not afford. One Saturday morning, docents explain, groups of women went to synagogues throughout the Lower East Side to encourage a boycott of kosher meat. At the Eldridge Street Synagogue, a pair of women ascended to the bimah at the front of the synagogue, in the men's section, and asked the congregation to officially support the boycott. When the president of the congregation and other male leaders attempted to dismiss their concerns and suggested that they buy only half of the kosher meat they needed, a commotion broke out from the gallery. Congregants above and below yelled, "No meat! No meat!" The following boycott of kosher meat succeeded in bringing down butchers' prices—at least for a little while.[70]

In telling these stories, the Museum at Eldridge Street encourages visitors to feel an empathetic and physical connection to the women of the early congregation, the "heroic housewives" who sat in the seats in which the visitors sit and saw a similar view of the sanctuary below.[71] This story serves to turn the women's balcony into a place of women's empowerment rather than oppression, addressing potential hostility from non-Orthodox visitors. It also links the synagogue to popular recollections of progressive political activism in the Lower East Side, itself an ostensibly secular object of American Jewish nostalgia.[72]

The Museum at Eldridge Street did not have to choose to present the women's gallery in this way. At other historic synagogues, women's galleries are considered out-of-the-way places, perfect for staff offices, as at the Jewish Museum of Florida in Miami Beach. Staff members there view the converted galleries as entirely secular spaces, while the main floor of the building—the men's space, where the primary ritual action of the service took place—is considered the primary artifact of the museum. In converting the women's galleries to staff offices, administrators are unconcerned that they have eliminated women's historic experience of the space and reinforced men's ritual experiences as "real" Judaism.[73] To be fair, these were not particularly lovely galleries, especially before they were converted to offices. But the question remains: What has the museum lost in deeming women's spaces unworthy of heritage tourism? The museum's utilitarian use of the balconies removes women's experience from the historical narrative of the synagogue. At this museum, visitors standing in the sanctuary feel elegiac nostalgia for a history of the synagogue that is told exclusively from the male vantage point. The choice underscores that even when staff members attempt to present a historic synagogue purely as a museum, they recognize the religiosity of parts of the building, in contrast to the supposedly secular office space.

In contrast, from the early days of the Eldridge Street Project's preservation efforts, staff members have used visitors' potentially ambivalent or negative feelings about the women's gallery as an opportunity to engage them in the ongoing work of shared nostalgia. In order to solicit funding to renovate the building, the Eldridge Street Project invited the public to view the building in various stages of disrepair and repair throughout its renovation. During this period, it invited a number of artists to display exhibits exploring the theme of the women's balcony, taking advantage of the creative ways they could use the space during the renovation. A number of innovative feminist installations made the Orthodox space palatable to non-Orthodox Jewish audiences.

In 1997, the Eldridge Street Project invited visual artist Carol Hamoy to create a version of her traveling *Welcome to America* installation to be displayed in the women's balcony of the synagogue. Born and raised in New York, Hamoy was the child of immigrant parents, and *Welcome to America* was originally designed for display at the Ellis Island National Museum of Immigration. For her installation at Eldridge Street, Hamoy studied the synagogue's archives and oral history collection to learn about the life stories of immigrant women in the synagogue's original congregation. She crafted ghostly dresses from wedding gowns, skirts, bed linens, scarves, and undergarments. The eighteen dresses that hung in the balcony at Eldridge Street represented twenty-five immigrant women who had worked in the garment industry, as Hamoy's relatives had.[74]

Hamoy tinted and stained the white garments and imprinted them in gold text with a quote from the woman or a brief, poignant description of a moment in her life. For Rose, whose baby had measles on the boat to America, Hamoy wrote, "She kept him wrapped in a pink blanket to offset his face," allowing him to pass through immigration inspections with an undetected illness. Another dress identified Chaye Soret as a "design prodigy from Pinsk."[75] Hanging from the ceiling and swaying in the breeze, the ghostly dresses materialized the absent, immigrant founding congregants. Visitors' movements through the maze of dresses and memories physically reinforced the connection between past and present. Reviewers saw spiritual meaning in the synagogue installation. A review in *Femspec*, an

Figure 3.7. Carol Hamoy, *Welcome to America*. Installation at the
Eldridge Street Synagogue, 1997. In the collection of the Eldridge Street
Project. Used with permission of Carol Hamoy and the Museum at
Eldridge Street.

interdisciplinary feminist journal, explained that the installation "invites the spirits who once frequented the synagogue to revisit their ancient abode. . . . Their presence among us . . . reminds us that our foremothers are ever present in our midst, especially when we pray."[76] Regardless of whether they were biologically connected to the women represented, visitors felt the guiding presence of their ancestors in this space.

A few years later, the Eldridge Street Project displayed Hana Iverson's *View from the Balcony*, which explored themes of distance from and reconciliation with the past in a site-specific video and sound installation from June 2000 through December 2003. *View from the Balcony* utilized an empty stairwell shaft that had once held the stairs leading from the main sanctuary to the women's balcony above. (After the building's renovation, this stairwell shaft held an elevator, making the building ADA compliant.) Visitors saw a film of the artist's hands sewing together pieces of Torah parchment projected onto this screen, which bridged the men's space and the women's balcony, while they heard a recording of women's voices in Hebrew, Yiddish, and English. In Hebrew, a woman's voice spoke the traditional Jewish woman's prayer blessing God for making her according to God's will. (In contrast, Jewish men traditionally thank God for not making them a woman.) In Yiddish, women recited folksy expressions and a recipe for strudel. Family stories about Jewish women's rituals played in English.[77]

When I interviewed Iverson, the artist described herself as "truly a secular Jew"—though she's familiar with Reform Jewish practices—and told me that she sees Orthodox Judaism as hurtful to women. According to Iverson, the installation metaphorically explored issues of healing and mending in Jewish history: the physical ruin of the Eldridge Street Synagogue during years of neglect; the synagogue's renovation, which at the time was ongoing; the physical distance between men and women in the synagogue; immigrants' separation from their countries of origin; and the American Jewish community's disconnect from the European traditions of their ancestors. Iverson told me that the empty stairwell "was like a ghost chamber because there had been an architectural structure there that was gone. . . . And ghosts live on that threshold."[78] In drawing connections between different historical periods, the installation served as a way to emotionally interact with the imagined ancestors through a liminal space. It performed the work of religion in building relationships

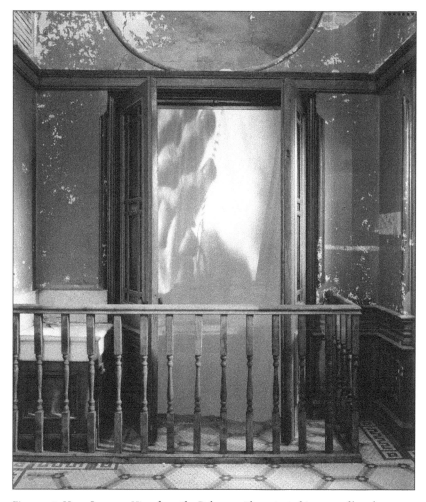

Figure 3.8. Hana Iverson, *View from the Balcony* with projected images of hands sewing. Installation at the Eldridge Street Synagogue, 2000–2004. Photo by Elliott Kaufman, 2000. Used with permission of Hana Iverson.

between the living and remembered ancestors. In its images of physical and metaphorical connection and disconnection from ancestors and from broader narratives about the Jewish immigrant past, *View from the Balcony* provided visitors an authorizing mechanism through which to explore conflicts they might feel about the space, even as they expressed a reverence for a historical space.

Figure 3.9. Hana Iverson, *View from the Balcony* installation in empty stairwell shaft. Installation at the Eldridge Street Synagogue, 2000–2004. Photo by Elliott Kaufman, 2000. Used with permission of Hana Iverson.

Through an active exploration of the past, Hamoy and Iverson drew together a community of visitors, artists, performers, and staff members affectively engaged with the synagogue gallery. These installations marked the synagogue, particularly the gallery, as a sacred space, in which conversations about the past were appropriate and necessary—a mitzvah, in the American sense of a good deed and an obligation. These events creatively used the synagogue's space to promote and teach elegiac nostalgia for a particular Jewish communal past. At the same time, they served as a creative advertisement for the Eldridge Street Project's restoration efforts.

By eliciting longing for particular Jewish pasts and reevaluating them through a contemporary feminist approach, Hamoy's and Iverson's exhibits demonstrated that the preservationist effort of the Eldridge Street Project was itself the work of a living religious space. In fact, for visitors who felt alienated by patriarchal Jewish traditions, these feminist exhibits could make the space more religiously meaningful than it had been when it only housed an Orthodox congregation. Hamoy's and Iverson's exhibits connected visitors to an elegiac nostalgia for the past that was both more broadly and more personally meaningful than the synagogue's history would have been on its own.

Our Immigrant Heritage

As staff members present historic synagogues as paradigmatic examples of a generic American immigrant experience, they expand the congregation of participants in their nostalgic narratives to include non-Jews. This inclusion is a performance of multiculturalism, a statement that the American melting pot "did not happen." Instead, in the multicultural viewpoint, the United States became a hodgepodge of ethnicities, all of which may be celebrated individually by all Americans.[79] Jewish nostalgia is a broadly recognizable American phenomenon within this multicultural celebration. Just as one does not have to be of Irish Catholic descent to participate in St. Patrick's Day celebrations in the United States, one does not have to be Jewish to participate in American Jewish nostalgia and to participate, however briefly, in the community in and around historic synagogues. But while St. Patrick's Day has largely been shorn of its religiosity, as recognizably religious spaces, historic synagogues that act as both synagogue and museum can simultaneously welcome non-Jewish participants in Eastern European Jewish nostalgia and retain specific Jewish religious qualities.

Speaking to an adult audience at the 2007 rededication of the Museum at Eldridge Street, Speaker of the New York State Assembly Sheldon Silver presented Jewish history as model for American political participation. "At this moment in history," Silver announced, "when the mere mention of the word 'immigrant' can evoke such bitterness and distress, it is wonderful to be together here on Eldridge Street and to be celebrating the restoration and re-dedication of this precious gem of our immigrant heritage."[80] Particularly because Silver is publicly known as an Orthodox Jew, his reference to "our immigrant heritage" is ambiguous, and it is unclear if he means that heritage belongs only to Jews or is the inheritance of all Americans; the politician may have been deliberately vague. Silver's remarks illustrate the ways that the conception of the United States as a "nation of immigrants" stands in for white ethnicity and whiteness itself, as Matthew Frye Jacobson has shown.[81] Significantly, the early twenty-first controversies over immigration to which Silver alludes are primarily about the immigration of Latinos and other non-white immigrants. In delivering these remarks at the Museum at Eldridge Street, Silver upheld the Jewish Eastern European immigrants of the Lower East Side as model immigrants, without regard to Chinese and other immigrants who currently live in the neighborhood and without attention to the ways in which Ashkenazi immigrants' whiteness helped them succeed in the twentieth century.[82]

Multiculturalism provides models to which others can relate. Non-Jewish visitors are an important part of the imagined communities of historic synagogues at all times, but their presence is particularly noteworthy at the signature events of the Touro Synagogue and the Museum at Eldridge Street: the George Washington Letter Reading and the Egg Rolls and Egg Creams Festival, respectively. Since its establishment in 1948, the Society of Friends of Touro Synagogue National Historic Shrine, now the Touro Synagogue Foundation, has held an annual observance commemorating George Washington's letter to the building's original congregation.[83] The Foundation invites local and national dignitaries to attend a ceremony on or about August 19, the day Washington penned his letter, and the small building is always filled to capacity with members of the Foundation, congregants, and others interested in the history of the building. Events of the George Washington Letter Reading include a ceremonial reading of Seixas's and Washington's letters, a keynote address by a public figure, and the presentation of awards to those who have worked to promote religious toleration, including the award of small college scholarships to two Rhode Island high school seniors—not necessarily Jews—for essays interpreting the contemporary relevance of Washington's letter. This is civil religion, an affirmation of national myths that attempts to unify Americans, but it is also a demonstration of the religious practice of American Jewish nostalgia, a reflection upon how Jewish pasts provide constitutive meaning and emotional relevance in the present.

The George Washington Letter Reading serves as an outlet for both patriotism and pride in the American Jewish community. When Supreme Court Justice Ruth Bader Ginsburg spoke in 2004, the year celebrated nationally as the 350th year of Jewish communal life in the United States, her presence and her words highlighted the success of American Jews. When the chair of the Touro Synagogue Foundation introduced Ginsburg as the personal "fulfillment of the American dream," he did not need to explain that he also meant the American *Jewish* dream. Ginsburg herself gave the Jews assembled reason to congratulate themselves and engage in elegiac nostalgia for the struggles of past generations of American Jews, particularly those who arrived in the early twentieth century. Describing her family history and her career, she asked rhetorically, "What's the difference between a Jewish bookkeeper and a Jewish Supreme Court judge? One generation."[84] Ginsburg's joke uses Jews to stand in for other American immigrant groups, who should imitate American Jews' apparent communal success in the public sphere, regardless of social, economic, or political differences in circumstances.

When I attended the George Washington Letter Reading in 2012, sixteen-year-old high school student Jessica Ahlquist was honored with the Teitz Award. That year, with the assistance of the American Civil Liberties Union, Ahlquist, an avowed atheist, had won a lawsuit against her public high school in Rhode Island, mandating the removal of a "school prayer" banner referencing "Our Heavenly Father" from the school's auditorium. The suit had brought verbal attacks, and even death threats, from her peers and from media outlets.[85] As I observed, the Touro Foundation praised Ahlquist as upholding Washington and Seixas's principles of religious freedom. While Ahlquist might be better described as fighting for freedom *from* religion rather than for free exercise *of* religion, representatives of the Foundation did not choose dwell on this distinction. Instead, for the Foundation, all defenders of American religious freedom are spiritual descendants of colonial Jews. These interpreters of American civil religion use Jewish particularity to stand in for all Americans, employing an emotional connection to the American Jewish past as a source of patriotic unity.

In a less ceremonial, more festive event, the Museum at Eldridge Street also explicitly extends the community of its participants in its signature event, the Egg Rolls and Egg Creams Festival. At this annual summer "block party" held since 2000, the museum celebrates Jewish and Chinese cultures, bringing together American Jewish memories of the former inhabitants of the Lower East Side and the traditions of the current Chinese American residents of the neighborhood, now recognizable as part of Chinatown. (In 2016, in a nod to Puerto Ricans in the neighborhood, this event became the Egg Rolls, Egg Creams, and Empanadas Festival.[86]) The festival has grown exponentially each year, and in June 2012, 10,000 people attended the festival, mobbing the street outside the synagogue and swarming in and out of the building. Festivities include a klezmer band performing traditional Jewish music followed by a performance of Chinese folk music. Kosher vegetarian egg rolls and egg creams are on hand.[87] Groups of women compete in both Chinese and American Jewish versions of mahjong, sometimes pausing to teach younger visitors how to play.[88] Inside the synagogue, specialists teach visitors how to tie tefillin and Chinese knots, how to write Hebrew and Chinese calligraphy, how to participate in a tea ceremony, and how to say basic words in Mandarin and Yiddish, among other activities. Children of all ethnicities can be seen wearing yarmulkes and Chinese opera masks that they have decorated.

This unique event is the creation of Hanna Griff-Sleven, a folklorist who served as the Director of Family History Center and Cultural Programs at the Museum at Eldridge Street. Griff-Sleven encouraged the Eldridge Street Project to interact with the local Chinese community even before she worked at Eldridge Street, when she reviewed the Project's application to the New York State Council on the Arts to hold a Jewish heritage festival. She advised a staff member who created the first Egg Rolls and Egg Creams Festival and then, when she joined the Project staff, further developed and expanded the festival herself.[89]

The event both draws on elegiac nostalgia for the neighborhood and complicates it. One museum intern wrote of the 2011 festival, "From the first emotive blast of the trumpet [of the klezmer band], I was filled with an odd sense of nostalgia for a time I never experienced. Something about the location of the synagogue took me to a different time, along with the entertainment, food, and activities that were provided at the festival."[90] But this nostalgia is not siloed. Griff-Sleven's festival is a community event, bringing together disparate residents and tourists in the neighborhood. Griff-Sleven takes pride in her connections with the local Chinese community, particularly through the Chinatown Senior Center, which connected her to many of the Chinese musicians and artisans who perform and display their work at the festival. Ken Lo, director of the China Arts Council, has worked at the Egg Rolls and Egg Creams festival for years, overseeing the tea ceremony. Lo grew up on the Lower East Side and remembers when a Jewish presence was more evident in the streets. Now, he says, "If there weren't any of these events at the synagogue, it would just be this strange building they don't know anything about."[91] The festival incorporates surprising—if local—actors into the religion of American Jewish nostalgia.

Not everyone immediately understands the festival, and some Jewish visitors would like to see it remain an exclusively Jewish affair. Griff-Sleven recounts that one Jewish woman attending the festival told her, "This is so weird. Why are you doing this?" Griff-Sleven laughs as she recounts her response. "Did you look around? We're a synagogue in Chinatown!"[92] The idea of the Lower East Side as a sacred Jewish space is so firmly planted in American Jewish cultural memory that such visitors have trouble accepting the evidence of Chinatown surrounding them.[93]

Still, Griff-Sleven's sense of obligation to the local neighborhood as well as to the Jewish past seems to be gaining ground. This vision, connecting the Jewish past to a non-Jewish present, may be easier to implement beyond the Lower East Side. While the Lower East Side bears a cultural burden to represent a broad, generalizable narrative about American Jewish history through the history of the neighborhood, beyond New York, Jewish heritage sites may have more freedom to create connections between a neighborhood's Jewish past and its present residents. In the Boyle Heights neighborhood in Los Angeles, the Breed Street Shul Project seeks to use the 1915 and 1922 buildings of the Breed Street Shul (Congregation Talmud Torah) as a community center focused on the needs of its neighbors. Boyle Heights was the center of Jewish Los Angeles from the 1920s through the 1950s and is now a low-income Latino neighborhood. Since the 1980s, the Shul "suffered neglect, vandalism, earthquake damage and abandonment, rendering it unusable and in real danger of demolition."[94] Preservationist efforts, led by the Jewish Historical Society of Southern California, saved the buildings from destruction and stabilized them. The Project is currently seeking funds for its restoration.

The Breed Street Shul Project plans to use the space as a center for a variety of non-profit organizations that will offer tutoring and afterschool activities for local school children, programming with Jewish youth groups, and a variety of adult education programs and social services. Stephen Sass, the longtime president of the Jewish Historical Society of Southern California who has led the effort to rehabilitate the Shul, says that the building "was born of a Jewish experience in a particular time and a particular place, and that is still meaningful, and we want to share that meaning and expand it and reinvent it."[95] Now established as a stable feature of American culture, American Jewish nostalgia is looking outward.

The message that nostalgia for the Eastern European immigrant experience belongs to a broader population is not only intended for adults. A coloring and activity book created by Eldridge Street staff members and sold in the museum gift shop teaches children the lesson that the turn-of-the-century Jewish immigrant experience is a paradigm for all American immigration. Narrated by a nameless child protagonist, the book contrasts the physical and economic difficulties of an immigrant past with the warmth of community, here represented by the grand Eldridge Street Synagogue. "Each week, when we stepped through the door, our dark tenement seemed far away. Inside, we found light and space and peace," says the narrator. Without a name or identifying features, the narrator is a friendly ghost of the children who once played in the synagogue building or fidgeted through services in the late nineteenth and early twentieth centuries, modeling emotional reactions to the building for young Jewish and non-Jewish visitors today.

The ghostly narrator of the Eldridge Street coloring book is disappointed to learn that the myth that American streets were paved with gold is false, but the synagogue revives his civic dreams: "Here at last, I found gold in America. Gold stars glowing from the highest, bluest ceiling I have ever seen. . . . Papa said they stood for freedom: the freedom to be ourselves in America."[96] Just as the Jewish immigrant stands in for a generic American experience, the Eldridge Street Synagogue becomes a place to learn broadly applicable American values. In this multicultural worldview, the Eastern European immigrant child is the model American immigrant, quickly recognizing that the ideals of American civil religion make up for the pain of dislocation and poverty. The narrator becomes American by finding the spiritual qualities of "light and space and peace" in this Jewish space of elegiac nostalgia.

Historic synagogues are points where Jews and non-Jews find religious meaning by connecting to the past through the authorizing process of emotional responses. These institutions of Eastern European immigrant nostalgia use longing for the past to teach a particular religious and civic vision of the future through a network of relationships involving Jews, non-Jews, and particular forms of ghostly ancestors. Negotiating the religious networks of elegiac nostalgia—in which both the living and the dead are invoked as active participants—individuals and organizations at historic synagogues participate in the dynamic religion of American Jews.

4

True Stories

Teaching Nostalgia to Children

"Sol, what are you telling that child?"
"A true story, just the way I remember it, Rose dear," Julie's
grandfather said.
—Linda Heller, *The Castle on Hester Street* (Philadelphia:
Jewish Publication Society of America, 1982)

In Linda Heller's *The Castle on Hester Street*, a children's book first
printed in 1982 and reissued in with new illustrations in 2007, the protagonist Julie listens to her grandparents tell warring stories of their days
on the Lower East Side. While Julie's grandfather spins magical fantasies
of golden baby carriages, goats who could leap over oceans, and castles
taller than pigeons could fly, her grandmother tells tales of poverty and
hardship. As Heller makes clear, both versions are "true" narratives that
effectively communicate nostalgia for the Jewish immigrant generation
of the early twentieth century to children several generations removed
from it. In *The Castle on Hester Street*, nostalgia offers a connection to an
imagined shared past, whether it is one of wonder or of melancholy. Less
important than the facts or even the feelings the past evokes is the sense
of connection itself. Illustrated books like Heller's teach children—and
their parents—that an emotional relationship to Central and Eastern
European immigration history is central to being an American Jew,
placing families within a narrative of American Jewish progress. In this
context, to perform the mitzvah of nostalgia is not only to engage with
the emotion but to share it with a younger generation.[1]

Illustrated children's books and collectible dolls depicting Eastern
European Jewish immigration to the United States reveal the nostalgic
attitudes that adults wish to pass on to the next generation, sometimes
subtly and sometimes didactically. They speak to the future of nostal-

gia.[2] Nostalgia is often assumed to be a condition of aging, collecting memories of prior experience, and it might seem counterintuitive to teach nostalgia to children, who are not expected to be old enough to experience longing for the past.[3] But American Jewish children's materials teach longing for familial and communal pasts that neither children nor adults have experienced. Instead, led by a variety of guides, parents and children learn to form their relationship to a particular imagined collective past together, as they develop their relationship with each other. While engaging with children's materials could be seen as an independent activity, audiences for Jewish children's books and dolls are directed by a host of institutions, including publishers, toy companies, and, increasingly, the philanthropic organization PJ Library. Reading certain children's books and playing with particular dolls connects families to the structures and worldviews that that comprise American Jewish religion, as parents and book creators and distributors teach children how to feel Jewish by longing for particular pasts.

Describing particular children's books and dolls as religious items provides a more comprehensive and more accurate view of where American Jews find meaning and truth claims. It also expands where we look for the most powerful institutions in their lives. Rather than turning to traditional religious institutions such as synagogues and religious schools—or turning only to those institutions—American Jews in the late twentieth and early twenty-first century have communicated Jewish values and ideas to their children by building on the work of Jewish and non-Jewish authors, illustrators, publishing companies, toy manufacturers, gift shops, and philanthropists.

While many scholars of children's literature restrict themselves to close analyses of published texts, both books and dolls are commodities that require multiple approaches in order to understand the intentions of those who created them as well as their reception history. As religious studies scholar Robert Orsi says, "The term 'reading' or even 'looking' does not exhaust what can be done with print."[4] Children— and adults reading to them and playing with them—*participate* in the worlds of books and toys. To understand these items as fully as possible, my analysis is based not only on the texts and illustrations of the books themselves, but also responses to the books and dolls in newspapers and online, as well as interviews with authors, illustrators, publishers, and others involved in creating and distributing American Jewish children's books.

In recent decades, nostalgia for Eastern European immigration to the United States at the turn of the twentieth century has become increasingly common in American children's materials about Jews. These nostalgic children's books largely came to fruition in the 1990s, following the development of Jewish genealogy in the 1970s and a turn toward Jewish historic preservation in the 1980s. In the multicultural milieu of the 1990s and early twenty-first century, nostalgic children's books about Jewish immigration history provide normative Jewish content that is more uplifting than Holocaust stories and less divisive than stories about Israel. Comparative literature scholar Jana Pohl identifies 78 English-language children's books dealing with the subject published by North American authors between 1970 and 2005, and many more have been published since that time.[5] These books tell optimistic stories about ethnic difference that holds particular meaning for American Jews but is accessible to all Americans.[6]

In the late twentieth and early twenty-first century, Jews not only told their children cheerful stories but also stories of suffering. In *Suffer the Little Children*, religious studies scholar Jodi Eichler-Levine importantly identifies the prevalence of stories of hardship and trauma in Jewish and African American children's literature. The books examined in this chapter offer a happier alternative, moving from a suffering immigrant past to a happy, normative American childhood. While the subjects of Eichler-Levine's study teach children and adult readers "whose lives are 'grievable,'" these nostalgic children's books teach children and adults whose stories are worth celebrating.[7] They allow children and adults to feel a comfortable affection for the hardships of past generations rather than a sense of guilt, bereavement, or responsibility for it.

The majority of nostalgic American Jewish children's materials feature stories about girls. American Jewish girls, real and imagined, have long been at the center of what it means to be an American Jews.[8] The stories examined in this chapter draw on the longstanding connections in English-language literature between white girlhood, sentimentality, and nostalgia. By the twentieth century, images of childhood, especially images of girlhood, became "an emblem of a lost past, of a lost self, and of memory itself," as historian Robin Bernstein writes.[9] Late twentieth-century and early twenty-first-century American Jewish children's books draw on these connections to use images of girls as a vehicle by which to access nostalgia for a lost time, rather than as the object of nostalgia themselves.

The immigrant nostalgia of American Jewish children's materials is an intimate affair. Like the nostalgia of genealogical research, it uses the idea of affectionate family relationships to connect Jewish readers with a transhistorical sense of community, a core feature of American Jewish religion. Manufacturers and distributors of nostalgic products for children and families intend to bring the imagined past to bear upon the immediate present and to direct values for the future. With authors speaking though readers' mouths and illustrators' work nestled in their laps, parents and children receive and share messages about how their connection to one another is related to their connection to a shared Jewish past. Ideally, the comfortable glow of present-day family relationships and remembrances of both real and imaged past family exchanges should enhance each other. In less ideal circumstances, when the lived experience fails to correspond with the model of warm family relationships, intimate nostalgia may be even more potent, intertwining longing for the inaccessible past with longing for exemplary family relationships. Intimate nostalgia not only employs the past and present to shape each other, but uses both to construct a particular kind of Jewish future.

We Are Neglecting Our Children

Stories about children have been used to address the issues American Jewish immigrants faced in the early twentieth century since the time of the immigration itself. Mary Antin's once widely read 1912 autobiography, *The Promised Land*, presented Antin as the quintessential American precisely because of her immigration as a child. Her autobiography begins with immigration to the United States as a religious rebirth: "I was born, I have lived, and I have been made over."[10] Writing against rising nativist tendencies, Antin declares, "I am the youngest of America's children, and into my hands is given all her priceless heritage."[11] America is "the promised land," and Antin is the promised child, the ideal immigrant as malleable youngster. Antin's work was intended for adult readers, not children. Still, following her model, images of children—especially girls—would be crucial to American Jewish self-fashioning for both Jewish and non-Jewish audiences over the following century.

American Jews have thought seriously and distinctively about educational materials for children since at least the early twentieth century, but an industry of materials for Jewish children's entertainment and informal education took off in the 1940s and 1950s as Jews reorganized their communities in the postwar suburbs, and it has grown significantly in the succeeding decades.[12] In the postwar years, middle-class migration from ethnic urban neighborhoods to newly developed suburbs had an indelible impact on the communal structures of American Judaism, including the development of American Jewish children's literature and playthings.[13] Following the Holocaust, the proper education and socialization of Jewish children in the United States—now undeniably the center of world Jewry—seemed ever more crucial to the continuation of Judaism. At the same time, during the Cold War, religious practice—especially that of Protestants, Catholics, and Jews—was seen as a hallmark of American exceptionalism, in contrast to the communism's antagonism to religion. Jewish leaders saw a strong religious upbringing as a way to form children into good Americans.[14]

But in their new suburban homes, mid-century American Jewish parents, largely the children of immigrants, relied heavily upon Jewish organizations to teach their children in Jewish rituals and historical narratives while they led home lives generally undifferentiated from those of their non-Jewish suburban counterparts. As a result, synagogue services, religious education, and other Jewish activities seemed divorced from their children's everyday American lives. Without the dynamic, continual ethnic reinforcement of Jewish neighborhoods in the city, Jewish community leaders worried that the maintenance of the Jewish identity of the next generation might be imperiled by suburban prosperity.[15] In this "era of the expert," parents were encouraged to turn to specialists' advice in every area of child-rearing, including religion.[16]

Jewish authors and educators attempted to fill the perceived Jewish gap at home by seeking fresh ways to interest American Jewish youth in Jewish religion and culture. Recognizing the limited value of formal religious education, too easily dismissed as stiflingly boring, they turned their attention to playtime.[17] In the 1940s and 1950s, American Jews created a variety of formal and informal educational materials for children, including "alphabet blocks, spelling games, coloring books, flip charts, film strips, fun books, cassettes, workbooks, and notebooks along with graduated texts," all designed to interest children in Jewish living and education.[18] These toys and activity books, along with new Jewish storybooks and biographies, were intended to foster a culture of Jewish childhood that communal leaders feared would not arise organically. Taken together, these items created a new canon of American Jewish children's materials outside the traditional adult realms of Jewish practice and study. In this context, the cheerful, seemingly innocuous genre of Jewish children's books bore heavy communal expectations.

Nonetheless, amidst all of these educational and entertainment books and toys, few works of Jewish children's fiction were published. In 1950, surveying the limited library of Jewish juvenile fiction, Jewish educator Jacob S. Golub concluded, "It is obvious that we are neglecting our children."[19] As an essential part of modern socialization, creating Jewish children's literature was a religious and communal obligation, a mitzvah that was essential to perpetuating Jews' ways of thinking about themselves, including their histories. For American Jews at mid-century and thereafter, children's literature was not merely a pastime, but an essential component in the development of children's—and thereby future adults'—religious identities.

The breakthrough Golub hoped for arrived within the year: First published in 1951, and continuously in print ever since, Sydney Taylor's *All-of-a-Kind Family* is generally acknowledged as the first mainstream American children's book to feature Jewish characters. The book set the tone for much of American Jewish children's literature that would follow. *All-of-a-Kind Family* and its sequels, which appeared from the 1950s through the 1970s, tell the story of an Eastern European immigrant Jewish family from 1912 through the interwar period. The first and most popular book in the series focuses on five "all-of-a-kind" sisters and their mischievous little brother living with their parents in a tenement on the Lower East Side, where their Papa runs a junk shop. Later books follow the family along a typical socioeconomic and geographic pattern of Jewish immigrant families, as they move to the new middle-class housing in the Bronx. Taylor's pioneering books paved the way for later children's literature featuring ethnic and religious minorities.

They validated young Jewish readers as they recognized characters like themselves and introduced Jewish characters to a mainstream American audience.

Since its publication, the All-of-a-Kind Family series has provided a model of how to effectively use the image of the Lower East Side as a site of nostalgia in American Jewish children's literature. In particular, the negative depictions of the physical conditions of the Lower East Side in the series provide a complex narrative of longing for the past and contentment with American Jews' upward mobility. Taylor sets the scene in the first book:

> The East Side was not pretty. There was no grass. Grass couldn't very well grow on slate sidewalks or in cobblestoned gutters. There were no flowers except those one saw in the shops of the few florists. There were no tall trees lining the streets. There were tall gas lampposts instead. There was no running brook in which children might splash on hot summer days. But there was the East River. Its waters stretched out wide and darkly green, and it smelt of fish, ships, and garbage.[20]

With this description, Taylor establishes what will become a well-worn pattern in Jewish children's literature: While poverty in Jewish immigrant characters' country of origin is represented as a reason for immigration, poverty in the United States is a temporary state that immigrants can overcome.[21] Taylor contrasts her characters' poverty and the unpleasant physical condition of the neighborhood with the sweetness of the intense relationships among the immigrant Jews who lived there.[22] This mythology both valorizes the American Jewish family and simultaneously suggests that in their subsequent upward mobility and move to the more disparate suburbs in the mid-twentieth century, American Jews lost a kind of authentic and unified Jewishness. At the same time, it suggests that American Jews still have the tools to replicate what they believe to be the best features of the past. Longing for the Jewish family of the past will create the Jewish family of present.[23]

While Taylor's books are less widely read now than in past decades, the stories still hold pride of place in the canon of American Jewish children's literature and in Jewish heritage work. On occasion, the Museum at Eldridge Street, located in the 1887 Eldridge Street Synagogue, offers an All-of-a-Kind Family walking tour of the Lower East Side. Staff members take children and their families to the remaining spots on the Lower East that resemble those that the characters would have encountered, including the local public school, the public library, a park, and a candy store. When I observed the tours, I found that many parents and children had not read the books before attending the tour, but, at the encouragement of the tour guide, several parents bought copies of the first book from the museum's gift shop afterward. Regardless of whether visitors are previously familiar with Taylor's series, repeating the stories and displaying images from the books helps museum staff members to encourage parents and children to feel an emotional and immediate connection to a landscape that is a cornerstone in American Jews' worldview.

Jewish children's literature developed slowly and steadily throughout the second half of the twentieth century, responding to the changing communal concerns of American Jews. In the 1960s, Jewish children's books about the Holocaust, modern life in Israel, retellings of folktales, and Jewish historical fiction appeared.[24] By the 1970s, as the roots movement and interest in white ethnic pride took hold—and Jewish genealogy began—mainstream and Jewish presses began to publish an increasing number of Jewish children's books.[25] Tentatively at first, and increasingly in the late twentieth century, children's books with Jewish themes were offered as part of the new multiculturalism. As multicultural materials became a standard part of many elementary school curricula in the 1980s through the early 2000s, Jewish-themed children's books began to have serious crossover appeal to non-Jewish audiences, and non-Jewish publishers became more likely to print Jewish books. Exemplifying this moment, Barbara Cook's classic *Molly's Pilgrim* appeared in 1983. Set in 1904, the book tells the story of Molly, the daughter of Russian immigrants whose elementary school classmates mock her accent. When Molly's mother helps her fulfill an assignment to make a "pilgrim" doll for her class's Thanksgiving Day celebration by making a Russian babushka doll, Molly learns that her family, too, are pilgrims. As Eichler-Levine observes, *Molly's Pilgrim* is a classic text of post-1960s multiculturalism. The Puritans are shorn of their colonial context and Eastern European Jews become the paradigmatic American immigrants. *Molly's Pilgrim* continues to be reprinted (and slightly revised over the years). It became a beloved staple in classrooms, and it inspired a play

and an Oscar-winning short film. "Remembering as an American becomes a means of being American," says Eichler-Levine.[26] Even more so,
remembering as an American Jew, descended from Eastern European
immigrants, becomes a means of being American.

In the mid-2000s, the slow and steady development of Jewish children's literature was entirely upended by the creation of the philanthropic organization PJ Library. The organization has both dramatically
expanded the Jewish children's book market and had an impact upon its
content. Currently, PJ Library is one of the most influential Jewish organizations in North America. Founded in 2005 by the real estate mogul
Harold Grinspoon, the North American iteration of PJ (for "pajama")
Library is a program of the Harold Grinspoon Foundation, which partners with local Jewish organizations including synagogues, Jewish community centers, and Jewish Federations to provide free books to Jewish
and interfaith families with children.

PJ Library purposefully uses children's books to influence Jewish families' values and practices. The program is one of a number of institutional
methods designed by Jewish communal leaders in the late twentieth and
early twenty-first centuries to fight against a perceived "continuity crisis," an overriding preoccupation with American Jewish birthrates and
concern about how interfaith families are changing American Judaism.[27]
Each month, through its affiliates throughout North America, PJ Library sends age-appropriate books or music to children ages six months
through eight years old. As parents are well aware, "The books are aimed
at children, but they are also aimed at teaching adults."[28] The organization prints special paperback copies of their book selections that include
unique commentary on books' front and back flaps to explain Jewish
concepts or values related the stories, as well as suggestions for conversations between adults and children or follow-up activities intended to
reinforce a particular Jewish value.[29] PJ Library encourages parents to
read and discuss the books with their children, even when their children could read them on their own. PJ Library's target is not parents or
children, but the Jewish family as a unit.[30] It is a thorough response to
Golub's 1950 lament that "we are neglecting our children."

For all that it is based on the seemingly lighthearted material of picture books, PJ Library demonstrates the burden that American Jewish
institutions place on popular culture to shape their communities. PJ

Library staff members are uncomfortable with the suggestion that PJ Library intends to influence families' religious lives and, in interviews, told me they preferred to talk about the "Jewish choices" that families might make within and beyond their homes. This reluctance to use the term "religion" might come either from staff members' own constrained definitions of religion or from a savvy understanding that labeling PJ Library's goals as religious ones would alienate a large part of their audience, which includes Jewish families who identify across and beyond the spectrum of Jewish denominations. Some of their recipients might avoid a program described as "religious" because they associate that term with formal organizations and mandated activities, such as belonging to a synagogue and following dietary laws. Nonetheless, despite staff members' protests to the contrary, the organization does, in fact, use children's books as a tool to shape American Jewish religion. The program is designed to draw families into organized Jewish life—not necessarily limited to synagogue membership—and to influence their values, both fundamental aspects of religion. Its books deliberately introduce families to or reinforce their connection with sacred rituals and Jewish customs. More broadly, PJ Library works to persuade American Jewish families to make Judaism an important part of their lives and to connect them, one illustrated book at a time, to networks that will help them do so.[31] Nearly all of the books examined in this chapter are distributed by PJ Library, and as such they have a wide audience across the United States.

The Eternal Grandparent

Many American Jewish children's books, including a number distributed by PJ Library, provide connections between young characters, who serve as stand-ins for real-life child readers, and the immigrant generation, who are almost invariably depicted as grandparents, as in *The Castle on Hester Street*. While children born in the twenty-first century are several generations removed from the era of Jewish immigration from Central and Eastern Europe, they are repeatedly encouraged to identify as the grandchildren of immigrants. At the same time, as authors depict the immigrant generation, they merge remembrances of their own grandparents and great-grandparents, blending the preceding generations into a single eternal grandparent figure. This imagined cross-generational familial connection teaches a sentimental nostalgia to the youngest American Jews and creates a link to multiple ancestral generations through a relationship with a single figure.

Dianne Hess, Executive Editor at Scholastic Press, has published a number of Jewish children's books, including several books distributed by PJ Library. While Scholastic primarily publishes mainstream materials aimed at children in public schools, Hess told me that she sees her work with Jewish books in the context of the changing American Jewish family. Hess, the daughter of European Jewish immigrants, told me, "the new generation in my family is East Indian, Chinese, German, half Jewish/half Lutheran, Puerto Rican, Columbian, et cetera. They're from all over the world." She explained:

> Most kids don't have a solid Jewish background now and don't have that nostalgia for the immigrant grandparents. And for me, it would be a great loss to break that connection with our past because that is the voice of a big piece of our history that held our dispersed community together for so many generations.[32]

Hess articulates how the grandparental immigrant experience of Eastern European Jews has become a central tenet of American Jewish identity politics, even as the demographics of Jews in the United States change. Without this narrative, in the view of Hess and others, Jewish children will be unmoored from the foundational narratives that bound earlier generations of American Jews. The genre of nostalgic children's books provides a connection with a timeless immigrant elders though an accessible, youthful protagonist.

In Amy Hest's *When Jessie Came Across the Sea* (1997), a young immigrant protagonist, the titular Jessie, serves as a stand-in for author and reader, and her relationship with her grandmother models an ideal relationship with familial and communal pasts. Longing for and honoring her distant grandmother, Jessie models the American mitzvah of nostalgia, performing an obligatory and praiseworthy religious act. Hest's straightforward narrative presents Jessie as an ageless orphan (presumably an adolescent) who lives with her grandmother in "a poor village far from here," the mythic shtetl of the American Jewish imagination.[33] When Jessie has the opportunity to immigrate to the United States, she reluctantly leaves her grandmother behind and settles on the Lower East Side. As she sews lace to sell she longs for grandmother, who taught her the skill: "Just to touch the soft lace was like touching Grandmother again."[34] In a satisfying end to the story, Jessie saves enough money to bring her grandmother to the United States, and the two are successfully reunited just before Jessie's wedding to Lou, also an immigrant.

Even though Jessie is herself an early-twentieth-century immigrant, the character still requires the complement of an immigrant grandparent figure. Material connections to her grandmother—the lace Jessie creates—eulogize a figure who is not yet dead in the story, but who is precious as living evidence of a lost past. While Jessie learns to adapt to her life in the United States, her unnamed grandmother undergoes no character development. She is a static Old-World character, defined by Jessie's love and longing for her. The character is an eternal grandparent, a relatable, timeless figure that draws connections between real and fictional generations.

Like many of the authors I spoke with, Hest drew upon her own experiences. *Jessie* is "really about my grandmother and myself," Hest told me. "I wrote this book as a way of telling about my own family history, and I blended the real family history with stories that I made up."[35] Hest's grandmother was born in the United States, and she used to tell Hest about her own parents, Jessie and Lou, who emigrated from Eastern Europe. The satisfying ending in which Jessie successfully brings her grandmother to join her in New York—the most historically unlikely part of the narrative—was, Hest told me, "my way of bringing back my grandmother, who died many years ago. It was my way of reconnecting with her and making a happy ending."[36] Jessie's longing for her grandmother mirrors the author's longing for her own grandmother and encourages the reader to long for the Eastern European immigrant past through the avatar of the eternal grandparent. In doing so, Hest's narrative also engages the twin homelands of American Jews, their Eastern European origins and urban ethnic neighborhoods of the early twentieth century. Hest brings Jessie's grandmother, a representative of one imagined communal past (the Eastern European Jewish town) to another (the Lower East Side). Jessie's reunion with her grandmother represents a moment where the past touches the present—one that is reenacted by reading the story.

The eternal grandparent figure is useful for the PJ Library, which uses the inside covers and inside flaps of the paperback books it distributes to explicitly teach about "Jewish values" that the organization wishes to highlight for parents and children. PJ Library's reading guide on the back flap of its paperback edition of *When Jessie Came Across the Sea* encourages deepening the connection between young readers and the protagonist. Connecting the story to the mitzvah of honoring the elderly, based on Leviticus 19:32, PJ Library encourages parents to "talk with your children about the Jewish values of respecting the elderly" and suggests that parents and children visit a local nursing home.[37] This instruction to visit a local institution rather than make a card or otherwise care for their own grandparents demonstrates that engaging with the eternal grandparent is an act of broader community continuity, not just the tracing of a specific family line.

PJ Library's connection between reader and protagonist strengthens the implicit lesson of nostalgia for the Eastern European Jewish immigrant pasts. This is a didactic project. "Teach your children about different kinds of value, including sentimental value," the reading guide instructs parents, encouraging adults to use this book as a jumping-off point for conversation with children about their own family histories.[38] Even if parents, grandparents, or other adult readers choose to discuss divergent family histories with juvenile readers or listeners, using *Jessie* to inspire these conversations still centers Eastern European heritage. PJ Library hopes to inspire conversations that make engagement with Eastern European Jewish nostalgia a personal experience, whether or not readers' own family histories mimic those of the story.

This Looks Like a Palace

One way that PJ Library draws families into the networks of organized Jewish life is through distributing books about markedly Jewish places, including historic synagogues. As emblems of a larger nostalgic movement for once-Jewish urban neighborhoods, historic synagogues often serve a symbolic role in children's books as in other Jewish nostalgic materials. Just as public history organizations use their historic synagogues to create a physically authentic relationship with the past through the medium of sacred space, illustrated children's books use images of

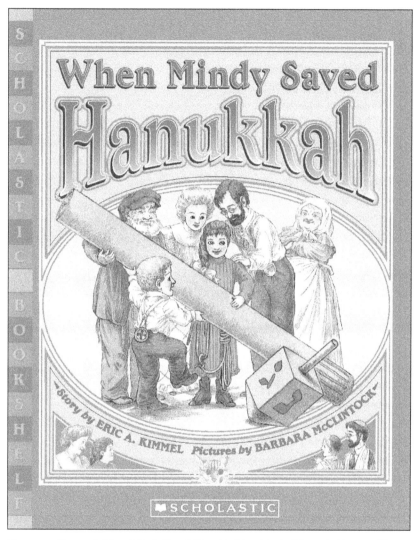

Figure 4.1. Cover of *When Mindy Saved Hanukkah* by Eric A. Kimmel, illustrated by Barbara McClintock. Scholastic Inc./Scholastic Press. Text © 1998 by Eric. A. Kimmel, illustrations © 1998 by Barbara McClintock. Used by permission.

historic synagogues as markers of an authentic, sacred Jewish past. The Eldridge Street Synagogue, located on the Lower East Side, appears in several children's books, including Eric Kimmel's *When Mindy Saved Hanukkah* (1998) and Elsa Okon Rael's *When Zaydeh Danced on Eldridge Street* (1997).[39] In these children's books, the historic synagogue appears as a symbol of a seemingly authentic Judaism, the religion of Eastern European immigrants in the early twentieth century. As in the practices of Jewish genealogy and the preservation of historic synagogues, Eastern European immigration to the United States appears as an indicator of authentic Jewish religion in children's literature. While staff members at historic synagogues used as heritage sites tell elegiac narratives about their sites' histories to demarcate them as sacred spaces, illustrated children's books present historic synagogues as magical places full of possibilities, an easy way to explain both religious spaces and heritage sites to children.

Eric Kimmel's *When Mindy Saved Hanukkah* is an endearing story of tiny, mouse-sized members of the Klein family who live behind the walls of the Eldridge Street Synagogue at the turn of the century, "borrowing" objects from the synagogue's human-sized inhabitants. *Mindy* was reprinted by Scholastic in 2005 and has been repeatedly distributed as a PJ Library book. The story consciously emulates Mary Norton's acclaimed chapter book, *The Borrowers* (1952). With tongue in cheek, Kimmel gave his protagonists a surname meaning "small" in Yiddish and German. At the end of the book, they host their friends, each representative of different groups of early twentieth-century Jews, also with names meaning "small": the Pequeños from Shearith Israel, the Spanish-Portuguese Synagogue in New York; the Littles from the Reform Temple Emanu-El; and the Katans from Jerusalem.

Kimmel, an acclaimed children's book author, has written several Hanukkah stories, including the Caldecott Honor-winning *Hershel and the Hanukkah Goblins* (1989). American Jews have often used Hanukkah to spur conversations about religious practices, education, authority, and public perception by non-Jews, both because of the holiday's proximity to Christmas and because its stories, home rituals, and public celebrations have long been adapted to make it relevant to the present day.[40] Like the Museum at Eldridge Street's appeal to both Jewish and non-

Jewish visitors, *Mindy* is designed to appeal to Jewish audiences familiar with the holiday and non-Jewish readers for whom this Hanukkah story will be an introduction to Jewish religion and history.

Kimmel's choice of the Eldridge Street Synagogue as the location for his characters, whose size associates them with myths about tiny creatures such as pixies and elves, conveys the message that the synagogue is a magical place. His biography on the back flap of the book adds to the mystique of the synagogue: "As soon as he began to write this story, he knew right away it was the perfect home for Mindy and her family."[41] Barbara McClintock's watercolor, black ink, and gouache paintings illustrating *Mindy*, featuring the synagogue building, complement the text's connection to the past by evoking early twentieth-century book illustrations. Setting the story in the historic Lower East Side synagogue asserts that history and heritage give rise to a certain kind of magic. The Museum at Eldridge Street, the public face of the Eldridge Street Synagogue, has repeatedly used the story as the basis for family treasure hunts within the historic synagogue, allowing children and parents to physically interact with the book and connecting multiple media of Jewish nostalgia.[42]

Mindy was created in conjunction with the restoration of the Eldridge Street Synagogue. When McClintock set out to illustrate the book in the late 1990s, the Eldridge Street Project's efforts to restore the historic synagogue were still underway. To prepare for her illustrations, McClintock did extensive research on the Lower East Side in general and the synagogue in particular. She spent time at the synagogue, photographing and sketching the interior and interviewing those involved in the restoration project. "At that point," McClintock told me, the synagogue "was really a mess. There were holes in the ceiling. It was really terribly degraded." McClintock was aware that "people were trying to renovate it, and they kept [running] out of money, and they'd have to find more grant funding, and then they'd come back. It was sort of in fits and starts, pulling the synagogue back together again."[43]

McClintock based her illustrations on the details she found on the remaining paintings on the walls and ceilings, the designs on the walls, the woodwork, and the intact pews, making a composite of the intact decorative elements. According to McClintock, she created what was the

Figure 4.2. Interior depicting the Eldridge Street Synagogue. From *When Mindy Saved Hanukkah* by Eric A. Kimmel, illustrated by Barbara McClintock. Scholastic Inc./ Scholastic Press. Text © 1998 by Eric. A. Kimmel, illustrations © 1998 by Barbara McClintock. Used by permission.

only picture of the original (or restored) sanctuary interior in existence at the time, which appears as a two-page spread in the book. McClintock is justifiably proud to recall that the Eldridge Street Project used her illustration in their presentations to potential donors to the Project and showed it to those who worked on the interior renovation—an interaction that demonstrates the intersection of the case studies in this book.[44]

When Elsa Okon Rael published *When Zaydeh Danced on Eldridge Street* in 1997, she and illustrator Marjorie Priceman would also have encountered the Eldridge Street Synagogue in a dilapidated condition. Like McClintock, Priceman created illustrations of the sanctuary, though her exuberant gouache and watercolor illustrations have a less detailed style than McClintock's. *Publishers Weekly* praised the artist for "captur[ing] the sacredness and beauty of religious symbolism without abandoning her playful, deceptively casual style."[45] Rael, for her part, provided child's-eye view of the sanctuary from the vantage of her young protagonist, Zeesie, who attends the synagogue with her grandfather on the holiday of Simchat Torah:

Zeesie had never seen so beautiful a synagogue. . . . Here the last of the sunset sparkled through brightly colored glass windows. Reds, greens, yellows, lavenders, and blues filtered in and cast a magical light across the pews. Wood carved in intricate patterns decorated the entire room. Zeesie spun around. This looks like a palace, she thought, and here I am, in the middle, like a princess![46]

The imaginative work of illustrators, piecing together images of the past, and engaging texts in the language of children, encourages young readers to place themselves within these scenes and to feel an emotional connection to these historic synagogues. These stories encourage children to adopt these scenes as part of their own experience and to connect them to their own religious lives, even if their experience (or lack of experience) of a synagogue differs from that of the characters. The elegiac nostalgia of historic synagogues used as heritage sites and the intimate nostalgia of children's books have been created in tandem, one influencing the other. In these works, children and adult readers are introduced to the longing for imagined pasts. As in the narratives of restoration told at historic synagogues, these books present the past glory of the synagogue as an active force in the present, and they use the childlike language of magic to do so, further sanctifying the historic synagogue as an awe-inspiring site.

Some Things Change and Some Things Don't

Children and parents are also drawn into books through stories about families, to which they are explicitly encouraged to relate. Intimately nostalgic themes of family memories and religious continuity are explicitly addressed in another PJ Library book, Sheldon Oberman's *The Always Prayer Shawl* (1994), illustrated by Ted Lewin, one of the few works of American Jewish nostalgic children's literature featuring a boy as a protagonist. This book demonstrates the way that family stories become religion, serving as myths and metaphors for deeply held communal values and connecting family history to communal histories. It does so through a story of a traditionally male religious garment passed down through the male line, alongside family stories and emotional responses to them.

Oberman's story of the book's creation, describing a unique familial reinterpretation of a standard ritual, speaks to a "rediscovery of tradition" popular in the 1990s. As adults, baby boomers—like generations before them—evaluated the religion of their parents and considered what they wanted to pass on to their children.[47] Using powerful, straightforward language, the book tells the story of Adam, "a Jewish boy in Russia many years ago," whose grandfather tells him the story of his name: "You are named after my grandfather whose name was Adam. He was named after his grandfather's grandfather whose name was Adam. That way there will always be an Adam." When Adam responds, "I am always Adam. That won't change!" his grandfather sagely replies, "Some things change. And some things don't."[48]

Adam and his parents leave their home for "a better place" that is "so far away that we can never come back," leaving his grandfather behind in Russia. Before the family emigrates, his grandfather gives Adam his prayer shawl, which his own grandfather had given to him. The narrative follows Adam's growth in his new country, as he continues to wear and repair his "always prayer shawl" throughout the years. The story concludes with Adam putting his prayer shawl on his own grandson and promising to give it him one day. Adam explains to his grandson that the prayer shawl has changed many times as it has been repaired. "But it is still my Always Prayer Shawl," he tells his grandson. "It is just like me. I have changed and changed and changed. But I am still Adam." In response, his grandson promises, "I am going to be just like you. I will have a grandson whose name will be Adam. And someday I will give him this Always Prayer Shawl." Now in the role of the grandfatherly sage, Adam replies, "Now I can teach you something that my grandfather taught me. He taught me that some things change and some things don't."[49] The generational transfer of the tallit (prayer shawl) and the name Adam provide both a tangible and symbolic connection to the past, while the wise, grandfatherly refrain—"some things change and some things don't"—elicits a nostalgic longing for that which is irrevocably past.

Published by Boyd Mills Press, the trade division of Highlights for Children, Inc., *The Always Prayer Shawl* was one of Oberman's most successful works. The Canadian writer, high school English teacher, sometime journalist, and filmmaker loosely based the story on his own family and set the story in Canada, but he also made the story generically North American so that it could be easily accepted by audiences in the United States. The book won numerous awards in both the United States and Canada, and it was distributed as a PJ Library book in 2012.[50] The book's success drew on its emotional appeal for audiences of all ages. At Oberman's public readings of *The Always Prayer Shawl*, wrote one journalist, "The effect on listeners is strong. Noses redden. Eyes rim. One man who heard Oberman on the radio had to pull his car off the road to compose himself." Children, too, found the book captivating: When he read the book at a Jewish school in Shaker Heights, Ohio, "Oberman's story caused second- and third-graders to stop swinging their high-tops and listen, even on the hot second day of school. A few thumbs found their way into mouths."[51] Shortly after the book's publication, Oberman turned his story into an hour-long play by the same title. It found ready performers and audiences at Jewish theater groups and Jewish festivals, particularly in Canada but also in the United States. As the *Winnipeg Free Press* reported in 1995, "Oberman's words seem to be everywhere these days."[52]

As Oberman later recounted, *The Always Prayer Shawl* had its roots in the author's memories of his own grandfather and in his relationship with his son. The book creates an imaginary and otherwise impossible connection between Oberman's grandfather, his zaida, who passed away in the 1960s, when Oberman was twelve, and Oberman's son, named Adam.[53] Oberman had inherited his tallit upon his grandfather's death. At the time, Oberman was entirely uninterested in both the inheritance and in Judaism. As he later recounted:

> The tallit seemed to represent . . . something that would bind me up with religious demands and restrictions: "Go to synagogue. Recite the prayers. Listen to the rabbi. Don't grow! Don't change!" So, I put the tallit away in a drawer and out of my mind.[54]

Decades later, Oberman came across his zaida's tallit as he prepared for his son Adam's bar mitzvah. By this point in his life, Oberman recounted, "I was craving peace of mind, wisdom, a faith in something beyond myself, and the quiet strength that my grandfather had drawn from his beliefs. I wondered if I might find it by honoring what he honored and by drawing upon its power."[55]

Oberman imagined that his father would give Adam his tallit and, as Adam put on his own grandfather's tallit, Oberman would put on his zaida's tallit. But Oberman's ex-wife Lee Anne objected—she had bought a new prayer shawl for Adam herself. Lee Anne, who had never had a bat mitzvah herself, wanted Adam to wear her gift, "so she could feel she was up there embracing and sheltering him just like that garment." With help from a rabbi, they arrived at a ritual compromise: Lee Anne removed the worn tzitzit (knotted ritual fringes) from Oberman's father's shawl and tied on the new ones from her shawl. Adam received a tallit comprised of the fabric of his grandfather's shawl and the tzitzit of his mother's gift, a ritual garment representing both sides of his family. "As for myself," Oberman concluded, "I was proud to finally wear my grandfather's tallit and soon afterwards, I wrote *The Always Prayer Shawl*." The illustrated book "was a final bar mitzvah gift for Adam which I gave on behalf of my grandfather, his great-grandfather, who had died so long before he was born."[56] Emphasizing direct transference on the male line, the book elides the ritual innovation—and a woman's interference—in Oberman's real-life family experience.

Like *When Jessie Came Across the Sea*, *The Always Prayer Shawl* simplifies intergenerational relationships. The four real-life generations—Oberman, his grandfather, his father, and his son—become three characters, only two of whom encounter each other at a time. (The immigrant Adam's parents have more of a role in the play.) The fictional Adam is an eternal grandparent *par excellence*, a link between generations and between Jewish life in pre-War Europe and modern life in North America. Oberman's representation of intimate nostalgia suggests a "desire for complete reconciliation of past and present."[57] *The Always Prayer Shawl* binds past, present, and future with the emotional intimacy and familial proprietorship of nostalgia.[58]

Oberman was well aware of the ways in which he conflated characters and rewrote history. He told a reporter, "I find myself writing stories in which old people are tremendously important to young people—the wisdom of older people is one of our greatest resources."[59] Nonetheless, the writer recognized that he dealt more with the idea of elderly wisdom than the reality. He freely admitted, "To be clear, there is a lot of wish-fulfillment that goes on in storytelling. Although I was close to my grandparents, I really didn't know them very well."[60] Reflecting upon the story's impact on readers and audiences, he said, "Even if you didn't know your grandparents, you know what you needed from them."[61] Oberman's comment underscores how important images of grandparents—far more than actual, living grandparents—are to Jewish nostalgia.

In *The Always Prayer Shawl*, Oberman added to the ritual of passing on the prayer shawl another ritual, a ritual of passing on the name Adam, his own son's name. In the book and the play, the immigrant Adam is named for his grandfather's grandfather, and Adam's grandson promises that his own grandson will be named Adam. This generational spread between Adams allows the transmission of the name to become a ritual link between fictional generations while respecting the Ashkenazi tradition of naming children only for deceased relatives.[62] The story, with its many-layered rituals and generational links, provides the emotional, nostalgic intimacy of what readers want from past generations—a comfortable nostalgia that assures them that, while the past is irrevocable, certain core values can be retrieved and passed on to future generations, and that objects passed from one generation to the next perform this work. By tying the familial story to religious ritual and garb, the book makes explicit the connection between intimate nostalgia and American Jewish religious life. The tallit exists in the story not as a symbol of religious law and ritual, but as a talisman of familial continuity. In this case, and often more broadly in American Judaism, religious practice is a vehicle for intergenerational connection, continuity, and recovery. Nostalgic religious practice bolsters this ultimate goal.

Ted Lewin's evocative pencil and watercolor illustrations of *The Always Prayer Shawl* complement Oberman's writing and storytelling, further emphasizing the connections between the author and his story and continuing Oberman's conflation of real and fictional generations. Lewin chose to illustrate the first half of the book, from Adam's childhood in Russia through the early years of his immigration, in black and white, and he illustrated the second half, which takes place closer to the present day, in color. The artist asked to borrow Oberman's grandfather's prayer shawl as he created the illustrations, and Oberman took pictures of himself wearing the prayer shawl so that Lewin would know how to depict it. Even though he had sent these pictures, Oberman recounted, "I was quite surprised when I opened the book to see that Ted had drawn me as the adult Adam wearing the shawl. I was also surprised at how much the model for [the young] Adam resembled my own son Adam at that age."[63] In a transitional two-page spread depicting the passage of time, Lewin depicted the young Adam in black and white next to a full-color adult Adam, who closely resembles Oberman. While Oberman and his grandfather were united by their shared physical experience of wearing the same tallit, the author and his grandfather-protagonist are conflated into a single character in this illustration.

In a fitting performance for a story about rituals, Oberman turned his public readings into a religious ritual by wearing his grandfather's tallit as he read his book. Larry Rosler, Oberman's editor, told me that watching Oberman recite *The Always Prayer Shawl* at his local synagogue while wearing the prayer shawl was "just spellbinding," and that it was one of the "great experiences" he had while working at Boyd Mills Press.[64] The act reinforced the portrayal of Jewish nostalgia as a mitzvah, a religious obligation born of imagined family connections. Oberman's act of wearing his grandfather's tallit also blended fact and fiction. Was he wearing the "always prayer shawl"? The line between his own family experiences and his narrative was deliberately obscured. The division between the religious activity of prayer and the ostensibly cultural activity of a public reading, too, has been made indistinct.

Oberman used his tallit as a prop to draw his audience into the story. Sheree Fitch, a fellow Canadian children's book author, recalled that when she first heard Oberman read *The Always Prayer Shawl*, she complimented him, and he responded by placing the tallit around her shoulders.[65] Recalling the moment, Rosler told me that he remembered Fitch saying, "'I wish I could tell stories like you. I could never tell them like you can.' And he took the prayer shawl and put it on her shoulders and said, 'Yes, you can. You can! You can do it.'"[66] Remembering Oberman after his death in 1994 at age 54, Fitch said, "The metaphor is apt. He wrapped us all in the embrace of his stories."[67] *The Always Prayer Shawl* and Oberman's tallit allowed him to tell a story that was at once intensely specific, familial, and male, but also inclusive of a broad audience. The intimate Jewish nostalgia of the story could provide existential meaning for the author and for his audiences, Jewish and otherwise.

A True Story, Just the Way I Remember It

In the 1980s and 1990s, books for American Jewish children increasingly expressed a self-consciousness about the communal myths that their pages told and retold. Linda Heller's acclaimed *The Castle on Hester Street*, with which this chapter opened, is an example of this trend in its focus on two eternal grandparent figures who debate their recollections of immigrant life on the Lower East Side.[68] First published in 1982 as part of an effort to increase the Jewish Publication Society's offerings for children, and reissued by Simon and Schuster with new illustrations in 2007, Heller's explicit, if lighthearted, focus on debates about American Jewish memory struck a chord with audiences.[69] The book suggests that intimate narratives and delightful stories are a kind of truth—one that can provide religious meaning even if it is not factually accurate.

In Heller's story, the young protagonist, Julie, hears radically different versions of the past from her grandfather and grandmother. Her grandfather, Sol, tells her extravagantly tall tales about his voyage from Russia to the United States and his life on the Lower East Side, beginning with Moishe the goat who pulled her grandfather's wagon from Russia to America, leaping across oceans "the way others jump over puddles." Julie's grandmother, Rose, counters with alternate, more realistic versions:

> Grandpa came on a boat, just like I did. It was terrible. Hundreds of families were crowded together. Babies were crying. Bundles were piled over. The boat rocked so much, I thought we would drown. But in Russia, life for Jews was very hard.[70]

When Sol recounts being greeted by President Theodore Roosevelt and tells Julie, "Everyone who came here was given a castle," Rose remembers the "horrible little room" he shared with several other boarders.

While it is clear that Rose's stories are intended to be more factual, it is important that both versions are presented as stories. Sol tells the more engaging tales, making the Lower East Side a place of magic and wonder. While Rose repeatedly corrects her husband—only infrequently conceding, "That part is true"—Sol defends his tales as "a true story, just the way I remember it."[71] Famed Holocaust survivor Elie Wiesel's advice to genealogists about evaluating family lore is relevant here: "What does it matter if they are true? . . . They're stories!"[72] Heller, like Wiesel, finds indispensable meaning in ancestors' imaginative alternate histories. Family legends are narratives that emotionally connect one generation to the next, communicating values and narratives that fashion family members' worldviews.

Heller's dual storyline offers an appealing way to depict the normative narrative of Eastern European immigration history that respects both popular memory and historical accounts. As one parent wrote in a glowing review of the book on Amazon, "I find this two-step process to be a clever way to teach children about the experience which their grandparents went through, first hooking them with a silly story, and then hitting them with the facts."[73] Like Jewish genealogists who honor their ancestors' seemingly fictional accounts while researching documented histories, Heller can have it both ways. The story valorizes both Julie's grandfather's fantastical account and her grandmother's more pragmatic tale of suffering, hard-working immigrants. While the narrative presents Sol's account as fictional and Rose's counterpoints as realistic, it also presents both as acts of memory-making. Both fact and fiction serve as forms of communal memory and as teaching tools for readers. Children learn not just a realistic portrait of the past but the way they might have reacted to it if they had lived through that period, emphasizing affection for the narrators and attention to recovering and sharing their feelings alongside—or even above—the facts of the story.

In the book's original publication, Heller, who had begun her career as an illustrator, illustrated her own narrative, using the limited color printing available in the early 1980s. The book received attention from Jewish audiences and won a number of awards, including the prestigious Sydney Taylor Book Award from the Association of Jewish Libraries in 1982.[74] Nonetheless, reviewers were not convinced of the book's broad appeal. A review for *School Library Journal* suggests the limited audience for books with Jewish history themes in the early 1980s. While the reviewer found the *Castle on Hester Street* "a good book to read and talk about while comfortably ensconced in a grandparent's lap" and conceded that it might have a place in "a class studying family origins," she believed would have limited interest for general audiences, and the quiet, haunting illustrations were not flashy enough to "attract the average browser."[75]

By the early 2000s, the Jewish book market had changed dramatically. *The Castle on Hester Street*, with its whimsical take on the immigrant Jewish past, may have been ahead of its time. In 2007, Simon and Schuster reissued the book with slight modifications to the text and replaced the author's illustrations with new ones by acclaimed illustrator Boris Kulikov. Kulikov's brightly colored, modern illustrations gave the book "new life," in the publisher's words.[76] The revised edition had mass appeal in the context of early twenty-first century multiculturalism, fitting neatly into some public schools' recently broadened curricula. *Booklist* called Heller's story "an elemental blend of magical dreams and harsh reality" and described Kulikov's illustrations as combining "the glowing tall-tale scenarios with realistic views of tenements and sweatshops to give listeners a sense of history without frightening them."[77] A *Kirkus* reviewer still found the text "a bit creaky"—especially its references to Theodore Roosevelt and Woodrow Wilson—but had nothing but praise for the new illustrations. Kulikov's illustrations "project an intimacy that will draw children in to this intergenerational interchange"—precisely what publishers and PJ Library realized would appeal to both Jewish and non-Jewish readers.[78]

In the readers' guide on the back flap of their paperback version of *The Castle on Hester Street*, PJ Library encourages young readers and their parents to reflect on Rose's grandparents' variant versions of the past. "Why might Grandpa have made up these scenarios? Why did Grandma Rose counter each of Grandpa's stories with one based in reality?" the PJ Library reading guide asks, introducing Jewish children to the self-conscious world of Jewish memory-making.[79] In the early twenty-first century, Heller's story usefully reconciles the difficulties faced by early twentieth-century Eastern European immigrants with their descendants' celebration of those experiences a century later. The majority of Jewish immigrants were working class, struggling economically and culturally in their new environment. Like Sydney Taylor's acclaimed All-of-a-Kind Family series, Heller celebrates the poverty and toil of earlier generations by representing it as a time of warm family relationships and a more authentic Judaism. Providing an alternative history of the period as a magical one helps bridge the gap between historical facts and the way later generations wish to remember the past. By the early twenty-first century, both grandparents' narratives could comfortably exist simultaneously, each providing an emotional "truth" for readers. While these emotional connections were to be taken seriously, they need not be a burden. They could be a fun romp through American Jewish history.

A Girl's-Eye View

The intimate nostalgia of American Jewish children's literature likely reached its largest national audience when, in the summer of 2009, Jewish immigration history was officially included in the Mattel-owned American Girl doll canon with the debut of its Rebecca Rubin character, the tenth character in its historical series. Rebecca was not the first Jewish doll created by American Girl. Lindsey Bergman, a contemporary character living in the Chicago area who loves animals and her laptop and wants to help out at her brother's bar mitzvah, was the first character in American Girl's limited-edition contemporary "Girl of the Year" doll and book series in 2001.[80] But, eight years later, the release of Rebecca, described as the child of Russian immigrants living on Lower East Side in 1914, garnered considerably more media and consumer excitement. Eighteen inches tall, with wavy, mid-tone brown hair and a smart red herringbone dress, the doll was accompanied by six slim chapter books describing a "spunky, conflicted, compassionate and determined" nine-year-old girl. The American Girl doll placed American Jewish heritage in the pantheon of American multiculturalism and invited all Americans to participate in the religious practice of Jewish nostalgia.

This exemplary iteration of nostalgia for early-twentieth-century Jewish immigration won approval from tween girls, Jewish feminists, and even Abraham Foxman, director of the Anti-Defamation League.[81] "Now we can discuss Jewish identity. . . . For this am I ever so grateful," one father wrote in an online review. "Thank you for this heritage treasure," a grandmother gushed in another.[82] As in the celebrations at historic synagogues used as heritage sites, Rebecca presents Eastern European Jewish immigrants as the ideal model of Americans immigrants. While non-Jewish purchasers of Rebecca may have a different connection to Eastern European Jewish heritage, they, too, have the opportunity to form meaningful relationships to Jewish immigration narratives as a way of being American.

Figure 4.3. Rebecca Rubin doll and *Meet Rebecca* book, American Girl. First edition doll, sold 2009–2014. Used with permission of American Girl Brands, LLC.

This accessible nostalgia does not come cheap. In 2009, following the same prices for all American Girl products, customers could purchase the Rebecca doll and one book for $105 or doll, accessories, and complete set of books for $152. A host of other tempting miniatures were available as additional purchases, including a "school set" with a tiny lunch box filled with cheese bagel, rugelach, and pickles ($36); a miniature Chanukah menorah, gelt, and dreidel ($36); a "Sabbath set" with doll-sized Sabbath candlesticks, challah, and a samovar ($68); as well as other outfits and furniture corresponding to Rebecca's adventures in the books, with prices ranging from $22 to $130 for individual items and sets.[83] As with other American Girl products, their high price signifies their value. As Lofton writes of American consumers, "We give spiritual

Figure 4.4. Rebecca's school set, American Girl, sold 2009–2015. Used with permission of American Girl Brands, LLC.

meaning to goods in order to express how much commodities mean to us, and also to reiterate that these goods distinguish us from others."[84] Spending money on American Girl materials signifies the stories families are willing to spend money on. Purchasing the Rebecca doll, books, and accessories allows consumers to possess—to take hold of— American Jewish nostalgia as both a plaything or a collectible item and as an emotional connection to an ancestral or shared American past.

The inclusion of American Jewish nostalgia in American Girl's history of the United States demonstrates its significant place in American public discourse by the early 2000s. Since the company's founding in 1986, and even after it became a subsidiary of Mattel in 1998, American Girl has reflected the vision of its founder, teacher and textbook author Pleasant Rowland.[85] Its products provide a semi-authoritative history of America for girls. As Rowland described the mission of the company, "We give girls chocolate cake with vitamins. Our books are exciting, our magazine is fun, and our dolls are pretty. But most importantly, they all give girls a sense of self and an understanding of where they came from and who they are today."[86] That is, American Girl's mission has been a project of defining Americans from its inception. American Girl's collection of historical fiction has become increasingly representative of Americans' historical racial diversity, including a girl escaping slavery in 1864, a Hispanic character living New Mexico in 1824, an American Indian of the Nez Perce in 1764, and a Chinese American in 1970s San Francisco. The popularity of American Girl products has made the racial diversity of their characters a subject of national discourse. To many consumers, these are not "just dolls," but a semi-official statement articulating different categories of Americans.[87]

As with all of American Girl's historical characters, the Rebecca doll is dressed in period clothing, and the doll, its accessories, and accompanying illustrated chapter books work in tandem to create a high-spirited, independent character grounded in "American values" associated with a particular tradition. Robin Bernstein identifies book-and-toy combinations as "scriptive things," directing children's imagination and play by tying a consumer product to a pre-established narrative. Scriptive things prompt behaviors and shape values.[88] Through its catalog and website, in its physical stores, and in publicity events, American Girl carefully markets the doll, accessories, and books as individual components that are part of the character that is Rebecca. The Rebecca accessories, like those of other American Girl characters, closely mirror the narrative and illustration of the books and encourage consumers to identify with Rebecca.[89] The branded character has had a powerful influence on how children—and the adults in their lives—imagine and interact with the American Jewish past. For consumers of American Girl dolls, early twentieth century immigration to New York is *the* formative moment of American Jewish history. American Girl's Rebecca provides a mainstream, child-centered script for longing for the period of Eastern European Jewish immigration.

In anticipation of their Jewish historical doll, American Girl commissioned children's book author Jacqueline Dembar Greene to write a series of books that would accompany the doll and provide the personality of her character. Greene had previously authored a number of children's books on both Jewish and non-Jewish themes.[90] Her Jewish historical fiction found its way to the desk of an editor at American Girl, who invited her to be one of several authors to submit proposals for books about an American Jewish girl set between 1880 and 1915; Greene's proposal was accepted and developed into a core set of six books to accompany the doll. (American Girl also published a number of additional Rebecca books, most but not all of which are written by Greene.)

American Girl specified only that the character should be among the first American-born generation of an immigrant family who came to the United States during the heyday of Jewish immigration, setting her in a recognizable historical context but not making her too foreign to be relatable to American-born consumers. Greene initially thought about writing a story about a Sephardi family, like her own ancestry. She lives outside of Boston, and she considered having the family immigrate through that city, as many ships were diverted there from New York when Ellis Island could not handle the influx of European immigrants. But she eventually jettisoned these initial ideas for a more mainstream story. As Greene recognized, for many of American Girl's target readership of eight to twelve-year-old girls, the American Girl books are "their first exposure to that phase of American history. And so it just seemed as though it made the most sense for it to be more mainstream and not some little sidebar that I came up with."[91] The normative history of Eastern European Ashkenazi immigration functions as monolithic precisely because it is understood that it must be told first, even if the author herself is Sephardi. Other stories receive later billing, if they are told at all.

Greene's Rebecca is a bold, energetic nine-year-old with big dreams of becoming a movie star. Appealing to the widest possible audience, Greene presents Judaism as an integral though occasional part of Rebecca's life that appears when it is relevant to her adventures but disappears when Rebecca pursues nondenominational activities such as acting in a movie or visiting Coney Island (which the family does to celebrate her brother's bar mitzvah). Like characters in other nostalgic Jewish children's books, Rebecca has grandparents who serve as representatives of the Old World, far more so than her parents, who are also immigrants. Her grandparents, unlike her parents, speak a stilted English. They uphold traditional Jewish rituals, preparing her brother for his bar mitzvah and objecting to her father's practice of working in the store on Saturdays.[92] Rebecca's Judaism and the eternal grandparents in her story are part of the package that makes her a familiar and appealing figure as an American Girl character.

American Girl celebrated Rebecca's debut with a program in which parents and girls could "meet" the new character and eat at the café in New York City's four-story American Girl Place on Fifth Avenue before being transported to a special tour of the Tenement Museum on the Lower East Side. There, girls, parents, and newly acquired dolls visited a recreated tenement apartment of 1916 where a costumed interpreter played its resident, fourteen-year-old Victoria Confino.[93] The following month, at a similar program, girls, parents, and dolls could enjoy a cruise in New York City's harbor and a "kosher-style" dinner.[94] Certified kosher food could be specially ordered. By participating in the American Girl activities, Jewish and non-Jewish girls and their parents could comfortably celebrate the dirt, noise, and poverty of the Lower East Side of the early twentieth century. (To be sure, Greene has made Rebecca's family financially comfortable, the better for affluent consumers to relate to her, while her cousin and best friend Ana fulfills the obligatory role of living in a tenement.) American Girl's celebration of Jewish nostalgia for the Lower East Side points to the ways in which historic sites, children's materials, and kosher-style food work together to form institutional networks of nostalgic longing.

Like Adam's experiences in *The Always Prayer Shawl*, Rebecca's adventures blend material from the period in which she is set, the childhood experiences of her creator, and the present day. *Candlelight for Rebecca*, which fulfills American Girl's regular Christmas or winter holiday book for its historical characters, centers around the drama of making Christmas decorations in Rebecca's public-school class. Greene's story follows a long history of American Jews using stories about children's Christmas and Hanukkah materials to articulate what it means to be a Jew in the United States at home and in public.[95] When Rebecca balks at making Christmas decorations, her teacher tells her that Christmas is a national holiday for all Americans to celebrate. Rebecca dutifully follows instructions but remains troubled by the assignment. Her inner conflict is resolved when she gives her Christmas centerpiece to her Italian neighbor. In doing so, Rebecca enacts values of generosity and religious pluralism, which are presented as both Jewish ethics and the standards of an "American Girl."[96] As Rebecca turns back to watch her neighbor light the candles in her centerpiece through his window, Greene reflects, "Mr. Rossi could enjoy his Christmas decoration from inside, and Rebecca could enjoy it from outside."[97] Greene told me that she based the story on her research on early twentieth-century public schools' efforts to Americanize immigrant children, but also on her own experience growing up Jewish in a small town in Connecticut in the 1950s. She recalled her inner torment when her class made Christmas centerpieces. Greene's mother resolved the conflict, suggesting that she give her project to a widowed neighbor, who expressed suitable admiration for Greene's work.[98]

Greene's story ultimately advances a multicultural agenda as a moral good, presenting tolerance and respect as Judaism's ultimate religious values as well as generic "American values."[99] Rebecca's Hanukkah adventure, conflating different periods in American history within a multicultural "girl's-eye view," encourages readers to use the scriptive book-and-doll combination to place themselves within what has become a timeless story. Longing for the Eastern European immigrant past is both a religious activity for American Jews and a means of expressing tolerance that is available to all consumers. While this may seem like a heavy load for a doll to bear, "competent performers"—as Bernstein calls users who understand the signs of doll and book combinations—will easily decode the layers of logic in this scriptive thing.[100] Readers accustomed to the didactic style of American Girl products are primed to interpret the present-day lessons in the Rebecca stories.

American Girl's Rebecca Rubin was not the first doll to depict American Jewish immigration history, though she is the most commercially successful and most fully developed character. One set of precursors, the Ellis Island Collection dolls, can be found in online and physical Judaica gift shops, including those in historic synagogues, such as the Jewish Museum of Florida. Jewish gift shops—often but not exclusively located in synagogue buildings—have shaped and expressed American Jewish religious values since the mid-twentieth century, as do their online counterparts.[101] In my ethnographic research at historic synagogues, I found that visitors not infrequently bought Ellis Island dolls for children—typically, older patrons bought them for their grandchildren—as well as for themselves.[102] Like Rebecca, these dolls inscribe American Jewish longing for the past onto the body of an imagined child. These dolls often act as ritual objects, sold alongside traditional ritual objects of kiddush cups and seder plates in synagogues' gifts shops run by sisterhoods (synagogue women's groups) as well as museum gift shops. They are often given as bat mitzvah presents, Chanukah presents, or to mark other Jewish occasions. For American Jews, purchasing, displaying, and playing with these dolls is a religious activity.

Copa Judaica, a Judaica wholesaler, began manufacturing these 20-inch porcelain dolls with stuffed bodies in the 1990s. Copa Judaica currently sells them online for $68; prices vary slightly among retailers.[103] According to the Copa Judaica website, the dolls "are inspired by the collected memories of the descendants of Eastern European Jews who immigrated to America through Ellis Island in the late 1800s."[104] In emphasizing memory, the manufacturer acknowledges that its focus is American Jewish nostalgia rather than historical accuracy. The name of the collection, too, is significant: Ellis Island, the onetime federal immigration station turned heritage shrine, is widely understood as a way station between worlds. Ellis Island serves to connect many Americans to their immigrant ancestors and allows them to reaffirm the myth of America as a haven for the world's "huddled masses." For Jews in particular, the commoditized sentimentality surrounding this onetime federal immigration station has transformed it into a locus of nostalgic longing for Jewish ethnic and religious pasts.[105]

Each Ellis Island doll comes with a "certificate of authenticity" and a card with a brief biography or inscription designed to place them in historical context: The "Leah Lili" doll "was from Bialystock [sic]. [S]he immigrated to America through Poland and Germany with her family in 1906 after the notorious June Pogroms in Bialystok during which her family's home an[d] grainery [sic] business were destroyed."[106] "Ruth" is accompanied by a short poem:

> In the shtetl the cold was fierce,
> damp snow and sleet were blowing.
> Then one day did Papa say,
> "Pack up your things, we're going!"[107]

The Ellis Island dolls' cards succinctly summarize American Jewish memories of Eastern Europe as miserable and the move to America as a dramatic change for the better. Ellis Island dolls help American Jews imagine the future of the past, placing themselves in the liminal moment of a child's immigration. Like Mary Antin's 1912 depiction of her childhood immigration in *The Promised Land*, these dolls and their owners can be reborn as Americans, through the passageway of Ellis Island.

Another collection of dolls celebrating Eastern European Jewish immigration, the Gali Girls, created by Aliza Stein, are also instructive toys that straddle the line between collectible items and toys. From 2004 until the demise of the company in 2013, Gali Girls sold Jewish history-themed soft-bodied 18-inch dolls that closely resembled those of American Girl and fit American Girl-branded doll clothing. Until 2009, American Girl customers who wanted "Jewish" 18-inch dolls were limited to Gali Girls or supplementing other dolls with American Girl's Hanukkah accessories. Stein also presented her dolls as an Orthodox-friendly alternative to Barbie and Bratz dolls, which she saw as sexually suggestive. Pre-Rebecca Rubin, Stein aimed to use the dolls to help Jewish girls "learn something about Jewish culture and communities in the past and in the parts of the world they may know little about." Stein told to a reporter, "We noted that it was a successful concept for American Girl, and we figured the formula could succeed for us."[108] Gali Girls's characters included Miriam Bloom, who immigrated from an unnamed "shtetl . . . surrounded by the persecuting Cossacks" through Ellis Island in 1913; Reyna Li, a merchant's daughter in twelfth-century Kaifeng, China; and Shoshana, a Sephardi girl in seventeenth-century colonial New Amsterdam who befriends a Native American girl, paralleling American Girl's Felicity character, whose story is set in colonial Virginia.[109]

Like the dolls, the Gali Girls chapter books, which first appeared in 2005, closely mirrored those of American Girl, though both the dolls and the books were of cheaper production quality than the upscale American Girl products. In a twist of American Jewish nostalgic fate, the author of the Gali Girls books, Robin Levinson, was introduced to founder Aliza Stein by Jewish genealogist Arthur Kurzweil after attending one of Kurzweil's writing workshops. While customers praised the books for providing "a great way to educate the children of today about the children of years gone by," the books were only loosely based on historical accounts. The Miriam book and doll, at least, was truly educating children in the religious longing of nostalgic intimacy.[110]

Gali Girls stories felt right to Jewish consumers, fitting in the normative narrative of American Jewish progress and uplift. In *Miriam's Journey: Discovering a New World*, Miriam and her sisters are unambiguously thrilled to leave Europe for America:

> "Guess what, girls!" Rose Bloom shouted, bursting through the door of their ramshackle house. . . . In Mama's right hand was Papa's latest letter, which had just arrived. . . . Mama waved the cards in the air and triumphantly proclaimed, "We're finally going to America!"
>
> "HOOOORAAAY!" Miriam, Ida, and Sophie yelled, jumping like monkeys on the mattress they shared.[111]

While many European Jews did regard America as a "goldene medina", or golden country, prospective emigrants—even children—would likely have had some ambivalence about leaving behind the world they knew and facing the prospects of a difficult trip to a port, an unpleasant transatlantic journey in steerage, and starting over in a new country with a new language and different mores to learn.[112] While American Girl's Rebecca is unabashedly patriotic, in keeping with the series, her immigrant cousin Ana expresses some reservation about the United States before Rebecca teaches her to love her new country. But like Antin's account in *The Promised Land*, Gali Girls characters feel no such hesitation. Using scriptive things, consumers could express longing not precisely for "the Old Country" but for the act of leaving it. These stories and dolls reiterate patriotic love for the United States and its present day through the form of nostalgic Jewish materials.

Some scholars and cultural critics have taken Jewish doll and book combinations to task for articulating a narrative of American Jewish progress. These stories, they claim, present oppression as a thing of the past, rather than instructing children in "the structures of inequality and prejudice that call us to solidarity with others in the present."[113] While the Ellis Island dolls and Gali Girls may warrant such criticisms, Greene's books address issues of economic disparity, labor rights, intergenerational conflict, and interfaith relations in a format accessible to young readers. Rebecca and her family live in a comfortable row house, but Rebecca expresses sympathy for their neighbors who live in crowded tenement buildings, including her cousin Ana and her family.[114] In

Changes for Rebecca, Rebecca is horrified by conditions at the factory where her uncle and cousin work and takes a stand at a factory strike.[115] In a historical explanation at the end of the book, Greene suggests that when Rebecca grew up, she "might have used her public-speaking skills to become a leader in the movement for workers' rights. . . . If Rebecca became a movie actress, she would likely have joined the screen actors' union so that she would be paid fairly by the movie studios."[116] As one reader wrote on Goodreads, *Changes for Rebecca* "teaches girls that they can make a difference and, even if it's scary, they should stand up for what's right."[117] Greene's books introduce readers to historical and political issues in an age-appropriate manner.

Moreover, all of the books and dolls discussed in this chapter provide a meaningful connection to the past that is independent of whether they become champions of social and political equality. One online reviewer commented, "My daughter loves to show [her doll] off and tell everyone she meets about being an immigrant and what life was like in NYC in 1914."[118] Another mother explained that her five-year-old daughter asked to make challah after reading about it in Greene's books, exemplifying the doll's role as scriptive thing directing play.[119] As children play with the doll, following American Girl's scripts or making up their own stories through play that include her, they build a connection to a particular, intimately nostalgic view of the American Jewish past. These children's materials simplify a historical narrative so that young consumers and the adults in their lives can easily understand it. But these books are not designed to be straightforward history lessons. Instead, they are designed to invoke particular emotions in their readers, inculcating in them the American Jewish narratives of nostalgic longing and uplift.

It's Their Story

While Jews are the primary creators and consumers of nostalgic Jewish material, non-Jews have long been involved in creating Jewish nostalgic materials and, more recently, have been an important part of the consumer base of Jewish children's materials. Non-Jewish artists frequently illustrate children's books with Jewish content published by mainstream publishers. Eric Kimmel, the acclaimed author of *When Mindy Saved Hanukkah*, told me that he saw having his books illustrated by non-Jewish artists as in part following in the tradition of the grand Jewish synagogues of Europe, which were often designed and created by non-Jewish architects and artisans, employing the best talent available, regardless of religion.[120] Through collaborations between authors, illustrators, and publishers, non-Jews have been integral in the production of American Jewish nostalgia at every level, shaping the way American Jews imagine their collective past.

Non-Jewish audiences are key to the reception of Jewish nostalgic children's materials. Attention to non-Jewish audiences allows Jewish producers of nostalgic materials to universalize their immigration stories. While both the book and the play versions of *The Always Prayer Shawl* depict Jewish immigrant experiences to North America, Sheldon Oberman and others involved in theater productions of the story encouraged generalizing its themes. "The story resonates universally with its exploration of tradition, heritage, and the immigrant experience," Rosler, the book's editor, explained.[121] While the original script for *The Always Prayer Shawl* references landmarks of Winnipeg's North End, the immigrant Jewish neighborhood, Oberman provided notes suggesting that future performances substitute local equivalents for landmarks, street names, and local industries of the early twentieth century, in order to make the story more relevant to future audiences.[122] The story is both particular and universal, becoming a kind of Mad Libs of local history.

As he read his book at schools and other venues in Canada and the United States, diverse audiences repeatedly told Oberman that it was as though he had told their family's immigration story. Audiences found the idea of inheriting heirlooms and connecting to the past through familial objects particularly appealing. "Whether it's the charm bracelet, the Chinese tapestry or whatever they received, it's still their story," Oberman told a reporter.[123] As when he encouraged writer Sheree Fitch, Oberman used his tallit—a Jewish ritual object and with particular personal meaning—to provide a material and emotional connection to the past that would encourage others to tell their stories, regardless of whether the stories were particularly Jewish.

Reporters, reviewers, and Oberman himself also broadened their interpretation of the play to encompass the general multicultural themes of immigration, toleration, and tradition. A CBC reviewer said of *The Always Prayer Shawl*, "You don't have to be Jewish to enjoy this play because it's about family and tradition and growing up. Anyone will enjoy it."[124] The play was designed to inspire audiences to relate to those who differed from them by custom, origin, or age: "The whole issue of tolerance is central to the play," Oberman told a reporter. "I want people to have an understanding of not only Jews, but of older people as well."[125] Like historic synagogues, *The Always Prayer Shawl* presents early twentieth-century Jewish immigrants and their descendants as model citizens to which others in a multicultural milieu should relate.

Greene, too, was happy to find that both Jewish and non-Jewish readers could relate to her American Girl Rebecca stories. Jewish parents told her that the books provided an accessible entry into discussions about their families' backgrounds, saying, "We always wanted to talk about it, but we never knew how to approach it."[126] On the rare occasions when Jewish readers objected to the Judaism she portrayed, Greene provided impromptu lessons on pluralism. As she signed books at the New York American Girl store, two Orthodox girls asked Greene why Rebecca's fourteen-year-old sisters lit Shabbat candles on Friday night, when their tradition was not to light Shabbat candles until they were married. Greene told me that she explained:

> The older you get and the more people you meet, the more you will discover that people do things sometimes differently than the way you do it in your family. That doesn't mean that it's wrong or right to do it just one way. It just means that different people do things in different ways and it's right for them. And it's interesting to know about it and to talk about it.[127]

Greene hoped that this brief introduction to the diversity of Jewish practices would broaden the girls' perspectives and encourage future conversations. Fictional Jewish children such as Rebecca serve as both articulations of the norm and as exemplars of diversity among Jews and among Americans more broadly.

Greene also heard from non-Jewish immigrant parents, including Latino families and an Indian family, that reading the book encouraged their children to express the difficulties they had encountered at school as immigrants or the children of immigrants, "because they didn't speak English perfectly or they looked a little different or they dressed a little different or they had slightly different foods or customs." As Greene explained to me, these parents told her that her books "gave my children a chance to open up and share their experiences and talk to us. And these were stories and experiences that they had had that we were hearing for the first time."[128] For Greene, these testimonies of dialogue between parents and children were "the very best outcomes of writing a book."[129] Jewish particularism was successfully used in the service of universalism, or at least in constructing a palatable multicultural American identity. Non-Jews can read themselves into a narrative that American Jews tell their children about themselves.

Through children's books and playthings, American Jews teach their children—and other people's children—nostalgia for Eastern European Jewish immigration as practice of American Jewish religion and American civic religion more broadly. Images of eternal grandparents and magical depictions of historical sites such as synagogues and ethnic neighborhoods create intimate connections to the imagined past. These themes are interwoven in a variety of stories and accompany the characters of dolls to encourage a connection to a particular American Jewish narrative, even for children whose family histories differ from the normative pattern, including Sephardi Jewish children, non-Jewish children, and Jewish children whose immigrant ancestors arrived in the United States long before their grandparents were born. The nostalgic structure by which American Jews are bound and connected to one another, to employ Lofton's definition of religion, is strong and flexible enough to encompass others.[130] Building on the intimacy of historical or imagined family relationships, American Jews employ an intimate nostalgia that uses the past and present to construct one another and to shape the future.

5

Referendum on the Jewish Deli Menu

A Culinary Revival

On Tuesday evening, February 9, 2010, the owners of Saul's Deli in Berkeley, California convened what they called a "Referendum on the Jewish Deli Menu." To the two hundred and fifty people assembled at their local Jewish Community Center and to those watching the live stream of the event from the comfort of their booths at Saul's, deli owners Karen Adelman and Peter Levitt announced that they had a problem: The standard Jewish deli menu was simply too long, at four pages and counting. The menu that deli patrons had come to expect relied on industrial meats and produce shipped from far-off regions, which the environmentally conscious owners of Saul's Deli wished to avoid. As Adelman explained to those assembled, "The idea is to get permission from our patrons to have the deli cuisine breathe like the seasons. And so perhaps you'll have a cold borscht in the summer and a hot borscht in the winter." Levitt jumped in, spelling out for their customers, "That means no chilled borscht in December."[1]

Adelman and Levitt had invited a few of their regular patrons and colleagues, including popular author and sustainable food advocate Michael Pollan, to join them in a public conversation on sustainability and the Jewish deli. With equal parts humor and seriousness, Adelman explained to the lovers of Jewish food who assembled there that a referendum is "when a body, in this case one deli, poses a question to people on issues that will affect them. Sometimes the results are binding; this is not one of those cases," she added, tongue in cheek, because Saul's was "not yet a fully democratic institution." She continued, "We are hoping that by opening up the conversation that we have around our deli to a wider audience, we may all contribute to this cuisine that we care so much about."[2] The owners of Saul's Deli wanted a forum to explain to their customers why they had been changing the menu at Saul's and why

Figure 5.1. Saul's Deli, Berkeley, California, 2019. © Stacy Ventura Photography.

they would continue to do so, in order to serve more sustainable, local, and artisanal products. But Adelman and Levitt aspired to change more than their own menu. They aimed "to make the Jewish deli cuisine actually a living, breathing cuisine. To drag it out of the museum."[3] Echoing preservationists' concerns that historic synagogue sites should resist the deadening effects of "museumification," Adelman and Levitt sought to strike a balance between honoring the past and accommodating modern usage. These conflicts are at the core of the project of American Jewish nostalgia, in which ostensibly non-religious institutions, like delis and historic buildings, guide American Jews' emotional and religious responses to familial and communal pasts.

In the early twenty-first century, there has been a nostalgic resurgence of interest in Ashkenazi Jewish cuisine, dishes brought by Central and Eastern European Jewish immigrants to the United States around the turn of the century and developed in the United States throughout the twentieth century. Journalists and restaurateurs often identify this trend as a Jewish culinary renaissance, a joyous rebirth of interest in Ashkenazi American cuisine. Revival is another apt metaphor for this trend, highlighting the religious and emotional nature of their work.

Rather than simply reproducing recipes from Ashkenazi Jews' Eastern European pasts and immigrant heritage in the United States, restaurateurs and purveyors of Jewish food are deliberately making American Jewish food fit for the twenty-first century. They have lost faith in the legitimacy of American Jewish culinary norms and their institutions, namely, mainstream Jewish restaurants, delis, and manufacturers. Their work emphasizes sustainability, reliance on local goods, and the slow food movement. They tout their artisanal production, culinary creativity, or a playful irony—all of which demonstrate a campy nostalgia that makes American Jewish history meaningful in the present.

The restaurateurs involved in this movement think carefully about the meaning that American Jews' pasts hold for them, expressing their reflections in edible form. Many American Jews, including some of the culinary revivalists, see engagement with Jewish food as a "cultural" or "secular" activity when not in the context of holiday or Sabbath rituals and festive meals. But the careful consideration that American Jews place on food practices outside of traditional religious contexts suggests a deeper significance to Jewish engagement with food, even in ostensibly secular contexts. American Jewish foodways provide individuals with a sense of community and belonging across time and space. In keeping with broader understandings of religious practice as meaning-making activities, it becomes clear that engagement with American Jewish cuisine is an example of lived religion, activities that practitioners might not recognize as religious but that provide meaningful structures to their lives. Preparing and eating certain types of food places American Jews in a nostalgic network of sacred relationships with family members, friends, and coreligionists living and dead, historical and mythical. Jewish culinary revivalists enthusiastically reaffirm their longing for their individual and communal pasts, and they proclaim that their approach to the past is as fresh as their ingredients.

While the Ashkenazi food revival includes both restaurant professionals and patrons, I focus here on the former, whose stories are more accessible, more deliberately curated, and more influential. To conduct this research, I pursued ethnographic research at restaurants; interviewed restaurateurs, entrepreneurs, and other food professionals; and conducted material and digital culture studies of their products. Making use of contemporary culinary trends, their own family stories, and establishing relationships to locations real and imagined, Jewish culinary revivalists create and sell the twenty-first century religion of Ashkenazi nostalgia. The revivalists present their Ashkenazi culinary nostalgia as both uniform and accessible to a broad audience even as it can be molded to fit the particulars of their own experiences and family histories as well as that of their patrons, forming the emotional bonds that are the basis of American Jewish religion.

Movements and Revivals

In May 2008, federal agents raided Agriprocessors, a kosher meat slaughtering and packaging plant in Postville, Iowa, arresting nearly four hundred undocumented immigrants. The raid and subsequent charges against Agriprocessors' owners, the Rubashkin family, made Jewish food production a topic of national debate and deep embarrassment for many American Jews. The Rubashkins had revolutionized and dominated the kosher meat industry, bringing modern industrial methods to the formerly negligible industry of glatt kosher meat, which adheres to the strictest standards of kashrut.[4] The raid drew attention to other denouncements of Agriprocessors, which was accused by various groups of having atrocious working conditions that violated health, safety, and labor laws, including hiring undocumented immigrants, intimidating workers, engaging in sexual coercion, abusing animals, and violating the ritual laws of kashrut. Regardless of whether they kept kosher, many American Jews were repulsed, angered, and deeply embarrassed to acknowledge that, as *The Forward* reported, "in the kosher certification process, working conditions are not a factor, according to the largest certifying agency, the Orthodox union." Postville became a rallying cry for Jewish activists who demanded that Jewish food industries—including but not limited to the kosher food industry—uphold ethical standards, giving them an opportunity to present their messages to wider and increasingly receptive Jewish audiences.[5]

As American Jews responded to the ethical and ritual questions raised by the Agriprocessors scandal, they built on the foundation of Jewish food activism that preceded the Postville crisis. That foundation rested on what has become known as the New Jewish Food Movement, an umbrella term for activists, organizers, farmers, and chefs suggesting new ways to think about food, environmentalism, and sustainability alongside Jewish traditions and new religious innovations. Though the New Jewish Food Movement is not necessarily recognized as religious by all of its participants and reporters on it today, it had an unabashedly religious origin in the 1970s Jewish Renewal movement, a mystically inflected, radically egalitarian, liturgically innovative denomination whose influence on mainstream Jewish denominations far exceeds its small number of members. Rabbi Zalman Schachter-Shalomi, a founder of the Renewal movement, coined the term "eco-kashrut" in the 1970s, and another Renewal leader, Rabbi Arthur Waskow, popularized the term in the 1980s. Eco-kashrut espoused workers' rights, animal rights, and equitable distribution of food resources. The New Jewish Food Movement has grown over subsequent decades, becoming more diverse and mainstream, but it has remained decentralized. In 2006, the Jewish communal leader and food activist Nigel Savage named the New Jewish Food Movement, an umbrella term encompassing a wide variety of Jewish food activists. Though the movement includes Jewish organizations in every denomination and those not affiliated with any denomination and Jews with a wide variety of practices, they are united by a religiously inflected idea of implementing what they see as "Jewish values" within the process of producing and consuming food.[6]

The Ashkenazi culinary revivalists examined in this chapter are a heritage-minded offshoot of the New Jewish Food Movement, applying the logic of Ashkenazi nostalgia to the movement. Jeffrey Yoskowitz, co-owner of Gefilteria, a purveyor of gefilte fish, horseradish, kvass, and other "Old World Jewish foods" made from sustainable ingredients, told me that he found something missing from New Jewish Food Movement organizations—an overt connection to Jewish history.[7] "It's the Jewish Food Movement, but the food wasn't Jewish," he told me. It was "Jews doing organic food" rather than Jews making and discussing organic *Jewish* food. The germ of his business was born when he began to ask, "Why aren't they doing gefilte fish? Why are they so focused on pasture-raised meats and yet they aren't talking about pasture-raised Jewish brisket? Why aren't they talking about pasture-raised pastrami in a deli and things like that?"[8] Yoskowitz and his compatriots take the Jewish-inflected environmental concerns of the New Jewish Food Movement and apply them to a longing for Jewish culinary pasts.

Ashkenazi culinary revivalists think carefully about the food they are creating, and others have been eager to think about it with them. The Referendum on the Jewish Deli Menu panel was among the first of what would be many public conversations about changes to the ways that traditional Ashkenazi food is bought and sold in the United States. Panels such as Gefilte Talk and Let's Brisket explored how Jewish food professionals are reconceiving humble staples of Ashkenazi cuisine.[9] Other events, such as Referendum on the Jewish Deli Menu, Deli Summit: The Renaissance, and The Future of Jewish Food addressed broad changes in the direction of Ashkenazi consumption and culinary presentation.[10] Mitchell Davis, executive vice president of the James Beard Foundation, a culinary non-profit organization, told me he had participated in eleven panels about Jewish food in 2013 alone.[11] In May 2020, during the COVID-19 pandemic, over 20,000 people attended virtual events at the online Great Big Jewish Food Fest, co-executive produced by Yoskowitz and entrepreneur Lisa Colton.[12]

As the names of the revivalist events indicate, the Jewish culinary revivalists enact and inspire conversations with a playful and campy nostalgia. The subject itself lends itself to a humorous approach. An American relationship between delis and humor dates back to the early twentieth century, as Jewish studies scholar Ted Merwin finds. Jewish comedy sketches took place in delis, a central meeting place for American Jews, and Ashkenazi food itself became a central theme in Jewish humor over the course of the twentieth century.[13] Appropriately, the nostalgia of the Ashkenazi culinary revival relies on a camp, the "sensibility of failed seriousness," as philosopher Susan Sontag defines it in her classic "Notes on Camp." Camp, explains Sontag, rejects the binary between highbrow and lowbrow and between traditional seriousness and frivolity.[14] The campy nostalgia of the Ashkenazi culinary revivalists honors the past with both whimsy and sincerity. Their work encourages playful reactions in consumers and reviewers, too. Reviewing Mile End, a Jewish deli in Brooklyn, *New York Times* food reviewer Ligaya Mishan writes, "This is the delicatessen, circa 2011: beautiful and earnest young people in architect eyeglasses sipping wine and eating chopped liver on pletzel like a canapé. Is that so wrong?"[15] The broad emotional range of camp provides revivalists and their audiences with an effective means of building an affective and sensory connection to the past, even as their ephemeral, palpable creations undeniably speak to the concerns of the present and suggest directions for the future.

Traditionally, the campy humor of the deli has taken a male voice. Like other restaurants, Jewish delis have been predominantly owned by men. The primary customers of the first American Jewish delis were likely single Jewish immigrant men, too.[16] Associations between women and dairy products date back to antiquity; females produce milk, so milk is coded "female." In the context of rabbinic dietary laws, which require ritual separation of meat and dairy products, masculine appetites are associated with meat, in contrast to female associations with dairy products. In the pre-rabbinic era of the Jerusalem Temple, meat was associated with formal sacrifices, controlled by male priests and male heads of households, and, as Talmud scholar David C. Kraemer argues, the gender dichotomy between milk and meat was upheld in the rabbinic period.[17] In the United States, the association between meat and men's appetites—as opposed to the daintier dishes women supposedly preferred—was well established in culinary discussions by the 1920s. In the postwar era, this gender dichotomy was demonstrated most strongly by descriptions of barbecuing as a manly outdoor activity, as opposed to women's work in the kitchen. In 1950s cookbooks otherwise directed at women, chapters on meat and outdoor cooking had titles like "Man's Job: Steak" and "Men Like Meat."[18] American purveyors of meat, including Jewish companies, have sometimes relied on gendered and sexualized images to sell their products. The 1950s advertisements of "Miss Hebrew National Salami" and "Miss Hebrew National Frankfurter" featured women wearing bikinis and crowns reclining among and cradling hot dogs, while Zion Meat Company's "Queen of National Hot Dog Week of 1955" wore a bikini top while frankfurters, sausages, and kielbasa formed her crown, short skirt, scarf, and bondage-like bracelets.[19] Associations between men, delis, and ribald humor have persisted into the twenty-first century, but there are a significant number of female entrepreneurs involved in the Ashkenazi culinary revival. While many of these women are business partners with men, the culinary revival provides women with an opportunity to alter the traditional script and insert a female voice—even a comedic female voice—into the story of commercial Ashkenazi foodways.

The campiness of the Ashkenazi culinary revival springs from broader trends in American consumption. Americans' interest in the aesthetics of earlier eras comes in waves, and the early twenty-first-century cycle of interest in an early twentieth-century aesthetic is often described as "hipster."[20] The hipster enjoyment of outdated styles is at once utterly ironic and utterly sincere. One cannot distinguish between consumers' sincere appreciation for the materials of the past and their employment of them ironically because they are one and the same.[21] Importantly, almost no one self-identifies as a hipster. It is a marketplace myth, a series of consumer practices united by the aesthetics of marketing strategies.[22] This makes the hipster no less real—American ethos has long been guided by retail—but it does mean that consumption is key to understanding the hipster mode of ironic living.

Highbrow critics excoriate ironic living, just as they do nostalgia in general. Writing in *The New York Times*, literature scholar Christy Wampole calls it "self-defensive mode, as it allows a person to dodge responsibility for his or her choices, aesthetic and otherwise."[23] Wampole's critique of hipsters echoes longstanding criticisms of nostalgia, sentimentality, and kitsch. But like earlier critiques of nostalgia, Wampole too easily dismisses methods of making meaning through emotional and consumer relationships with images of the past. One can be sincere and playful at the same time, seriously engaging images of the past while reviewing them from an ironic or campy distance—and while making or spending money on the venture. Ashkenazi culinary revivalists are among many entrepreneurs capitalizing on the broader interest in the materials, aesthetics, and tastes associated with the early twentieth century. This in no way means that they and their customers are not thoughtful about their moral obligations. In fact, they use their campy cuisine to articulate their view of the proper relationships to their families and communities and to the Jewish and American past, present, and future.

While the Ashkenazi culinary revival includes people of all and no Jewish practices, their collective efforts should be understood as religious. In American religious traditions, revivals involve restructuring institutions and redefining social goals. The food professionals examined in this chapter are reconsidering the American food industry's reliance on manufactured and processed goods and accepted ways of making American Jewish cuisine.[24] They have lost faith in the legitimacy of American Jewish culinary norms and their institutions, namely, restaurants, delis, and manufacturers. They are leading the call to redefine

American Jewish cuisine according to values of the New Jewish Food Movement and the sustainable food movement. This is American Jewish religion—the institutional networks of individual and communal efforts to create meaning and pursue values through everyday actions, including producing, distributing, and consuming food.

An Unjustified S(ch)mear Campaign

While the New Jewish Food Movement focuses on environmental and ethical concerns in general, Ashkenazi culinary revivalists tell a specific story about the history of American Jewish food. Theirs is a declension narrative, a story of decline that is essential to revivals, not unlike the salvation stories told about the reconstruction of historical synagogues. In the declension narrative of American Jewish food, manufacturers and the mid-century desire for culinary convenience play the bad guy. Mitchell Davis writes in the introduction to his cookbook *The Mensch Chef: Or Why Delicious Jewish Food Isn't an Oxymoron*:

> Somewhere between the Exodus from Egypt and the migration to New York's Upper West Side, Jewish food got a bad rap. Perceived as old-fashioned, greasy, and overcooked beyond recognition, Jewish food has suffered from an unjustified s(ch)mear campaign begun by Borscht Belt comedians and perpetuated by guilt-stricken *bubbes* with heavy hands in the kitchen.[25]

Others simply declare Jewish food to be bad altogether. In a 2011 *Time* magazine article, food writer Josh Ozersky declared, "I'm going to just blurt it out. Jewish food is awful." He enumerated what he has in mind:

> Dry and flavorless brisket, cooked in a salty fluid of Campbell's beef broth and Lipton onion soup mix . . . tasteless matzoh balls . . . pasty, cold chopped liver with inexplicable pieces of hard boiled egg implanted in it; dense lokshon kugels, sweet noodle casseroles as unappetizing as a Christmas fruitcake; and of course, the always terrifying herring in cream sauces, a food so vile in appearance that it could turn a glutton anorexic overnight.[26]

Tellingly, Ozersky largely conflates Ashkenazi Jewish food with pro-cessed American food, mentioning the brands Campbell's and Lipton by name; it probably goes without saying that Manischewitz manufactured the matzah meal in his matzah balls. When critics speak of Jewish food as bad food, their image of Jewish food is tied to particular moments in mid-twentieth century America.

More historically minded critics of Jewish foodways talk explicitly of the effect of the industrialization of American food on American Jew-ish food, associated with American Jews' desire to eat like other Ameri-cans. In the late nineteenth century, proponents of scientific cooking and cooking school experts had urged immigrant families to give up the dishes of their homelands for a more uniformly "American" diet con-sisting of bland New England fare. But by the 1950s, American culinary trends broadened to accept adaptations of immigrants' foodways. The *Complete American Cookbook* (1957), included recipes for chow mein, Javanese rice, tamale pie, egg foo young, and Italian sausage in cabbage leaves.[27]

As ethnic foods, including Jewish foods, were incorporated into the American palate, they were also subject to the enthusiastic reliance on manufactured goods sweeping the nation at mid-century. As David Sax writes in *Save the Deli*, a popular book documenting his exploration of Jewish delis in North America and worldwide, "By the late 1950s, a housewife on Long Island could fill her cart with prepared, preserved, frozen or canned kosher Jewish foods ranging from Crisco vegetable shortening (eliminating the need for *schmaltz*), to Manischewitz bottled *gefilte* fish and powdered *matzo* ball soup mix (eliminating the need to cook)."[28] These manufacturers changed the way Jewish food tasted, smelled, felt, and looked. They also standardized expectations about Jewish food, making it more homogenized and centered on certain rec-ognizable, iconic dishes such as matzah balls and gefilte fish. At the same time, as Sax's account makes clear, the declension narrative of Jewish food blames mid century women in particular for acquiescing to these market trends.

The declension narrative of Jewish food is also inseparable from the fate of the iconic American Jewish restaurant, the deli. The uniquely American innovation of the delicatessen has its roots in the grocery stores of Jewish and non-Jewish immigrants from the Germanic states to the United States, particularly to New York, beginning in the 1840s. Delicatessen stores selling sausages, smoked meat, jams, cakes, and other German delicacies were especially popular around Christmas.[29] Eastern European Jews who immigrated to New York in later decades built upon the establishments of their German predecessors, incorporating their own Romanian, Polish, and Russian foodways into an American commercial synthesis. Jews had a long history of owning taverns in Eastern Europe and, in their hands, the American delicatessen completed the transition from store to restaurant.[30] The Works Progress Administration (WPA) estimated that there were about five thousand Jewish-style delicatessens in the New York metropolitan area in 1936, at the height of the deli's heyday. But as the deli became more ubiquitous, its fare became more standardized. The quality of meat and breads in delis declined as high food and labor costs made cooking, curing, and slicing their own meat an economic challenge for delis. By the end of the twentieth century, delis had lost much of their client base as American Jews' palates shifted. Along with other Americans, they sought diets with less fat and then those with fewer carbohydrates. By 2000, there were only about thirty-five delis left in the New York area, including only a dozen in Manhattan.[31]

As Sax told me, when he set out to write about American Jewish delis in 2005, the working title of his manuscript was "The Death of the Deli."[32] As Sax traveled from one deli to another, attitudes toward Jewish cuisine were changing in response to shifting trends in the broader American culinary world. Jewish chefs drew upon the innovations of Italian and Asian chefs who had reimagined their fare, celebrating American versions of those cuisines and creatively adapting standard dishes. At their Manhattan restaurants, chefs Rich Torrisi and Mario Carbone have paid homage to "their own true culinary heritage, as children more of New York than of Italy." The pair are famous for "applying haute technique and the best local, seasonal ingredients they can find to the tired tropes of Italian-American cooking."[33] Chef David Chang, another Manhattan restaurateur, has done similar work for Korean cuisine.[34] Jewish chefs soon followed the culinary zeitgeist. By 2011, when Ozersky declared, "Nobody is giving Jewish food the Torrisi treatment, raising [it] up to a world-class level and celebrating its flavor profiles," he had clearly missed major changes in American Jewish cuisine.[35] In fact, the Torrisi treatment is exactly what the Jewish culinary revivalists have been attempting to do.

Jeremiads about American Jewish food now end on an exultant note. "Posterity will show that the real savior [of the Jewish deli] will be the handful of second-wave Jewish delis that have opened since the dawn of the new millennium," write Michael Zusman and Nick Zukin; the latter co-founded the Jewish deli Kenny & Zuke's in Portland, Oregon. The owners of these new delis, crow Zusman and Zukin, "are seeking to learn the traditional ways, some nearly forgotten. But they are neither naïve nor enslaved by the past. . . . The modern Jewish deli artisans are updating and altering traditional forms."[36] Mile End, Saul's Deli, Gefilteria, Kenny & Zuke's, and other restaurants and small businesses are elevating a folk cuisine to a higher culinary level and asserting a sense of place in their food, making a connection to an imagined authentic cuisine of Eastern Europe and Jewish immigrants as well as boldly embracing its adaptation in the United States. "It's a late identity politics playing out in the form of a knish," Mitchell Davis told me.[37] The declension-and-revival narrative of Jewish American food has been heralded in Jewish and mainstream media, with dozens of exuberant article titles—"Haimish to Haute in New York," "The Gentrification of the Gefilte," "The Great American Deli Rescue," "The New Golden Age of Jewish-American Deli Food"—proclaiming the rise of a new American Jewish cuisine, one that would return to an ideal Eastern European past and recreate it according to contemporary American tastes.[38]

Family Stories and Recipes

"What we set out to do at Mile End was nothing if not a way for us to connect with our own pasts and families," Rae Bernamoff explains about the Brooklyn deli she and her husband, Noah Bernamoff, founded. She writes that "Noah's Nana Lee was the ultimate home-maker, while my Grandma Bea was (and still is) a high powered professional. . . . We wanted to take a cue from Nana's old-world, made-from-scratch ethic and meld it with the forward-thinking ambition of my own grandmother."[39] Black-and-white photographs of both grandmothers accompany her words in *The Mile End Cookbook*, a carefully designed hardcover with a bright cover reminiscent of mid-twentieth-century aesthetics and filled with large, high quality photographs. Photographs of the Bernamoffs' grandparents accompany Rae's introduction, juxtaposed with a photograph of the young restaurateurs and their deli. Noah wears trendy, plastic-framed glasses and is fashionably if effortlessly scruffy; Rae wears attractive cat-eye glasses and has fashionably long bangs, pulling some of her hair back in a retro hairstyle. The textual and visual depiction of the Bernamoffs and their grandmothers illustrates how the Ashkenazi culinary revival draws together both individual and communal nostalgias. The Bernamoffs want to connect with their family histories, but they are also nostalgic for the imagined world of their grandmothers. Just as authors of Jewish children's books draw on their own memories of grandparents to create an eternal grandparent figure to which young readers can relate, revivalists' memories of their grandmothers makes their work more meaningful to themselves while helping customers identify with their restaurants' stories.

Jewish culinary nostalgia is cool, and it sells. At Mile End, Noah and Rae Bernamoff playfully model an engagement with their family histories and nostalgia about past generations, both for personal satisfaction and as a successful marketing strategy. They model for patrons the search for authenticity in the connection between their family stories and the larger narratives of American Jewish history. As historian Hasia Diner describes, nostalgic foodways often involve the recollection of "iconic meals" that represent dishes as "the treasured recipes of someplace called 'back home,'" wherever that might have been.[40] Retelling the story of American Jewish commercial decline, Ashkenazi culinary revivalists emphasize their culinary origins in Jewish home cooking, especially of past generations. In many cases, as at Mile End, they use the story of a woman cooking at home to lend a certain kind of homey authenticity, often to the work of a male restaurateur who elevates home cooking to an authoritative business model.

Noah Bernamoff grew up in Montreal, and he named his restaurant after the Montreal neighborhood in which Jewish immigrants settled in the early twentieth century. (Like New York's Lower East Side and Brooklyn, Mile End is now undergoing urban revitalization.) Originally, Bernamoff intended to serve Montreal cuisine, such as poutine, smoked meat, and Montreal-style bagels. But his vision changed:

> My Nana Lee died a few months before we planned to open. This woman was the glue that held my family together. . . . Her food, and her huge Friday-night dinners, gave structure and substance to our lives. . . . Maybe I overreacted, but when she died I thought to myself: Is this the end? Will this food find someplace to live on in our lives?
>
> Suddenly everything shifted into focus. This restaurant we were about to open had to be a Jewish restaurant.[41]

Bernamoff's rhetorical questions—"Is this the end? Will this food find someplace to live on in our lives?"—are not only reflections about his own family but imply broader concerns about the passing of the first and second generations of American Jews. His own personal story is presented as a synecdoche for the broader story of North American Jews. Nostalgia for family histories and for larger American Jewish narratives cannot be disentangled.

Through their restaurant, the Bernamoffs communicate their personal, familial nostalgias to their customers, who may enter the restaurant with their own nostalgic attitudes toward Jewish food. Like the staff and visitors of historic synagogues, restaurateurs and their patrons have a shared nostalgia rather than a collective nostalgia. Architectural historian Giovanni Galli defines shared nostalgia as "a spiritual community of individuals, sharing just the sentiment per se and not its object."[42] At restaurants like Mile End, owners and patrons may share nostalgic sentiments springing from individual sources while, at the same time, participating in a distinct narrative about Ashkenazi American pasts in Eastern Europe and in immigrant neighborhoods.

When I spoke with Noah Bernamoff over breakfast at Mile End—I had the "mish-mash," eggs with onions, greens, and salmon; he had a platter of whitefish salad, egg salad, and lox with a bialy—Bernamoff told me:

> It was sort of in her passing that I felt more comfortable labeling this huge life-changing project that I was maybe doing "Jewish." I didn't have the confidence or inspiration until that point to feel proud to call this thing Jewish. But then I did, and it's important that I did, because it's been a large part of the narrative that we've been able to tell and part of narrative within which we've been able to create.[43]

At a public panel, Bernamoff elaborated, "I felt it was an obligation; I felt a sense of responsibility for my future children, that I should be able to provide that warmth and that Shabbos table for them."[44] The incorporation of his family story, both in the past and in the imagined future, into the broader Jewish narrative became a religious obligation, a mitzvah. This religious obligation cannot be disentangled from his commercial enterprise, nor should it be—the Bernamoffs and their customers earnestly engage in a shared nostalgia that is complicated but not diminished by the financial exchange.

Family memories also inspired Shoshanna Gross, the millennial co-owner of Challah, a food truck in Columbus. To Gross, deli items like corned beef sandwiches are more than just symbols of comfort. "Jewish food is soul food to me," she explained. "It reminds me of my childhood, sitting in the kitchen with my mom and sister talking about our personal histories and traditions."[45] Before opening Challah in 2013, Gross spent time thinking about her roots and her connection to the past. Jewish food, she came to realize, was "the thread connecting all of it."[46]

The Mile End Cookbook provided direction for Gross and her non-Jewish business partner, chef Catie Randazzo, another millennial. From their food truck, they serve sandwiches made from seasonal and local ingredients that reimagine Jewish deli cuisine, like their house-smoked whitefish salad with fresh dill and horseradish aioli, served with a potato latke and pickled beets on a challah roll. Their menu draws upon Gross's family background and Randazzo's culinary training in restaurants in Brooklyn and Portland, Oregon, where Randazzo learned to brine pickles and butcher her own fish and meat.[47] The food truck represents "a combination of those two lifestyles, which I like to call the Captain Planet effect," explains Gross, referencing the early 1990s television show *Captain Planet and the Planeteers*. Just as Captain Planet could only be summoned by the combined efforts of the Planeteers, Gross and Randazzo saw themselves as improving their menu by merging Ashkenazi culinary traditions with contemporary food trends.

Gross and Randazzo's campy nostalgia is summed up in the name of their truck, Challah, sometimes spelled with an exclamation mark. The name is a pun on the exclamation "holla!" and the truck's distinctive logo is in the shape of a megaphone. "With food trucks, you have to have a sense of humor. We wanted something that was fun," says Gross.

Figure 5.2. Challah food truck at a wedding. Photo by Dan Buckley Photography, 2016. Used with permission of Dan Buckley.

Randazzo's sister suggested the name Challah. "We immediately liked the camp and kitsch of it. We liked that it described our point of view," Gross told a reporter.[48] In both name and deed, Challah brings together Gross's emotional connections to her family's Jewish traditions and contemporary culinary and marketing trends in a campy nostalgia that reinterprets traditional foodways for the present day.[49]

The family stories of the Bernamoffs and of Shoshanna Gross, retold and packaged as campy nostalgia, are in line with the declension narrative of American Jewish food. While critics deride commercial Jewish food as overly processed and industrial, new restaurants emphasize their culinary origins in Jewish home cooking. Owners' familial nostalgic tales provide credibility when they compete for business with Jewish delis that have existed for decades. David Sax explained to me that in his research for *Save the Deli*, he found that stories about owners' nostalgia for their families' meals provide a sense of authenticity that appeals to patrons and the media. "It creates a story around a dish. . . . It's like, this is something that's real. We're getting the real deal now," Sax said. With a family origin story, "this isn't just some restaurant concept and some guy just taking a bunch of recipes."[50] Restaurateurs' family stories serve the same purpose as the family photographs that traditionally lined the walls of Jewish delis. Indeed, Sax found that many new Jewish deli owners adorned the walls of their restaurants with "their grandparents' photographs and the old Yiddish newspapers and their bar mitzvah photos." This décor, and the stories that accompany it, convey the message to customers that "there is a real family behind this place."[51] Nonetheless, being good for business does not necessarily make a story less sincere. As always with camp, the Ashkenazi revivalists' approaches to their familial and communal pasts are at once sincere and serious, humorous and reflective. The culinary revivalists earnestly honor their predecessors even as they change their recipes, even as they laugh at them, and even when they profit from their stories.

Noah Arenstein, a lawyer and proprietor of the New York food stand Scharf & Zoyer (Yiddish for sharp and sour), was also inspired by family recipes and the desire to put his own campy spin on the culinary traditions of his childhood. Arenstein grew up in Cincinnati, raised on his grandmother's baking, his grandfather's love of pickles, and tales of the fish store his grandfather had owned.[52] On Saturday and Sunday afternoons, his family went to a pair of shops for fresh bagels and lox. "It was a ritual, a weekend ritual, and that was the stuff I grew up loving," Arenstein explained.[53] He decided to pay tribute to these dairy and vegetarian Ashkenazi American culinary traditions by changing them, serving what he calls "global Jewish sandwiches" inspired by the food of Arenstein's childhood as well as "the Jewish cooking of Georgia, North Africa and Spain, among others."[54]

In 2013, Scharf & Zoyer's signature dish was the "kugel double down," a Jewish take on KFC's Double Down, a sandwich of bacon and melted cheese and "secret sauce" between two fried chicken fillets. One version Arenstein created contained maple-flavored farmers cheese and a slaw of apples and onions between two pan-fried slices of noodle kugel.[55] Arenstein explained to me, "It's all very tongue in cheek. A lot of the stuff on the menu is a joke, tongue-in-cheek kind of riff on what I enjoyed eating growing up."[56] Arenstein's riff on the rituals of his childhood rests upon the playful juxtaposition of the traditional family dish of Ashkenazi noodle kugel and contemporary fast food. In reinterpreting familial and beloved cuisine in the style of a decidedly lowbrow contemporary dish, the Kugel Double Down expresses love for Ashkenazi culinary traditions in the style of campy, nostalgic appreciation.

Not all of revivalists' campy reinterpretations of family stories fit the expected mold. Julia Hungerford is the proprietor of the vegetarian Jewish food trailer in Austin, Texas that she named Shhmaltz, ironically referring to rendered chicken fat, a traditional staple of Ashkenazi cuisine, and its popular American referent of kitschy sentimentality.[57] She serves vegetarian and vegan adaptations of classic deli sandwiches named after American Jewish figures like the Harvey Pekar Reuben, a homemade seitan and cabbage sandwich with vegan Russian dressing and optional Swiss cheese on rye bread, named for the comic book writer. Hungerford's application of the names of writers, artists, and actors to her dishes—including a Gertrude Stein goat cheese sandwich and Gilda Radner mock tuna salad—is quintessential commercial camp. Hungerford's tributes to outlandish personalities resonate with Sontag's observation that "as a taste in persons, camp responds particularly to the markedly attenuated and to the strongly exaggerated."[58] Hungerford's choice to irreverently apply the names of larger-than-life celebrities to her sandwiches follows the playful logic of a campy sensibility.

While Hungerford's sandwiches are inventive takes on Jewish culinary heritage "with a modern, Austin flair," her vegetarianism is in line with her family tradition.[59] Hungerford was raised vegetarian in Tennessee, and her vegetarian grandmother, a Polish Holocaust survivor, influences her cooking. "My grandmother is a great cook—the holidays that we celebrated were always around food such as Passover and Rosh Hashanah. She didn't have recipes, you just put these things together," Hungerford told a reporter.[60] A Jewish newspaper reassured readers, "Hungerford's grandmother, now 91, is kvelling over her granddaughter's new trailer, and called the other day from Tennessee to let her know."[61]

Even as restaurateurs build on their own family backgrounds, they are also constantly competing with Jewish customers' nostalgic memories. Ken Gordon, owner of the artisan deli Kenny & Zuke's, which features house-made pastrami, told me, "Everyone is an expert on Jewish Deli—or they think they are—and no one is shy about letting us know about it."[62] He told a reporter:

Everybody has a frame of reference for delis. Everybody was either in a city with good delis, of which there are many [or] everybody has had pastrami, or rye bread, or pickles, or whatever it is, and it's something everybody has an opinion on. Or they taste something we make and it's not like their grandmother made it. Oh, when was the last time you had your grandmother's blintzes? "Oh, it was when I was four." Oh, so you remember that real well, don't you?[63]

American Jewish customers' personal nostalgic attachment to Jewish food can be an impediment to change in the cuisine. Zach Kutsher, owner of Kutsher's Tribeca, named for his family's famed Jewish resort in the Catskill mountains in upstate New York, complained to me about customers coming into his restaurant "with a bad attitude." He was frustrated with those who expected the food they remembered from the restaurant's eponym and were disappointed by his restaurant's changes to traditional dishes.[64] As Gordon said, Jewish restaurants are compared to "one's ideal, not necessarily reality. It's this fuzzy-lensed memory of something a lot of people had as a child—like their grandma's matzo ball soup. Which may or may not be worthy of the adulation." Gordon works to maintain a sense of humor about customers' expectations. He finds expanding their notions of established cuisines "both incredibly annoying and frustrating, and a lot of fun!"[65]

The successful Jewish culinary revivalist manages to strike a balance between personal nostalgia and culinary innovation. As Theo Peck, owner of the Brooklyn market Peck's Specialty Foods (and descendent of the owners of the famed Lower East Side Jewish restaurant Ratner's) explained, revivalists' food must "look familiar and taste familiar and smell familiar, but also taste delicious."[66] Gefilteria's creators have served as Peck's "in-house picklers," a position that seems both archaic and novel.[67] For its most ardent admirers, Gefilteria finds the balance Peck describes. Writer Rose Surnow described patrons sampling wares from Gefilteria's booth at the Hester Street Fair on the Lower East Side in 2012:

A woman named Hillary McGrath took one bite of the gefilte crostini and seemingly went into a trance. I've never seen fish affect someone like that.

"This was the first time in fifty years that I had that same exact sensory feeling as I had eating my grandparents' gefilte. It really brought me back to my childhood," she said.[68]

Reflecting on this nostalgia, Surnow said, customers "were practically having a religious experience." While Surnow likely meant this description to be tongue in cheek, engaging with Gefilteria's gustatory interplay between innovation and nostalgia can, in fact, be a religious activity. Connecting Jewish culinary traditions to contemporary sustainability trends and to the campiness of the hipster aesthetic provides their products with a particular kind of authenticity. Combined with the sensory experiences of personal memories, Gefilteria's products can help customers engage with the sacred relationships between past and present that form American Jewish religion—and, its owners hope, provide a market for a boutique purveyor at the same time.

Kosher-Style and Other Standards

Whether or not Jewish culinary revivalists serve kosher food, they continue to think about kashrut. For Jewish culinary revivalists, kashrut remains a standard of culinary authenticity, even as it is one that they continually challenge. Even if they profess no interest in kashrut, potential Jewish customers' complaints ensure that the revivalists continue to think about the category. (A typical comment on a Jewish newspaper's online article about kosher-style restaurants reads, "I can't get past the fact that for anything to be concidered [*sic*] real Jewish food it should be KOSHER."[69]) Despite these complaints, a long history of non-kosher Jewish American cuisine exists, and standards and popular expectations of kashrut have changed dramatically over the course of American Jewish history. Fervent discussions about kashrut, "kosher-style" cuisine, and other standards point to concerns about authenticity and authority within the Ashkenazi culinary revival.

Kashrut itself has never been stable; it has changed a great deal over time and has had considerable regional variation. Before the emancipation of European Jews, most Jews lived in largely self-regulated Jewish communities. They ate according to regional and communal religious standards, which led to variations in practice, as in requirements for kosher slaughter and the number of hours one should wait between eating meat products and dairy products. Following Jewish emancipation in the long nineteenth century, an increasing number of European Jews, now able to enter mainstream non-Jewish societies, began to question the legitimacy of kashrut entirely. In nineteenth-century America, Reform Jews questioned culinary practices that set them apart from other Americans. They did their best to reframe Judaism as a matter of belief and moral behavior, associated with men, rather than of cooking and consumption, associated with women. Radical reformers regularly accused their traditional opponents of practicing "kitchen Judaism" which should be relegated to "the antique cabinet where it belongs." The term "kitchen Judaism" dismissed kashrut as both an "unthinking folk religion" and as women's work, and therefore not worthy of modern religious practice, which was the domain of rational men.[70] For other American Jews, not caught up in these highbrow debates, "growing apathy or indifference, rather than fervent ideology" led to the abandonment of inconvenient restrictions on consumption.[71]

Nonetheless, even as a growing number of modern Jews came to disregard the laws of kashrut, many retained the culinary preferences that had been shaped by it. Many American Jews have avoided pork and other overtly non-kosher food products. At the same time, they have indulged in foods like Chinese cuisine, in which the traif (non-kosher) products were less overt. In the early to mid-twentieth century, Chinese food, in which meat is minced and disguised in sauces, became "safe traif," less threatening and more attractive than other non-Jewish or traif cuisines.[72] Still, as historian Jenna Weissman Joselit writes, American Jews "held on to their affinity for gefilte fish, brisket, and blintzes, chipping away at the identification between 'Jewish' and 'kosher' in the process." Food that engaged Jewish culinary traditions but was not kosher came to be known as "kosher style," a term whose precise definition varies among restaurateurs and consumers. "The gastronomic equivalent of ethnicity," in Joselit's words, kosher style separated culinary traditions from ritual requirements.[73] Preparing, purchasing, and eating kosher-style food provides a means of "'consuming' Jewishness, or Jewish culture," argues food studies scholar Jennifer Berg. She writes, "Elevated to a new status, what we once thought of as lowly Jewish fare, now suggests a heightened sense of group belonging."[74] What became known as kosher-style or Jewish-style deli food changed as American Jews' practices shifted. The decidedly non-kosher Reuben sandwich, attributed to the German Jewish immigrant Arnold Reuben, has become a staple of the "Jewish

Figure 5.3. Gefilteria gefilte fish slice and box. Photo by Lauren Volo. Used with permission of Jeffrey Yoskowitz.

deli" menu, even as the sandwich of sour rye with Russian dressing, sauerkraut, corned beef, and Swiss cheese boldly violates kosher prohibitions against mixing meat and dairy products.[75] At the same time, kosher-style restaurants brought Jewish cuisine into a general marketplace, introducing non-Jews to Jewish food as their owners competed with other non-kosher restaurants for both Jewish and non-Jewish customers.

Some Jewish revivalists eschew kashrut altogether, seeing a stark division between kosher restaurants and non-kosher restaurants. Ken Gordon of Kenny & Zuke's explained to a reporter that he began serving bacon because there were so many requests for bacon and eggs by his patrons, most of whom are not Jewish. "If you're not Kosher, you're not Kosher," Gordon said. "There's no in between."[76] Gordon believes that biblical kashrut laws "were instituted for some very real health and sanitation concerns" that no longer exist. "I think one of the things that draws me to Judaism is not the orthodoxy or the strictness of the laws, but its tolerance and acceptance of change," he told me.[77] Despite Gordon's assertion about the black-and-white nature of kashrut—with which some who keep and regulate kashrut would likely agree—there is, in fact, a wide spectrum of "in between," which includes American Jews who respond to the tradition of kashrut regulations in different, and sometimes seemingly contradictory, ways.

As I conducted my research, the restaurateurs and food experts with whom I spoke frequently held up Jeffrey Yoskowitz as the revivalist concerned with kashrut and as their Jewishly observant colleague. Yet even Yoskowitz and his business partners in Gefilteria, Elizabeth Alpern and Jackie Lilinshtein, have a complicated relationship to certified kashrut. Producing a kosher product was important to Yoskowitz, since he wanted to be able to serve his fish at meals with his family, who keep a kosher home. When Gefilteria began in early 2012, it was too small to pay the fees for a heksher (kashrut certification by an agency, denoted by a symbol) and its required supervision by a mashgiach. Its creators attempted to compromise by operating their small business out of the kosher kitchen of an Orthodox synagogue in Manhattan's East Village.[78] By the following year, Gefilteria had grown sufficiently to pay for kosher certification by the world's largest kosher certification agency, the Orthodox Union (OU), for its gefilte fish and horseradishes. Nonetheless, kosher certification is expensive and difficult to manage for a small organization, particularly when dealing with a major certifier such as the OU. Gefilteria's team chose to certify their beet kvass and other products through a local certifier, the Vaad Harabonim (rabbinic council) of Queens. Yoskowitz praised his experience with the Vaad of Queens, but he refused to go into detail about his dealings with the OU and made clear that this relationship was not altogether pleasant. Because of the niche nature of its business, kosher certification makes sense for Gefilteria's packaged goods; the lack of certification would probably eliminate a significant segment of its market. At the same time, because of the small scale of its operation, when it sells fresh food such as cheese blintzes at pop-up markets in New York, as it did at Paper Magazine's pop-up Super Duper Market in August 2013, Gefilteria does not pay for a mashgiach to certify that its products are kosher. For most of their audience, it is the company's connection to traditional Ashkenazi foodways and their emphasis on local and sustainable ingredients that certifies their food's Jewish authenticity.

Gefilteria's kosher certification is the exception in the field. Julia Hungerford, proprietor of the Austin, Texas food truck Shhmaltz, sees the vegetarian, non-hekshered food she serves as in line with Jewish American tradition. She told a reporter that American Jews' varieties of kashrut practice have inspired vegetarian recipes. "If you keep kosher," explained Hungerford, "you can't eat milk and meat together, and you have to use separate sets of dishes for the two. It's a hassle, and you can imagine a lot of vegetarian food came out of that."[79] Hungerford's vegetarian menu nods to kashrut laws but is not bound by them, equally drawing Jews who observe some form of kashrut, such as eating vegetarian food in restaurant that are not certified as kosher, and contemporary vegetarians and vegans more generally, making it appealing to both Jewish and non-Jewish customers in food-conscious Austin.

The Bernamoffs' emphasis on sustainability as an alternative to kashrut is more common for revivalists than Hungerford's vegetarian approach. Over breakfast at Mile End, Noah Bernamoff told me that "as a Jew who believes in the Jewish tradition as the most powerful element of our people and our nation [rather] than the religious aspects, I feel like I can very much rationalize the non-kosher food that I serve" in terms of environmental and ethical concerns. "I'm sourcing incredible ingredients; we're buying products from farms, we're buying products from cattle that's been raised with respect for the animal, respect for the earth; fish that have been caught in a sustainable fashion, not with nets, not where you . . . keep half the fish." Customers at Mile End are not fed meat from animals treated with hormones and antibiotics. For Bernamoff, environmental sustainability is a universal concern; at the same time, he believes that as a Jew he has a special responsibility to maintain the earth, a commitment that he demonstrates through the food served at Mile End. "To serve matzah ball soup with unkosher chicken that's pastured and raised by an Amish family in Lancaster County, Pennsylvania, to me is a better chicken soup than buying kosher chicken which is factory farmed, where the chickens are shitting all over each other. That's kosher [but] that's not Jewish to me. That doesn't fall in line with what I think are my Jewish ethics."[80] For Bernamoff, Mile End respects Jewish traditions because of the meat it serves, not in spite of it. True Jewish religion, for Bernamoff, is a sincere connection to familial and communal pasts pursued with respect to ethical concerns.

Kosher meat is typically more expensive than non-hekshered meat, and sustainable kosher meat is extremely expensive. "Kosher meat basically sucks," Ken Gordon told me, speaking of non-sustainable kosher meat:

It's not of the highest quality, is charged a ridiculous premium for, and the local, natural beef we use is far superior. So the question is—do we adhere to some outdated and unnecessary dietary laws and eat inferior quality beef, or do we produce a superior quality product that's—in fact—healthier and doesn't deplete the Earth's resources in transporting it, something that we need to consider as the caretakers of this planet[?][81]

For Jewish chefs like Gordon and Bernamoff, serving sustainable meat is a Jewish obligation. Eating kosher meat is not part of their Jewish practice, and serving it at their restaurants is out of the question.

In discussions about kosher-style cuisine, language quickly becomes confused, even for professionals in the Jewish food industry. In the same interview, Kutsher told me that his restaurant was not kosher and that it does not serve traif meat. In these seemingly antithetical declarations, he meant that it served meat only from kosher animals (beef, chicken, and duck) but that it did not buy meat that had been slaughtered and certified as kosher, nor was the restaurant itself certified as kosher.[82] His business partner, the entrepreneur, philanthropist, and semi-professional race car driver Alan Wilzig, asserted on a blog in advance of the restaurant's opening, "There will be a GREAT many items on the menu for 'all but the most Glatt' of Kosher guests."[83] Wilzig explained that since most American Jews do not keep kosher, the menu would be approachable for most American Jews, even those who keep a variation of kashrut, such as eating only meat from kosher animals, regardless of whether it was properly slaughtered and certified a kosher. There would also be options for the smaller number of Jews who "eat dairy out," eating only fish and vegetarian items at non-kosher restaurants.

Nonetheless, despite confusion of language, restaurateurs have a sense of what fits and what does not fit within their cuisine. "I'm not serving people bacon-wrapped matzah balls," Bernamoff told me, referencing Jewish chef Ilan Hall, winner of the second season of reality TV show *Top Chef*, who serves bacon-wrapped matzah balls at his Los Angeles restaurant, the Gorbals.[84] "I don't believe in that from a food concept," Bernamoff continued. He is insistent that even as his restaurant is innovative, it remains true to the spirit of the cuisine. "You wouldn't go to a great Italian restaurant and get steak and egg lasagna. Lasagna is lasagna and matzah ball soup is matzah ball soup." At the same time,

Bernamoff has no problem serving bacon, the quintessential non-kosher item, within the confines of a breakfast sandwich. "What is special about that breakfast sandwich to me," he told me, is "that's the breakfast sandwich I ate every Sunday morning with my dad. That's the bacon and eggs that I had that to me became religion in some way, in that sort of routine."[85] A bacon, egg, and cheese sandwich represents his Jewish family experience, without contradiction, and his experience is representative of many American Jews. For Bernamoff, a non-kosher sandwich is religion not merely because of the routine, but because of its association with family traditions. In contrast, bacon-wrapped matzah balls, which pair a traditional dish with a forbidden one for shock value, are an inappropriate innovation that goes beyond what he sees as the boundaries of the cuisine.

Some Ashkenazi revivalists aim for such shock value. In the middle of Passover, Jewish chef Jason Marcus and his non-Jewish girlfriend, Heather Heuser, opened a restaurant in Brooklyn's Williamsburg neighborhood that they named Traif, the Hebrew and Yiddish word for non-kosher. As *The New York Times* reported, Traif is located "in the valley of the shadow of the Brooklyn-Queens Expressway, where bearded Hasidim cross paths with mustachioed steam punks."[86] Hasidim had moved to Williamsburg along with other Jews leaving New York's crowded Lower East Side in the years before World War II, and, after the war, they were joined by large numbers of Hasidic Jews from Hungary and Romania who had survived the Holocaust. In recent decades, artists and musicians have moved to the neighborhood, and the culture clash between Hasidim and hipsters has been widely reported and parodied, as on the Tumblr blog *Hasid or Hipster*, largely a compilation of photographs of bearded men in hats of uncertain designation.[87] With Traif, Marcus and Heuser took the juxtaposition of cultures a provocative step further, creating a restaurant "celebrating pork, shellfish and globally-inspired soul food"[88] on Broadway Avenue, the current dividing line between the two residential communities. The restaurant's striking icon is a silhouette of a pig inscribed with a heart. As Traif's owners surely expected, the restaurant's opening generated plenty of buzz.[89]

Traif's engagement with Jewish food traditions is not a simple rejection of religious dietary laws, but a particular form of Jewish culinary camp.[90] As queer theorist Eve Sedgwick explains, "Unlike kitsch-attribution . . . camp-recognition doesn't ask, 'What kind of debased creature could possibly be the right audience for this spectacle?' Instead it says what if: What if the right audience for this were exactly me?"[91] Traif and similar works of American Jewish camp, such as Bad Jew BBQ sauce—"It takes a bad Jew to make good BBQ," as the tagline goes—are post-nostalgic materials, negative but playful reactions to the sentimentality of nostalgia.[92] Post-nostalgic camp ostensibly rejects the sentiments of nostalgia and mainstream American Jewish practice—often along with traditional religious requirements—but nonetheless engages in a relationship with them, maintaining the nostalgic attitude toward the past even as it refines it. As blasphemy always engages the power of the sacred, these examples of post-nostalgic camp still engage the religious meaning of Ashkenazi nostalgia.[93] It is no coincidence that these appeared in New York, the American Jewish Zion.[94] Blasphemy requires the right audience to be appreciated, and camp must be performed at home, among friends, or at least amidst a friendly crowd. Not everyone who eats at Traif gets the joke, or cares about it, but those who do become part of the joke itself.

New York and Other Places

As in other cases of Jewish nostalgia, New York looms large in American Jewish cuisine. Many American Jews see New York as the American Jewish Zion; those living outside the New York region are in the American Jewish diaspora.[95] Physical and imagined connections to New York, like connections to the traditional Zion, are religious ones, structuring the process of individual and communal meaning-making. In the realm of foodways, a "New York deli" is roughly equivalent to a kosher-style or Jewish deli, a manifestation of Jewish identity having been subsumed into the melting pot of New York ethnicities. "The sights, sounds, and tastes that tell us we are inside a Jewish delicatessen were all formed over the past century and a half as the delicatessen emerged and evolved in New York City," says Sax.[96] As Jews who had first settled in New York left that city for other parts of the country, they opened "New York style" delis in major cities as a way to market Jewish food without restricting their clientele solely to Jewish customers.[97] For both Jewish and non-Jewish customers, the descriptor "New York" serves as a mark of authentication, pointing to the development of American Jewish cuisine in New York and, beyond that, to its origins in Eastern Europe. For non-Jewish customers in other parts of the country, a New York deli serves as comfortable way to act as a culinary tourist, more accessible and familiar than a kosher-style or Jewish deli. For Jews outside of New York, the label explicitly ties American Jewish eating habits to the dominant narrative of American Jewish migration history.

In marketing their sustainable gefilte fish, the co-owners of Gefilteria have drawn upon the commercial vintage aesthetic and nostalgic images of the Lower East Side and Brooklyn. At the Gefilte Talk panel, Jeffrey Yoskowitz described Gefilteria as having a "Lower East Side, 1920s, pushcart aesthetic." He and his co-owners began the company by initially envisioning "a pushcart on every corner." Conflating the Lower East Side with the Eastern European origins of Jewish immigrants, Mitchell Davis, moderating the panel, described the company's image as "shtetl chic." Gesturing at Yoskowitz, who was wearing suspenders, Davis invoked "the hats, the beards, the suspenders" of the style.[98] These vague images blend nostalgia for images of early twentieth-century Jews, associated with the Lower East Side, with contemporary hipster appeal, associated with particular parts of Brooklyn. Beyond the physical location of their production in Brooklyn, both Gefilteria's hipster aesthetic and their sincere connection to Jewish pasts place them ideologically in New York.

In the San Francisco Bay Area, baker Emily Winston created Boichik Bagels, first as a pop-up shop and then as a brick-and-mortar store in the East Bay. Winston is explicitly trying to recreate the taste of the bagels of the beloved Manhattan bagel chain H&H, which she ate growing up in New Jersey. H&H closed in 2012, and when she heard the news, Winston said, "It was like someone died and no one bothered to tell me." Winston wryly named her business after her grandmother's response to her butch personal style. "Oy, such a boychik!" her grandmother said in response to Winston's short hair, using a Yiddish term of endearment for a young boy. "Tell me, will you be having your bar mitzvah soon?" her grandmother teased.[99] Winston explains, "In a big way, I'm selling nostalgia, and the name suggests that." This is a nostalgia not for Ashkenazi Jews' European origins, but for past generations of New York Jews, reinterpreted to suit Winston's present-day identity.[100]

Other culinary revivalists, located outside of New York, find the pervasive association with that city to be more of a problem. By now, Ken Gordon told me, customers' ideas of the New York deli are "the friggin' gorilla in the room!" at his Portland Jewish deli. Customers constantly compare Kenny & Zuke's to their ideal of a New York deli, even if they have not been to an actual New York deli in years. Reviewers do not hesitate to do the same. While the majority of Yelp reviews for his restaurant are positive, a typical negative review reads, "They think they are like a REAL NY Deli—me-thinks not. Being a NYer I feel qualified to make that assessment."[101] Yet, as Gordon wrote to me in an emphatic email, "in the 7+ years we've been doing this, not once . . . not one single time . . . have we ever referred to ourselves as a NY Deli. Or a NY-style Deli! Never . . . Ever!"[102] Likewise, Adelman and Levitt list "Why isn't there a good New York deli in the Bay Area?" as a frequently asked question on Saul's website. They explain to customers, "Saul's is not a New York deli, and its non-New Yorker, 21st century audience has a different palate and different cultures and politics informing their dining desires. . . . Recreating the New York deli is not our charge. Food, authenticity, flavor, sustainability, survival, and being true to the values of our culinary roots are our first priority."[103] Gordon, Adelman, and Levitt, like other revivalists, attempt to alter customers' framework of authenticity from emulation of an ideal place to contemporary concerns about the taste and origins of the food they consume.

When Adelman and Levitt bought Saul's from its founding owners, many of the restaurant's ingredients were shipped from New York to Berkeley. The building has housed a continuous series of delis since the 1950s. It has been Saul's since 1986, and Adelman and Levitt bought the deli from the founding owners in 1996.[104] Seeking to improve the quality of the food they served and reduce the impact on the environment in the early 2000s, Adelman and Levitt began to buy more of their ingredients from local sources, including rye bread from the Berkeley-based Acme Bread and fish from Bay Area sources. As they began to serve more seasonal foods, they ran into a pickle problem. As Levitt explained to those assembled at the Referendum on the Jewish Deli Menu, regular customers of Jewish delis expect a half-sour pickle to be consistently available, though they probably do not know about the short period of time a half-sour pickle remains half sour before turning into a full-sour pickle. A half-sour pickle is made from a fresh cucumber and eaten six to twenty days after pickling. Levitt and Adelman had chosen to serve pickles made from local cucumbers, grown between June and November, offering what they saw as a more authentic iteration of traditional Ashkenazi cuisine, as well as one more in line with their culinary concerns. But, as a result, they would only be able to serve half-sour pickles alongside their sandwiches for a short time, and at greater expense. Levitt explained, "We've become ossified. The Jewish deli has to have a half-sour pickle all year. But what happens in the middle of winter? There are no [fresh] pickles close to New York or L.A. or Berkeley" at that time.[105] A year later, at the Deli Summit, she added, "If you eat pickles in February, you know they come from Costa Rica and they're pumped full of chemicals. You shouldn't be eating pickles in February, and I hope you'll start seeing that in all the new delis."[106] For some time, customers had to put up with only having half-sour pickles at Saul's in seasonally appropriate months, along with a lesson in agriculture and geography. (Ultimately, customers' loyalty to the standard American Jewish deli fare won this battle, and one can now eat half-sour pickles at Saul's year-round.)

As Adelman told me, she and Levitt are broadening the geographic and historical scope purview of their Jewish delicatessen. "We see ourselves in a continuum," she said. The deli's "principal story is Ashkenazi Jews from the Old World and then New York, and then they continue going west," until they reach California, where Saul's is located. She continued:

> We absolutely recognize and use as a major resource Poland and Russia and the whole Ashkenazi Jewish experience. And then we also quote and use and revel in New York, although we don't feel it's necessary to fly our ingredients out from there—although there are a couple products that for nostalgia's sake we will, like Fox's U-Bet syrup.[107]

The food served at Saul's tells a story of the relationship between emotions, community, geography, and memory. But Adelman and Levitt are expanding the Jewish pasts represented at their deli, too. While their menu remains focused on Eastern European inspirations, they also offer a number of dishes from Middle Eastern cuisine, inspired by Sephardi and Mizrachi Jewish pasts. Serving selective Middle Eastern dishes

allows Saul's to serve more vegan and vegetarian entrees, which is important for a restaurant in Berkeley but can be challenging for a Jewish deli.
"Broadening that story a little bit . . . [is] a little sidestep that's inclusive"
of both more Jewish pasts and more customers and allows Saul's to "continue to tell the story" of Jewish cultures and Jewish food beyond the
monolithic narrative of Ashkenazi American food, Adelman told me.[108]
At the same time, this very inclusion also folds non-Ashkenazi Jewish
histories into the narrative of Ashkenazi nostalgia. The side dish may be
Mizrachi, but the larger platter—and the deli itself—remains focused on
Central and Eastern European heritage.

Even within New York, some revivalists are de-emphasizing the idea
of that city, though change remains difficult. Montreal-born Noah Bernamoff's creation of Mile End in Brooklyn began with his "quest to
make smoked meat, the most sacred of Montreal delicatessen foods.
It started out as homesickness, a longing for familiar flavors that New
York's pastrami and corned beef couldn't quite replicate."[109] Bernamoff
ultimately chose to emphasize the Jewish nature of his restaurant over
its Canadian roots, both because of personal convictions and economic
considerations, though he maintained its Montreal theme, too. "There's
a million Jews in the city, and there's only a couple thousand Canadian
[Jews]," Bernamoff told me, laughing at his original naiveté.[110] Still, Mile
End presented smoked meat as an iconic *Jewish* food within New York
culinary pantheon, multiplying the geographic referents of Ashkenazi
culinary nostalgia.[111] New York remains a powerful symbol of Ashkenazi culinary authenticity, but alternative approaches that broaden its
narrative and religious possibilities are developing. Revivalist restaurateurs are both reinvigorating and reimagining their emotional relationships to the city's Jewish histories and, in doing so, building on and
shifting the practice of American Jewish religion.

A Knish Going Glam

In July 2013, writer A. Pontius reviewed the Brooklyn restaurant Potatobird, which serves updated versions of knishes, on the website *Tables for
One*. "The knish," declared Pontius, "feels like a weird relic of New York,
although unlike most relics, you can eat it with mustard." Potatobird
offers knishes to be eaten with other condiments, too, serving knishes

made with maple syrup and bacon, wasabi knishes, pulled pork barbe-
cue knishes, hushpuppy knishes, and aloo gobi knishes, among others.
"These are decidedly non-kosher knishes," Pontius concluded. Katherine Bernof, the proprietor of the Potatobird, explained her restaurant
concept, saying, "I like the idea of the knish going glam for a day. It's like
dressing up your grandmother in your leather jacket and adding some
sparkly sunglasses."[112] Though the review referred to knishes as a New
York food, they are one of a number of iconic Ashkenazi Jewish foods
that have been symbolically tied to New York; Berg identifies knishes as
the "most ethnic and least assimilated" iconic Jewish food.[113] In merging
the knish with the cuisines of other cultures, Potatobird made explicit
the culinary fusion of American and European Jewish cuisines that had
occurred gradually throughout twentieth century.

I planned to visit Potatobird and interview Bernof for this book, but,
strangely, while I could locate the address of Potatobird provided in the
review on Google Maps, I could not find Potatobird's website or any
other reviews. To my increasing frustration, I was also unable to locate
Bernof's contact information, no matter how many times I typed various combinations of the search terms "Katherine Bernof," "Potatobird,"
and "knish" into Google's search engine. After spending an embarrass-
ingly long time searching for traces of Potatobird and Bernof online,
I finally realized that the website *Tables for One* posts reviews of fake
restaurants. The creation of designer Evan Johnston, the blog served as a
"little world," snapshots of "another New York City," in which Johnston,
under the nom de plume A. Pontius, reviewed restaurants of his own
imagining.[114]

While this review seems to be a practical joke at my expense, it also
signifies how widespread a phenomenon Jewish culinary nostalgia has
become. It is so recognizable that websites like *Tables for One* can parody
it, imagining an entirely plausible restaurant that playfully reimagined
the knish "dressed up" in the guise of other recognizable cuisines. In
fact, Potatobird was not so far off. Knishery NYC, the creation of Noah
Wildman, offers sweet and savory knishes at booths at street fairs and
at specialty shops such as Malt and Mold on the Lower East Side.[115]
Wildman told a reporter, "It's time for the knish to get a modern up-
date."[116] While his knishes are not quite as outlandish as those of the
imaginary Potatobird, Wildman has been known to make mushroom

quinoa, curry sweet potato, broccoli cheddar, and hazelnut chocolate cheese knishes.[117]

The campy and ironic nostalgias of the Jewish culinary revival have become a widespread phenomenon, as the Potatobird review demonstrates. Jewish culinary revivalists engage nostalgia even as they push back against it, forming dynamic relationships with imagined pasts and complex religious communities in the present. Nostalgia calls attention to what no longer exists, longing for an irrevocable past. But even in its melancholy, religious nostalgia can be playful and celebratory, not only of the past, but of the emotional effect of the past upon the present, like a knish going glam for the day.

Conclusion

The Limits and Possibilities of Nostalgia

On a Saturday evening in May 2018, Courtney Byrne-Mitchell and Mattie Ettenheim were married at the Golden Unicorn, a dim sum restaurant in Manhattan's Chinatown, just down the street from the Museum at Eldridge Street, located in the historic Lower East Side synagogue. Byrne-Mitchell and Ettenheim met when they were both working at the museum. Byrne-Mitchell began as an intern at the museum and worked her way up to director of visitor services; Ettenheim was the educational manager, and I interviewed her when I conducted research at the museum. Their wedding, and their reception and ketubah signing at the museum the next morning, reveal the possibilities—and some of the limits—of the institutions of American Jewish nostalgia.

Ettenheim is Jewish, and Byrne-Mitchell's family is Irish Catholic; their wedding was, in Byrne-Mitchell's words, a "big gay interfaith wedding." The couple—who go by the Byrneheims after their marriage—were married by folklorist Hanna Griff-Sleven, who had been a mentor to both of them at Eldridge Street. Griff-Sleven had shaped much of the direction of the museum, creating its signature Egg Rolls and Egg Creams (now Egg Rolls, Egg Creams, and Empanadas) Festival, a street festival that celebrates the multiple immigrant heritages, past and present, of the neighborhood, discussed in Chapter 3. Like Griff-Sleven's street festival, the wedding ceremony was a celebration of multiple heritages with a Jewish overlay. The dim sum restaurant was a large, affordable space serving one of many types of New York ethnic food that the couple loved. The Byrneheims thoughtfully reshaped the standard Jewish wedding ceremony to reflect them, their family and communities, and their values.[1] In place of the sheva brachot (seven blessings) of the traditional Jewish wedding ceremony, the couple's friends presented reinterpretations of themes from the Jewish wedding blessings, including saying an Irish blessing and singing an Alleluia, echoing a Catholic Mass.

Outside, the couple had a professional photograph taken of the two of them gazing at each other—Byrne-Mitchell in a flowy white jumpsuit and Ettenheim in a white halter-top dress—in the middle of the street outside the Eldridge Street Synagogue, fire escapes and Chinese signs in the background. Byrne-Mitchell posted it on Instagram with the caption "Where it all began . . ." She referred, of course, to the beginning of their relationship, but the caption might also identify the Lower East Side as a nostalgic birthplace, in the general imagination, of American Jewish history, and their connection to that history as a couple.

Though families can and do rent out the Eldridge Street Synagogue for weddings and bar and bat mitzvah ceremonies, the Byrneheims did not. An Orthodox congregation still meets in the building, and museum staff continually work to balance their institutional needs and the sensibilities of visitors with those of the congregation. The Byrneheims' choice of a Saturday evening wedding—beginning before the end of Shabbat on Saturday night—precluded their use of the space for their ceremony, as Orthodox Jewish weddings are not held on Shabbat. And as former employees of the museum, Byrne-Mitchell told me, the couple avoided confronting the congregation and the museum with the question of whether a gay and interfaith wedding would be permitted in the space. Their choice to sidestep conflict about interfaith and gay Jewish weddings exemplifies the negotiation of contested institutional goals discussed in Chapter 3.

Yet, despite their assumption that their marriage would not be welcomed by the congregation that meets in the space, the Byrneheims wanted to include the Eldridge Street Synagogue in their wedding somehow because that space is sacred to them. On the morning following their wedding ceremony, the Byrneheims hosted a Sunday morning brunch at the Museum at Eldridge Street. All of the museum's volunteers were invited, including those who had not met each of the brides. Some of the couple's friends had never been to the museum before, a regrettable fact the couple thought should be amended. The museum is "such an important space to us that we wanted everyone to be there," Byrne-Mitchell told me. It is "a space that will always be part of our lives."[2] It felt right to celebrate their marriage with their community in that space and in the context of the nostalgic story told by the Museum at Eldridge Street. This location linked the story of the beginning of their relationship and marriage with a particular story of the genesis of American Jewish communities, bringing together the optimism and affection they felt for their personal pasts and the emotions that the Museum at Eldridge Street evokes of love for the past and hope for the future. It was both fitting and praiseworthy—an American Jewish mitzvah—to celebrate their marriage there.

It matters that the Byrneheims are gay and interfaith, that they were married by a female folklorist rather than a male rabbi, and that they expressed their union in relation to a primary site of the standard narrative of American Jewish nostalgia. While some might see theirs as a singular and individualistic wedding, diverging from the standard practices of American Jews, the Byrneheims are deeply and intentionally tied to their communities, including Jewish communities and American Jewish narratives. They are representative of an increasing number of people in American Jewish communities in the twenty-first century who are creatively exploring and expanding American Jewish religious life while productively, lovingly, and yearningly engaging with its past.

The Byrnheims' wedding, like the stories of other people told throughout this book, refutes claims by Jewish academics and Jewish community professionals that American Jewish religion is declining. Looking for American Jewish religion in synagogues, Jewish community centers, and Jewish Federations, they fail to see it flourishing in unconventional religious institutions like museums and restaurants. And, in lamenting the loss of normatively constituted American Jewish families—the so-called "continuity crisis" or "marriage crisis" of American Judaism—they fail to see, and fail to study, the new places and new communal practices where American Jewish religion is thriving. These new religious places and practices include institutions and activities inspiring nostalgic longing and affection for Eastern European Jewish immigration history, like the Museum at Eldridge Street.

Nostalgic institutions, like the mitzvah of nostalgia itself, are products of the late twentieth- and twenty-first centuries. As these institutions have developed, they have increasingly standardized the ways American Jews think they *should* feel and respond to Eastern European immigration history. Beginning in the 1970s, Jews who were inspired by the white ethnic identity movement that formed in response to movements to positively identify African American and other minority histories and experiences turned to researching their family histories.[3] As they found each other, they created local, national, and international societies, journals, and databases. Preservationists took an interest in restoring historic synagogues located in former Jewish urban neighborhoods in the 1980s, creating organizations and foundations that would support their efforts to present the buildings as museums to the public. As public interest in multiculturalism picked up, Jewish and non-Jewish authors, illustrators, and publishers of children's books produced children's books representing Eastern European Jewish immigration in the 1990s. By the early 2000s, as hipster nostalgia trended, Jewish chefs, restaurateurs, and other "foodies" turned their attention to reinvigorating the deli and other forms of Ashkenazi American cuisine.

Each of these forms adds something new to the rhetoric of Jewish nostalgia: Genealogy directs researchers toward an intimate and authoritative nostalgia, emphasizing the power of the family historian. Historic synagogues guide visitors toward an elegiac nostalgia. Children's books and dolls teach a playful and affectionate nostalgia, and the culinary revival offers a campy or ironic nostalgia. Different materials suggest different emotional registers for nostalgia. At the same time, each of these forms has built on the logic of the others. Family historians support the restoration of historic synagogues and patronize delis that remind them of family traditions. Historic synagogues host meetings of genealogists, readings of nostalgic children's books, and get catering from Jewish culinary revivalists. Children's books reference historic synagogues and Eastern European foodways. Culinary revivalists draw upon their family histories for inspiration and claims of authenticity. These connections and relationships have provided outlets for creative reflection on the past as well as reinforcing the standards of nostalgia.

There are other important forms of American Jewish nostalgia for the immigration era in the late twentieth and early twenty-first centuries, including the creation and endless revivals of *Fiddler on the Roof*; postvernacular interest in Yiddish, including a growing number of Yiddish speakers; and the second life of klezmer music, among others.[4] But each of the four case studies in this book exemplifies a particular kind of material culture that infuses the everyday activities of Jews' lives with nostalgia. They are not singular events like attending a concert. Rather, they construct a sensibility that profoundly shapes people's lives. Even those who engage with these materials may not see, without an interpretive frame like the one presented in this book, the ways that these objects and spaces constitute and shape their religious identities, senses of self, and feelings of belonging. These four cases are also generally overlooked by scholars examining American Jewish religion and American Jewish organizations, who see them as light or fun and therefore fail to take them seriously as part of the religious fabric of American Jewish life.

These are also organizations that are dynamic and constantly addressing new trends. As DNA testing becomes ever more affordable and accessible, discussions on online Jewish genealogy forums have an increasing focus on understanding and interpreting the results of DNA tests. Even as conversations about race continue to make many Ashkenazi American Jews squirm—many are equally uncomfortable with identifying as simply "white" and with descriptions of Jews as a distinct race—conversations about Jews, DNA, and genealogy rely on racialized notions of Jewishness. In analyzing what they call "gene talk" among Jewish genealogists, religious studies scholars Sarah Imhoff and Hillary Kaell find, "gene talk reinforces the idea of a Jewish people both by building a community of genealogists helping one another and by offering apparent scientific support for the 'objective' reality of Jewish lineage."[5] As DNA tests improve, Jewish genealogists have ever more avenues of overcoming "brick walls," dead ends blocking their research that they could not overcome with older research avenues of oral history, material culture, and archival documents alone. One the one hand, an overriding focus on Ashkenazi Jewish genes in home testing reinforces the idea that Ashkenazi heritage is *Jewish* heritage and bolsters a focus on nostalgia for Eastern European pasts. On the other hand, as those who identify as Jews find a range of non-Ashkenazi genetic markers and as those who do not identify as Jews are told they have "Jewish genes," conversations about Jewish heritage may widen.[6] For now, many Americans who do not identify as Jews but learn of Jewish ancestry through DNA testing are quickly pulled into conversations about American Jewish nostalgia for Ashkenazi heritage. While these new Jews are often warmly welcomed by normative Jews on Jewish genealogy social media platforms, such as the Tracing the Tribe Facebook group, they can be seen as threatening, too, especially if they continue to profess another religion.[7]

Historic synagogues continue to become incorporated into mainstream American immigration narratives, solidifying American Jewish nostalgia as part of American discourse. The Jewish Museum of Florida, housed in two historic synagogues in Miami Beach, became part of Florida International University in 2012, enabling it to draw on the university's resources without substantially changing its mission.[8] The Vilna Shul in Boston has been undergoing long-needed renovations, restoring the building's badly degraded murals and upgrading the space, including making the building more accessible. Part of its funding came from the Boston City Council and the Mass Cultural Council, a Massachusetts state agency. Boston city councilor Josh Zakim told a reporter that "the restoration of the Vilna is important to the history of Boston, and to the history of immigration in our city and our country."[9] Both developments demonstrate the increasing inclusion of American Jewish nostalgia in local civic histories. While American Jews have long pushed civic institutions to include American Jewish history, these sites of Jewish nostalgia use their spaces to teach visitors to have a certain kind of emotional reaction to American Jewish immigration history.[10]

The Museum at Eldridge Street has continued to use its space in creative ways to tell stories of loss, longing, and revival. In 2018, it hosted the site-specific exhibit *Below the Horizon: Kiki Smith at Eldridge*, partnering with the artist who designed its new stained-glass east window. In the most dramatic part of the exhibit, gold leaf-covered birds perched on aluminum chairs in the women's gallery, recalling the pigeons that flew through the sanctuary during its decrepitude. One of the chairs balanced impossibly on another, and another was suspended like another chandelier between the original west rose window and Smith and Gans's new window. Like the feminist installations the Eldridge Street Project hosted in the women's gallery during the building's renovation, Smith's exhibit recalled the synagogue's absent founding congregants of the early twentieth century, especially the women. It evoked the synagogue building's ruin and the hope of its restoration. Some reviewers saw the empty chairs as symbols of the absence of Jews murdered in the

Figure C.1. Kiki Smith, *Below the Horizon: Kiki Smith at Eldridge*. Installation at the Eldridge Street Synagogue, 2018. Photo by author.

Holocaust, once again drawing connections between empty American synagogues and the Holocaust. Others saw "real joy" in the birds flapping their wings and emphasized the way the art interacted with the "serene, lambent mood" of the synagogue building.[11]

Children's books featuring themes of American Jewish nostalgia receive an ever-widening audience through PJ Library, the non-profit organization distributing free children's books to Jewish and interfaith families. The organization continues to expand its influence on Jewish and interfaith families in the United States and throughout the world, with quantifiable effects.[12] In 2018, the Association of Jewish Libraries gave its prestigious Sydney Taylor Body of Work Award to PJ Library and its founding philanthropist, Harold Grinspoon. PJ Library continues to include children's books with nostalgic themes in its repertoire. The Jewish Book Council awarded Lesléa Newman's *Gittel's Journey: An Ellis Island Story*, an illustrated PJ Library book about a Jewish girl's immigration from an unnamed Eastern European country, the 2019 National Jewish Book Award for Children's Literature.[13] Another popular new book distributed by PJ Library, Joanne Oppenheim's *The Knish War on Rivington Street*, is based on a true story of competing bakeries selling knishes on the Lower East Side.[14] The book does not mention Jews, Judaism, or any Jewish signifiers other than knishes, pushcarts, and Rivington Street. Readers who are American Jewish insiders may know that Rivington Street is located in Lower Manhattan, in what once was a Jewish immigrant neighborhood filled with pushcarts, and that knishes are an Eastern European Jewish food that has become part of New York street food. The absence of explicit reference to Jews allows this to be a nostalgic Jewish story for self-selecting readers. For others, this can be a generic story of immigrant small-business owners and a lesson in tolerance.

Not all nostalgic endeavors are successful. Some of the sites of Jewish foodways discussed in this book have closed. Food trucks are a lower-cost way for chefs and restaurateurs to try out new ideas—and the Ashkenazi culinary revival lends itself to experimentation—but they are also notoriously difficult businesses. The food trucks Challah in Columbus and Shhmaltz in Austin have closed, though Shhmaltz has made a reappearance as a vegan deli pop-up restaurant.[15] The restaurant Kutsher's Tribeca, in lower Manhattan, closed too. Zach Kutsher, the owner, had told me explicitly that, rather than pursuing a passion for reimagined

Ashkenazi cuisine, he hoped to capitalize on a trend by using his family's name, remembered by some American Jews for his family's former resort in the Catskill mountains.[16] Kutsher's Tribeca was on the pricier side for Ashkenazi culinary revivalist ventures, and perhaps he misjudged the price point.

But other Ashkenazi culinary revivalists are thriving. The owners of Gefilteria, Jeffrey Yoskowitz and Liz Alpern, continue to sell their mail-order frozen gefilte fish and packaged goods, but they have also branched out. Their cookbook, named *The Gefilte Manifesto* after their initial business platform, received a great deal of favorable press from Jewish and national outlets.[17] The pair continue to give classes, talks, and workshops individually and together throughout North America and Europe. Kenny & Zuke's filed for bankruptcy in 2019 and closed one location, but its locations in downtown Portland and Portland International Airport remain open.[18] Noah and Rae Bernamoff have left Mile End Deli, but the deli continues under the ownership of Joel Tietolman and Adam Grusin, who have expanded to a location in Birmingham, Alabama.[19] Wise Sons Jewish Deli, a revivalist deli and bagel venture in San Francisco that "pairs classic Jewish recipes with the best Californian ingredients," now has five locations in the Bay Area and has expanded even further afield, with an overseas outlet in Tokyo.[20]

While nostalgia is often thought of as feminine, all of these ventures include people of all genders. They pursue Jewish genealogy, are staff members and visitors to historic synagogues, write and create Jewish children's books, and are reimagining Ashkenazi cuisine. Often, men and women do so in partnership with one another, as in Sallyann Amdur Sack and Gary Mokotoff co-founding and editing the Jewish genealogy journal *Avotaynu* or Jeffrey Yoskowitz and Liz Alpern co-founding the Jewish food venture the Gefilteria. American Jewish nostalgia is gendered, but it is gendered in the way that Holocaust remembrance and identification with Israel are gendered. That is, these activities, like all human activities, are performed by gendered people who have gendered experiences, but are not in themselves performed more by people of a certain gender.

Still, perceptions of gender differences persist. At a 2018 panel on the Jewish deli revival in San Francisco, one woman asked of the all-male panel, "Why aren't there women on this panel? Is it that there aren't women in this field?" Evan Bloom, a co-founder of Wise Sons, pointed to a few women in the field—including Karen Adelman of Saul's Deli in Berkeley and Liz Alpern of Gefilteria, both of whom work with male business partners—but suggested that it was a male-dominated field.[21] I would point to the same women and suggest that the Ashkenazi culinary revival has a surprising number of women, considering how difficult the food industry is for women in general.[22] Furthermore, though several food trucks featuring Ashkenazi revivalist food that were owned by women have closed, their onetime presence points to the attraction of this work for women.

More strikingly, I have found a gendered difference not in the practices of nostalgia itself but in the reception of my work. When I presented my research on Jewish genealogists to a meeting of the San Francisco Bay Area Jewish Genealogy Society, men tended to respectfully disagree with my conclusions about nostalgia and religion, preferring to emphasize the archival and academic aspects of their work over the emotional, while women heard me naming something that resonated with them. "We're doing more than recording names," one woman told me. I have tried to name that "more."

The genealogical researcher who spoke to me of the "more" recognized in my research an acknowledgment of the affective work she performs through genealogy. It is a religious practice that helps her to express her honor, reverence, and longing for the past and to understand her place in her family narrative and, through it, her place in the world. Though they would not necessarily use these words, Byrne-Mitchell and Ettenheim's wedding was also one example of individuals connecting ideas of American Jewish pasts and futures in through communal rituals and institutions. Theirs is not a story of cultural loss, but of a generative relationship to American Jewish histories and stories in order to identify themselves as a couple and situate themselves as a family with ties to the past that reach into the present in ever-widening circles. The Byrneheim wedding ceremony on the Lower East Side and their brunch at the Eldridge Street Synagogue meaningfully placed their new family unit within the context of their immediate families; their communities; their religious institutions, beliefs, and practices; and the narratives to which they were drawn.

When I began this project, I thought I was writing a book about institutions, including genealogical societies, museums, publishing companies, PJ Library, and restaurants. It turns out I also wrote a book about families—or the ways that these institutions help us navigate feelings about our families. Institutions and communities help people understand and interpret their family relationships and histories by placing them in larger social and historical contexts, and the institutions of American Jewish nostalgia are particularly designed to do so. They allow people to make sense of unwieldly family stories, and they help guide and structure individuals' feelings about their families by fitting them into larger, more widely recognizable narratives. This is precisely the work of religion—structuring individual experiences into broader narratives of meaning.

Like families, the narratives of nostalgia exclude certain people and certain stories. Nostalgia is a norm, and as such it encourages the most simplistic, streamlined versions of any story. The nostalgic longing of American Jews for stories of Eastern European immigration at the turn of the century and for Eastern European pasts—expressed through genealogy research, historic synagogues, children's materials, and food practices—deliberately centers certain Ashkenazi experiences and marginalizes other Jewish stories. The story of Eastern European Jewish nostalgia is big and bold enough to encompass and incorporate other stories, the way the colonial Sephardi Touro Synagogue gets retold in the pattern of Eastern European immigration and Middle Eastern Jewish cuisine becomes a side dish at delis, but this inclusion, too, can be a form of erasure.

Both families and communal institutions rely on boundaries. However one defines "family," says Kathryn Lofton, it is a means of defining intimate boundaries. "Family is a claim of differentiating dependency: this *us* exists in part by how it distinguishes itself from all the other *they*."[23] "Whatever families do," agrees anthropologist Jonathan Boyarin, "they are in the business of inclusion and exclusion—and the exclusions, more often than not, are done silently."[24] Religious norms like nostalgia can help families go about the business of those silent exclusions. One might argue that in not pushing the issue of whether they could hold their wedding ceremony at the Eldridge Street Synagogue, the Byrneheims permitted a particular kind of silent exclusion. But the Byrneheims' wedding also exemplifies the ways that people can work within nostalgia to change the boundaries of such norms. By laying claim to the practices of American Jewish nostalgia, individuals can partake in and exercise Jewish religious identity in ways that are more expansive than Jewish ritual law might otherwise permit.

It is easy to dismiss nostalgia as excessively sentimental, feminized, and thus unworthy of attention, or, alternatively, actively harmful in that it valorizes and simplifies complicated histories. But nostalgia is a fundamentally significant part of many people's lives and therefore must be taken seriously. American Jewish nostalgia has become part of the mainstream institutional landscape, accepted and understood as part of what it means to feel Jewish. For many American Jews, to engage with nostalgic materials is a positive engagement with community that fulfills a mandate to honor ancestors both real and imagined and conveys desires for the future. Or, as cultural critic Rokhl Kafrissen declared exasperatedly on Twitter, there are many kinds of continuity other than reproductive ones.[25] As a mitzvah, nostalgia for immigrant pasts accommodates the diverse religious needs of American Jews, providing meaning on personal, familial, communal, and institutional levels. At the same time, as an emotion and a practice, nostalgia remains intensely personal. Nostalgic practices make American Jews feel a connection to the past that creates community in the present and imagines a particular kind of future.

Recognizing the dynamic practices, desires, pleasures, and play of American Jewish nostalgia as religious ones points us to the wide variety of ways that Americans find constitutive meaning in their lives beyond traditional denominational structures, in institutions and through practices generally considered secular. Redefining American Jewish religion expands where we see Americans finding meaning and which institutions we recognize as most powerful in their lives. Americans are shaped by norms and values articulated not only by their synagogues, churches, mosques, and temples, but also by restaurants, publishing companies, toy manufacturers, gift shops, museums, and philanthropic organizations, which teach them not only how to behave but also how to feel.

ACKNOWLEDGMENTS

The ancient Jewish text Pirkei Avot (Ethics of the Fathers) famously advises the reader to appoint a teacher for oneself and to acquire a friend. I have been extraordinarily lucky in receiving support from the overlapping categories of teachers, colleagues, research subjects, and friends in the many years of this book's development.

Chapter 3 began as a master's thesis at the University of Virginia. I am grateful to the U.Va. Jewish Studies faculty members, especially my thesis advisors, Asher D. Biemann and Vanessa L. Ochs. Vanessa opened my eyes to looking at Jews' lives and the objects they use to construct those lives. Rachel Minkin, thank you for the Great Rhode Trip, one of my first forays into ethnographic research.

As a Ph.D. student, I found a remarkably warm and supportive intellectual community at the Department of Religion at Princeton University. There are few places like it. Thank you to Wallace Best, Jessica L. Delgado, Eddie Glaude, R. Marie Griffith, Kathi Kern, Kathryn Gin Lum, Leigh Schmidt, Jeffrey Stout, and Judith Weisenfeld for your exceptional teaching and mentorship. The Religion in the Americas workshop is simply the best, and that group helped shape this project in multiple stages. April C. Armstrong, Alda Bathrop-Lewis, Annie Blazer, Kijan Bloomfield, Vaughn Booker, Andrew Walker-Cornetta, Ryan Harper, Nicole C. Kirk, Jenny Wiley Legath, Rachel McBride Lindsey, Emily Mace, Alyssa Maldonado, Caleb Maskell, Kelsey Moss, Anthony Petro, Lindsay Reckson, Leslie Ribovich, Harvey Stark, Irene Beth Stroud, James Young, and Grace Yukich—you have helped me think about religion and therefore about everything. Jenna Weissman Joselit taught me to see humor and play in Jewish objects early in the formation of this book. R. Marie Griffith and Judith Weisenfeld, my Ph.D. advisors—how can I begin to thank you? You have shaped the way I see the world and you have made scholarship a joy.

I am grateful to have received support from many sources over the years. The Program in Judaic Studies at Princeton University provided support in graduate school from 2008 to 2013. The Berman Foundation awarded me a dissertation fellowship administered by the Association for Jewish Studies in 2012 to 2013, which allowed me to pursue research in New York, Miami Beach, Boston, and Newport, Rhode Island. The Berman Foundation fellowship led to a fortuitous writing group with Joshua Friedman, Moshe Kornfeld, and Laura Limonic. I am grateful to the Myer and Rosaline Feinstein Center for American Jewish History at Temple University for a summer research grant in 2014. Participants at a 2016 workshop at the Feinstein Center provided valuable responses to the introduction and Chapter 1.

The graduate workshop in American Jewish history at the Jean and Samuel Frankel Center for Judaic Studies at the University of Michigan in 2013 was a memorable and formative moment in the development of this book. Thank you to April C. Armstrong, Rachel Deblinger, Rachel Feinmark, Joshua Jay Furman, Jaclyn Granick, Markus Krah, Deborah Dash Moore, Shari Rabin, Katie Rosenblatt, Rachel L. Rothstein, Ronit Y. Stahl, Britt Tevis, and Beth Wenger for comments on Chapter 3.

The John C. Danforth Center on Religion and Politics at Washington University in St. Louis provided me with an in-residence dissertation completion fellowship and a wonderful academic community in 2013 to 2014. Thank you to Anne Blankenship, Darren Dochuk, Emily Suzanne Johnson, Mark D. Jordan, R. Marie Griffith, Suzanna Krivulskaya, Rachel McBride Lindsey, Laurie Maffly-Kipp, Lerone Martin, Leigh Schmidt, and Karen Skinner.

The Department of Religion and Culture at Virginia Tech provided a home for me and my manuscript for two years as a Visiting Assistant Professor. Aaron Ansell, Brian Britt, Zach Dresser, Kim Kutz Elliott, Matthew Gabriele, and Ashley Reed helped me think about the subject of this book in broader contexts.

The 2016–2017 Young Scholars in American Religion cohort—Brandon Bayne, Cara Burnidge, Emily Suzanne Clark, Brett Grainger, Justine Howe, M. Cooper Harriss, Elizabeth Jemison, Nicole Meyers Turner, and Daniel Vaca, and our valiant mentors, Leigh Schmidt and Kathryn Lofton—provided feedback on many parts of this book. Thank you for being my people. Nicole Meyers Turner, our virtual writing dates make things happen.

I am grateful for the responses I have received at workshops, conferences, and public talks over the years from both scholars and Jewish community members. Thank you to feedback from folks at the Bay Area Academic Consortium for Jewish Studies in 2017. In the Department of Religious Studies at Stanford University, Esiteli Hafoka, jem Jebbia, Hajin Jun, Kathryn Gin Lum, and Adeana McNicholl provided important feedback on Chapter 3. Colleen McDannell, Joseph Stuart, and other members of the Rocky Mountain American Religion Seminar provided useful advice on my introduction and Chapter 1 in 2018. Miriam Udel gave me generative comments on Chapter 4 at the 2019 Childhood in the Jewish Imagination symposium at the Graduate Theological Union.

In the Department of Jewish Studies at San Francisco State University, my colleagues Fred Astren, Marc Dollinger, Eran Kaplan, and Kitty Millet have provided invaluable encouragement. The John and Marcia Goldman Chair in American Jewish Studies and a Presidential Award for Professional Development of Probationary Faculty have helped me finish this book. I have discussed many of the ideas in this book with my students at SF State, and I am appreciative of their insightful and often surprising responses.

Many colleagues read many pieces of this book, often multiple times over the years. Lila Corwin Berman, Rebecca L. Davis, Sarah Imhoff, Ken Koltun-Fromm, Jodi Eichler Levine, Samira K. Mehta, and Anthony Petro provided thorough and crucial comments at various points of this project. Thank you to Jennifer Hammer at NYU Press and the North American Religions series editors, Tracy Fessenden, Laura Levitt, and David Harrington Watt, who have shepherded this book for some time. This book was completed during the COVID-19 pandemic, and I am grateful to everyone at NYU Press for their diligent work during a difficult time. Thank you to Jennifer Margulies, author of the poem *Timepiece* that I used at the beginning of the book. This poem previously appeared in Issue 32 of *Borderlands: Texas Poetry Review*.

Rachel McBride Lindsey, Nicole C. Kirk, and Jessica Kirzane read and discussed many parts of this book many times; Emily Suzanne Johnson, my fellow dissertation fellow, read this book cover to cover. It is a blessing to be your friend and to work alongside you, even from afar, in joyful days and in more challenging times. Rachel Minkin and Fannie Bialek are exceptional hostesses, and I'm lucky that they hosted me on research trips in Massachusetts and Rhode Island, respectively. Ashley Reed helps me think about sentimentality and affection in scholarship and life. Daniel Crane Kirzane sharpens my thinking, especially when we disagree. David A. M. Wilensky provided an editor's eye and a friend's encouragement. Laura Eve Engel gave epigraphical emotional support. Shaina Hammerman, I am grateful for your insights and your friendship. Shayna Weiss has been my most constant conversation partner about serious matters and silly ones—usually both—since Miriam Udel's introductory Talmud class in the Drisha Summer High School Program, and she has helped me think through every part of this book. Thank you.

I owe an immense debt of gratitude to the many people who generously gave their time to speak with me about their work as well as to those who allowed me to pursue ethnographic research at their institutions. It has been a great pleasure to spend time with people who were willing to tell me about their work and their passions. Some of these conversation partners may not agree with my conclusions, but I hope that the respect I have for their work is apparent. I thank genealogists Linda Cantor, Jo David, Alex Feller, Jessica Friedlander, Robert Friedman, Bennett Greenspan, Tammy Hepps, Susan King, David M. Kleiman (may his memory be a blessing), Kate Kleiman, Arthur Kurzweil, Steven Lasky, David Mink, Gary Mokotoff, Roni Leibowitz, Jeffrey Levin, Hadassah Lipsius, Marla Raucher Osborn, Sallyann Amdur Sack-Pikus, Samantha Katz Seal, and Pamela Weisberger (may her memory be a blessing). I also thank the other members of the Jewish Genealogical Society and the Computers and Genealogy Special Interest Group, both in New York, for letting me observe them. Rachel Eskin Fisher, thank you for speaking to me about your scholarship on Jewish genealogists and your work as founding director of the Genealogy Institute at the Center for Jewish History. Thank you to Jessica Cooperman for speaking with me about the Samberg Family History Program at the Center for Jewish History. I thank members of the San Francisco Bay Area Jewish Genealogical Society for feedback on a presentation. Tammy Hepps provided invaluable feedback on Chapter 2.

For speaking with me about their work in relation to historic synagogues, I thank Jessica Antoline, Allan Arkush, Jo Ann Arnowitz, Courtney Byrnehiem, Mattie Byrneheim, Meryle Cawley, Bonnie Dimun,

Michael Feldberg, Annette Fromm, Steven Greenberg, Judy Greenspan, Steven Grossman, Hanna Griff-Sleven, Abie Ingber, Nancy Johnson, Dallas Kennedy, David M. Kleiman, Sara Lowenburg, Marc Mandel, Amy Stein Milford, Mark Nystedt, Bea Ross, Barry Shrage, Sam Seicol, Mary Jo Valdez, Sarah Verity, and Marcia Jo Zerivitz. I also thank artists Carol Hamoy and Hana Iverson for speaking to me about their installations at the Eldridge Street Synagogue and allowing me to use images of their work. I thank as well the dedicated educators and docents at the Jewish Museum of Florida, the Museum at Eldridge Street, Touro Synagogue's Congregation Jeshuat Israel and the Ambassador John L. Loeb Jr. Visitors Center, and the Vilna Shul, who allowed me to shadow their tours and took the time to chat with me on their breaks.

Thank you to Jacqueline Dembar Greene, Dianne Hess, Linda Heller, Amy Hest, Eric Kimmel, Barbara McClintock, and Larry Rosler for speaking with me about their work writing, illustrating, and editing children's books. Thank you to Julie Parks at American Girl for her assistance. For conversations about PJ Library, thank you to Tamar Fox, Meredith Lewis, Jennifer Baer Lotsoff, Erika Meitner, Vivian Newman, and Marcie Greenfield Simons. My thanks to the University of Manitoba Archives for their assistance with the Sheldon Oberman Collection.

In the dynamic world of American Jewish food, I thank Karen Adelman, Noah Arenstein, Noah Bernamoff, Mitchell Davis, Debra Ferst, Ken Gordon, Emunah Hauser, Josh Lebewohl, Peter Levitt, Ilyse Lerner, Zach Kutsher, David Sax, Jeffrey Yoskowitz, and Alix Wall.

The connections between my case studies were embodied in the extraordinary person of David M. Kleiman, who passed away in 2014. Publisher, public historian, genealogist, educator, and Jewish food enthusiast, Kleiman served on the Executive Council of the Jewish Genealogical Society in New York and was deeply involved in genealogy networks in New York and elsewhere, both Jewish and non-Jewish, as a member of the Association of Professional Genealogists and the Genealogical Speakers Guild and as the co-founder and chair of the New York Computers and Genealogy Special Interest Group. After working with Ambassador John L. Loeb Jr. on a number of projects related to Loeb's family history, Kleiman became the curator of the Ambassador John L. Loeb Jr. Visitors Center at the Touro Synagogue in Newport, Rhode Island. I am deeply saddened that I cannot share this book with him.

The roots of this book are in family trips to historic synagogues as I was growing up. My parents, Andrea and Jerry Gross, taught me to love books, history, and fellow Jews, even when one vehemently disagrees with them. My mother is always my first and last editor. My siblings, Sam Gross, Lisa Gross, and Mia Gross are simply my favorites. Lisa and my brother-in-law, Jordan Keitelman, saw me through the completion of this book, when the arrival of my nephew, Ezra Keitelman, was a wonderfully welcome distraction. Ezra, may you bring only what is useful from the past into your future.

NOTES

INTRODUCTION

1 Based on the author's observations from summer 2012.

2 Haroun K., review on Yelp.com, March 20, 2008.

3 Roberta Berken, "Footprints of History," *Museum at Eldridge Street*, September 17, 2013, www.eldridgestreet.org.

4 Hasia Diner, "'Buying and Selling 'Jewish': The Historical Impact of Commerce on Jewish Communal Life," in *Imagining the American Jewish Community*, ed. Jack Wertheimer (Waltham, Massachusetts: Brandeis University Press, 2007), 28–46. Holly Snyder, "Rethinking the Definition of 'Community' for a Migratory Age: 1654–1830," in *Imagining the American Jewish Community*, ed. Jack Wertheimer (Waltham, Massachusetts: Brandeis University Press, 2007), 3–27.

5 68 percent of American Jews say one can be Jewish without believing in God. Pew Research Center, *A Portrait of Jewish Americans: Findings from a Pew Research Center Survey of U.S. Jews*, October 1, 2013, 58.

6 Vanessa L. Ochs, *Inventing Jewish Ritual* (Philadelphia: Jewish Publication Society, 2007), 5–7. Sally M. Promey, "The Public Display of Religion," in *The Visual Culture of American Religions*, eds. David Morgan and Sally M. Promey (Berkeley: University of California Press, 2001), 27–48.

7 Lila Corwin Berman, *Speaking of Jews: Rabbis, Intellectuals, and the Creation of an American Public Identity* (Berkeley: University of California Press, 2009). Kate Rosenblatt, Lila Corwin Berman, and Ronit Stahl, "How Jewish Academia Created A #MeToo Disaster," *The Forward*, July 19, 2018, https://forward.com. On Jewish-Christian intermarriage, see Samira K. Mehta, *Beyond Chrismukkah: The Christian-Jewish Interfaith Family in the United States* (Chapel Hill: University of North Carolina Press, 2018).

8 Shelly Tenenbaum, "Good or Bad for the Jews? Moving Beyond the Continuity Debate," *Contemporary Jewry* 21, no. 1 (January 2000): 92.

9 Robert A. Orsi, *Between Heaven and Earth: The Religious Worlds People Make and the Scholars Who Study Them* (Princeton, New Jersey: Princeton University Press, 2005), 2.

10 Kathryn Lofton, *Consuming Religion* (Chicago: University of Chicago Press, 2017), 5.

11 David D. Hall, ed., *Lived Religion in America: Toward a Theory of Practice* (Princeton, New Jersey: Princeton University Press, 1997).

12 Colleen McDannell, *Material Christianity: Religion and Popular Culture* (New Haven: Yale University Press, 1995), 4.

13 Compiled lists of the mitzvot vary, though they have been standardized over time, and no single person in any particular historical moment would be expected to fulfill all of them.

14 Yehuda Kurzter, *Shuva: The Future of the Jewish Past* (Waltham, Massachusetts: Brandeis University Press, 2012), 29.

15 Kurzter, 29.

16 Steven M. Cohen and Arnold M. Eisen, *The Jew Within: Self, Family, and Community in America* (Bloomington: Indiana University Press, 2000).

17 In 2018, Cohen was accused of sexual harassment of female colleagues. Cohen did not deny the allegations, apologized for a pattern of "inappropriate behavior," and later resigned from his position as a full professor at Hebrew Union College–Jewish Institute of Religion as well as other affiliations. See Hannah Dreyfus, "Harassment Allegations Mount Against Leading Jewish Sociologist," *New York Jewish Week*, July 19, 2018, https://jewishweek.timesofisrael.com. "Hebrew Union College-Jewish Institute of Religion," *Jewish Telegraphic Agency*, August 22, 2018, www.jta.org. Some scholars argue that there is a relationship between Cohen's harassment of women and his articulation of the continuity crisis. According to Rosenblatt et al., Jewish communal leaders' focus on social scientific research and statistics about families and children have been a means of articulating what Jewish families should look like, and when and how Jewish women should marry and bear children. For a study of the religiosity of Jewish-Christian interfaith families that does not see them declining in religiosity, see Mehta.

18 Cohen and Eisen, 2. A Jewish Federation is a local confederation of Jewish social agencies, volunteer programs, educational bodies, and other organizations. The umbrella Jewish Federations of North America is one of the most powerful organizations in American Jewish life, representing 146 Jewish Federations and over three hundred communities, which annually raise and distribute more than three billion dollars. The Jewish Federations of North America, https://jewishfederations.org.

19 Pew Research Center.

20 Tisa Wenger, *Religious Freedom: The Contested History of an American Ideal* (Chapel Hill: The University of North Carolina Press, 2017), 17–18. Tisa Wenger, *We Have a Religion: The 1920s Pueblo Indian Dance Controversy and American Religious Freedom* (Chapel Hill: The University of North Carolina Press, 2009). Curtis J. Evans, *The Burden of Black Religion* (New York: Oxford University Press, 2008).

21 Vanessa Ochs distinguishes between categories of "articulate objects," which are commonly recognized Jewish markers; "Jewish signifying-objects," which function to express a Jewish value; and "ordinary objects transformed," which include a range of materials that become religious objects depending on their use. Vanessa L. Ochs, "What Makes a Jewish Home Jewish?" *Cross Currents* 49, no. 4 (Winter 1999/2000), www.crosscurrents.org. David Chidester, *Authentic Fakes: Religion*

and American Popular Culture (Berkeley: University of California Press, 2005). R. Marie Griffith, *Born Again Bodies: Flesh and Spirit in American Christianity* (Berkeley: University of California Press, 2008). Lofton, xi.

22 Yosef Hayim Yerushalmi, *Zakhor: Jewish History and Jewish Memory* (New York: Schocken Books, 1989), 94.

23 Yerushalmi. See Peter Novick, *That Noble Dream: The "Objectivity Question" and the American Historical Profession* (Cambridge, United Kingdom: Cambridge University Press, 1988). Amos Funkenstein, "Collective Memory and Historical Consciousness," *History and Memory* 1, no. 1 (Spring–Summer 1989): 5–26. Michael Schudson, "The Present in the Past versus the Past in the Present," *Communication* 11 (1989): 105–113. David Lowenthal, *The Heritage Crusade and the Spoils of History* (London: Methuen, 1987). David N. Meyers, *The Stakes of History: On the Use and Abuse of Jewish History for Life* (New Haven: Yale University Press, 2018).

24 Ann Cvetkovich, *Depression: A Public Feeling* (Durham, North Carolina: Duke University Press, 2012), 4. Erika Doss, *Memorial Mania: Public Feeling in America* (Chicago: University of Chicago Press, 2010).

25 For American Jews and the Holocaust, see Deborah E. Lipstadt, *Holocaust: An American Understanding* (New Brunswick, New Jersey: Rutgers University Press, 2016), Laura Levitt, *American Jewish Loss after the Holocaust* (New York: New York University Press, 2007), Jennifer Hansen-Gluklich, *Holocaust Memory Reframed: Museums and the Challenges of Representation* (New Brunswick, New Jersey: Rutgers University Press, 2014), and Avril Alba, *The Holocaust Memorial as Sacred Space* (Basingstoke: Palgrave Macmillan, 2015), among others. For Israel in American Jewish culture, see Michelle Mart, *Eye on Israel: How America Came to View Israel as an Ally* (Albany: State University of New York Press, 2006), Shaul Kelner, *Tours That Bind: Diaspora, Pilgrimage, and Israeli Birthright Tourism* (New York: New York University Press, 2010), Emily Alice Katz, *Bringing Zion Home: Israel in American Jewish Culture, 1948–1967* (Albany, New York: State University of New York Press, 2015), and Shaul Mitelpunkt, *Israel in the American Mind: The Cultural Politics of US–Israeli Relations, 1958–1988* (New York: Cambridge University Press, 2018), among others.

26 David D. Hall, introduction to *Lived Religion in America: Toward a Theory of Practice*, ed. David D. Hall (Princeton, New Jersey: Princeton University Press, 1997), ix.

27 Sally M. Promey, "Religion, Sensation, and Materiality: An Introduction," in *Sensational Religion: Sensory Cultures in Material Practice* (New Haven: Yale University Press, 2014), 14–15.

28 Ken Koltun-Fromm, *Imagining Jewish Authenticity: Vision and Text in American Jewish Thought* (Bloomington: Indiana University Press, 2015), 6. Stuart Z. Charmé, "Varieties of Authenticity in Contemporary Jewish Identity," *Jewish Social Studies* 6, no. 2 (Winter 2000): 133–155.

29 See David Glassberg, *Sense of History: The Place of the Past in American Life* (Amherst: University of Massachusetts Press, 2001), 7.

30 Arthur Kurzweil, interview by author, May 1, 2012. Kurzweil includes a chapter on "What If You Were Adopted?" in his *From Generation to Generation*, 74–75.

31 Jo David, interview by author, June 5, 2012. This story is also recounted in Jo David, *How to Trace Your Jewish Roots: Discovering Your Unique History* (New York: Citadel Press, 2000), 7.

32 Sallyann Amdur Sack, interview by author, April 28, 2012.

CHAPTER 1. HOW DO YOU SOLVE A PROBLEM LIKE NOSTALGIA?

1 *Jewish Museum of Florida—FIU*, https://jmof.fiu.edu.

2 A mezuzah is a small decorative case containing a parchment bearing verses from the Torah on it. Some Jews place a mezuzah only on the doorpost of the outer door of their homes. Others also place a mezuzah on every interior doorpost except the bathroom door.

3 Steven Lasky, "The Museum of Family History: An Overview," *Dorot: The Journal of the Jewish Genealogical Society* 29, no. 1 (Fall 2007): 1.

4 Lila Corwin Berman, "Sociology, Jews, and Intermarriage in Twentieth-Century America," *Jewish Social Studies: History, Culture, Society* 14, no. 2 (Winter 2008): 32–60.

5 Pew Research Center, *A Portrait of Jewish Americans: Findings from a Pew Research Center Survey of U.S. Jews*, October 1, 2013.

6 Laurie Goodstein, "Poll Shows Major Shift in Identity of U.S. Jews," *New York Times*, October 1, 2013, www.nytimes.com.

7 Cary Funk and Greg Smith, *"Nones" on the Rise: One-in-Five Adults Have No Religious Affiliation*, Pew Research Center, October 9, 2012.

8 For example, Herbert J. Gans, "Jews of No Religion and the Future of American Jewry," *eJewish Philanthropy*, June 23, 2015, http://ejewishphilanthropy.com.

9 Pew Research Center, *A Portrait of Jewish Americans*, 7.

10 See Pew Research Center's review of Jewish denominational switching in *A Portrait of Jewish Americans*.

11 For the construction of religion as a category, see Jonathan Z. Smith, *Relating Religion: Essays in the Study of Religion* (Chicago: University of Chicago Press, 2004). For the construction of Judaism as a religion, see Leora Batnitzky, *How Judaism Became a Religion: An Introduction to Modern Jewish Thought* (Princeton, New Jersey: Princeton University Press, 2011). For the construction of American religions, see Robert Orsi, *Between Heaven and Earth: The Religious Worlds People Make and the Scholars Who Study Them* (Princeton, New Jersey: Princeton University Press, 2005).

12 Laura Levitt, "Impossible Assimilations, American Liberalism, and Jewish Difference: Revisiting Jewish Secularism," *American Quarterly* 59, no. 3 (September 2007): 807–832.

13 Samira K. Mehta, *Beyond Chrismukkah: The Christian-Jewish Interfaith Family in the United States* (Chapel Hill: University of North Carolina Press, 2018).

14 Jessica Cooperman, *Making Judaism Safe for America: World War I and the Origins of Religious Pluralism* (New York: New York University Press, 2018). Kevin M.

Schultz, *Tri-Faith America: How Catholics and Jews Held Postwar America to Its Protestant Promise* (Oxford: Oxford University Press, 2011). Deborah Dash Moore, "Jewish GIs and the Creation of the Judeo-Christian Tradition," *Religion and American Culture: A Journal of Interpretation* 8, no. 1 (Winter 1998): 31–53. Laura Levitt, "Interrogating the Judeo-Christian Tradition: Will Herberg's Construction of American Religion, Religious Pluralism, and the Problem of Inclusion," in *The Cambridge History of Religions in America*, vol. 3 (Cambridge: Cambridge University Press 2009), 283–307.

15 Tisa Wenger, *Religious Freedom: The Contested History of an American Ideal* (Chapel Hill: The University of North Carolina Press, 2017).

16 Arthur A. Goren, "A 'Golden Decade' for American Jews: 1945–1955," in *The American Jewish Experience*, ed. Jonathan D. Sarna (New York: Holmes & Meier, 1997), 300.

17 Goren, 310.

18 Hasia Diner has demonstrated that organized commemoration of the Holocaust began shortly after World War II rather than in the 1960s as previously held. Hasia Diner, *We Remember with Reverence and Love: American Jews and the Myth of Silence after the Holocaust, 1945–1962* (New York: New York University Press, 2010).

19 Goren. Rachel Kranson, "'To Be a Jew on America's Terms Is Not to Be a Jew at All': The Jewish Counterculture's Critique of Middle-Class Affluence," *Journal of Jewish Identities* 8, no. 2 (July 2015): 59–84.

20 Jack Wertheimer, "The American Synagogue: Recent Issues and Trends," in *American Jewish Year Book 2005*, vol. 105, eds. David Singer and Lawrence Grossman (New York: American Jewish Committee, 2005), 3–86. Wertheimer cites the 1945 survey of the National Opinion Research Center (NORC) and the 1970 National Jewish Population Survey, 11–12.

21 Wertheimer, "American Synagogue."

22 Pew Research Center, *A Portrait of Jewish Americans*, Chapter 3, "Jewish Identity." Pew researchers provided a series of topics and asked respondents, "Is that essential, OR important but NOT essential, OR not an important part of what BEING JEWISH means to you?" Pew Research Center, *A Portrait of Jewish Americans*, "Appendix B: Topline Survey Results," 167.

23 Tracy Fessenden, *Culture and Redemption: Religion, the Secular, and American Literature* (Princeton, New Jersey: Princeton University Press, 2007).

24 Susan King, interview by author, May 2, 2012.

25 Robert J. Friedman, interview by author, August 8, 2012.

26 For the ways in which Holocaust narratives provide emotional and commemorative norms that serve religious purposes for American Jews, see Jodi Eichler-Levine, *Suffer the Little Children: Uses of the Past in Jewish and African American Children's Literature* (New York: York University Press, 2013).

27 Svetlana Boym, *The Future of Nostalgia* (New York: Basic Books, 2001), 338. Michael Tanner, "Sentimentality," in *Art and Morality*, ed. José Luis Bermúdez (New

York: Routledge, 2003), 106–107. On the sentimental and issues of taste and class, see Barbara Kirshenblatt-Gimblett, *Destination Culture: Tourism, Museums, and Heritage* (Berkeley: University of California Press, 1998) and Colleen McDannell, *Material Christianity: Religion and Popular Culture in America* (New Haven: Yale University Press, 1995).

28 Tanner, 106–107.

29 Charles S. Maier, "The End of Longing? (Notes Toward a History of Postwar German National Longing)," in *The Postwar Transformation of Germany: Democracy, Prosperity, and Nationhood*, eds. John S. Brady, Beverly Crawford, and Sarah Elise Wiliarty (Ann Arbor: The University of Michigan Press, 1999), 273.

30 Raymond Williams, *Marxism and Literature* (New York: Oxford University Press, 1977).

31 Boym, 5.

32 Jean Starobinski, "The Idea of Nostalgia," *Diogenes* 54 (1966): 81–103. David Lowenthal, *The Past Is a Foreign Country* (New York: Cambridge University Press, 1985), 10–11.

33 Susan J. Matt, *Homesickness: An American History* (New York: Oxford University Press, 2011), 252.

34 Lowenthal, *The Past Is a Foreign Country*, 11.

35 Todd M. Brenneman, *Homespun Gospel: The Triumph of Sentimentality in Contemporary American Evangelicalism* (New York: Oxford University Press, 2014), 6–7.

36 Claudia Stokes, *The Altar at Home: Sentimental Literature and Nineteenth-Century American Religion* (Philadelphia: University of Pennsylvania Press, 2014).

37 Brenneman.

38 Jeffrey Shandler, *Shtetl: A Vernacular Intellectual History* (New Brunswick, New Jersey: Rutgers University Press, 2014).

39 Arnold Eisen, *Rethinking Modern Judaism: Ritual, Commandment, Community* (Chicago: University of Chicago Press, 1998), 158.

40 Paula Hyman, "Traditionalism and Village Jews in 19th Century Western and Central Europe: Local Persistence and Urban Nostalgia," in *The Uses of Tradition: Jewish Continuity in the Modern Era*, ed. Jack Wertheimer (New York: The Jewish Theological Seminary of America, 1992), 191–202. Linda Nochlin, "Introduction: Starting with the Self: Jewish Identity and Its Representation," in *The Jew in the Text: Modernity and the Construction of Identity*, eds. Linda Nochlin and Tamar Garb (New York: Thames and Hudson, 1996), 7–19.

41 Shandler.

42 Hasia R. Diner, *Lower East Side Memories: A Jewish Place in America* (Princeton, New Jersey: Princeton University Press, 2000), 18.

43 Shlomo Katz, quoted in Hasia Diner, *We Remember*, 334.

44 Matthew Frye Jacobson, *Roots Too: White Ethnic Revival in Post-Civil Rights America* (Cambridge, Massachusetts: Harvard University Press, 2006).

45 For American Jews and whiteness, see Eric L. Goldstein, *The Price of Whiteness: Jews, Race, and American Identity* (Princeton, New Jersey: Princeton University

Press, 2006) and Karen Brodkin, *How Jews Became White Folks and What That Says about Race in America* (New Brunswick, New Jersey: Rutgers University Press, 1998). Today, Ashkenazi Jews are about 62 percent of the worldwide Jewish population and about eighty percent of the American Jewish population. Aaron J. Hahn Tapper, *Judaisms: A Twenty-First-Century Introduction to Jews and Jewish Identities* (Oakland, California: University of California Press, 2016), 19.

46 Jacobson, 4.

47 Caryn Aviv and David Shneer, *New Jews: The End of the Jewish Diaspora* (New York: New York University Press, 2005), 3, 12.

48 Joellyn Wallen Zollman, "The Gifts of the Jews: Ideology and Material Culture in the American Synagogue Gift Shop," *American Jewish Archives* 58 (2006): 66. Mezuzot is the Hebrew plural of mezuzah.

49 Shaul Kelner, *Tours That Bind: Diaspora, Pilgrimage, and Israeli Birthright Tourism* (New York: New York University Press, 2010).

50 See Pew Research Center, *A Portrait of Jewish Americans*, Chapter 5, "Connection with and Attitudes Toward Israel."

51 Vanessa L. Ochs, *Inventing Jewish Ritual* (Philadelphia: Jewish Publication Society, 2007), 96.

52 Colleen McDannell, *Material Christianity: Religion and Popular Culture* (New Haven: Yale University Press, 1995), 4.

53 Beth Wenger, *History Lessons: The Creation of American Jewish Heritage* (Princeton: Princeton University Press, 2010).

54 M. J. Rymsza-Pawlowska, *History Comes Alive: Public History and Popular Culture in the 1970s* (Chapel Hill: The University of North Carolina Press, 2017), 4–5.

55 "Museum Membership," *Jewish Museum of Florida*, www.jewishmuseum.com. Accessed November 1, 2013. (The museum's website has changed since its acquisition by Florida International University.)

56 Alisa Solomon, "Tradition! The Indestructible 'Fiddler on the Roof,'" *New Yorker*, October 8, 2015, www.newyorker.com.

57 Alisa Solomon, "Balancing Act: Fiddler's Bottle Dance and the Transformation of 'Tradition,'" *TDR: The Drama Review* 55, no. 3 (Fall 2011): 21–30.

58 Ronald L. Grimes, *Rite out of Place: Ritual, Media, and the Arts* (New York, Oxford University Press, 2006), 53.

59 In the film, Tevye does not ask this question of the rabbi; an unnamed young man does. Harold Rhode, "The Importance of Jewish Religion, Culture, and History," in *Avotaynu Guide to Jewish Genealogy*, eds. Gary Mokotoff and Sallyann Amdur Sack (Bergenfeld, New Jersey: Avotaynu, 2004), 43. Rhode follows a Jewish convention of writing "G-d" to avoid desecrating God's name.

60 For the image of the Hasid as a reference to lost Jewish worlds, see Shaina Hammerman, *Silver Screen, Hasidic Jews* (Bloomington: Indiana University Press, 2018).

61 Dianne Hess, telephone interview by author, December 2, 2013.

62 Eichler-Levine.

63 David Beriss, "Haute, Fast, and Historic: Restaurants and Rise of Popular Culture," in *The Bloomsbury Handbook of Food and Popular Culture*, eds. Kathleen LeBesco and Peter Naccarato (London: Bloomsbury Academic, 2018), 124–125.

64 Maura Judkis, "On Rye Review: Deli That Doesn't Put You Down for a Nap," *Washington Post*, February 17, 2017, www.washingtonpost.com. Ilyse Lerner, interview by author, November 25, 2016. On Rye has since closed.

CHAPTER 2. GIVE US OUR NAME

1 Arthur Kurzweil, *From Generation to Generation: How to Trace Your Jewish Genealogy and Family History* (New York: Morrow, 1980).

2 The haggadah quotes from Exodus 13:8. Adapted from *Passover Haggadah*, Deluxe Edition, The Coffees of Maxwell House (Kraft General Foods, Inc. 1991), 25. Created as an advertisement for the coffee company, the Maxwell House haggadah is the most widely-circulated haggadah in the world, with over fifty million copies printed since its creation in 1934.

3 Kurzweil, *Generation to Generation*, 11. The shtetl, the small town of Eastern Europe where Jews were the majority in the population and set the tone of life, has become an idealized archetype of idyllic pre-modern Jewish life. See Jeffrey Shandler, *Shtetl: A Vernacular Intellectual History* (New Brunswick, New Jersey: Rutgers University Press, 2014).

4 Troy Messenger, *Holy Leisure: Recreation and Religion in God's Square Mile* (Philadelphia: Temple University Press, 1999).

5 I draw on Robert Orsi's understanding of religion as sacred relationships. Robert Anthony Orsi, *The Madonna of 115th Street: Faith and Community in Italian Harlem, 1880–1950*, 2nd ed. (New Haven: Yale University Press, 2002). Robert A. Orsi, *Between Heaven and Earth: The Religious Worlds People Make and the Scholars Who Study Them* (Princeton, New Jersey: Princeton University Press, 2005).

6 Jews traditionally used patronymic names in Hebrew and other Jewish languages, with a first name followed by "son of" or "daughter of" one's father's name. Today, although Jews use surnames in everyday life, many still employ Jewish patronymics—sometimes with an alternative first name in a Jewish language—for religious rituals, including inscribing them on tombstones.

7 Bill Gladstone, review of *Every Family Has a Story: Tales from the Pages of Avotaynu*, ed. Gary Mokotoff, *Avotaynu* 24, no. 2 (Summer 2008): 65. "Avotaynu" is Hebrew for "our fathers" or "our ancestors." The term is frequently used in Jewish liturgy to refer to the biblical patriarchs and to communal ancestors more broadly.

8 Tammy Hepps, email to author, December 26, 2018.

9 Jeanne Kay Guelke and Dallen J. Timothy, "Locating Personal Pasts: An Introduction," in *Geography and Genealogy: Locating Personal Pasts*, eds. Dallen J. Timothy and Jeanne Kay Guelke (Burlington, Vermont: Ashgate Publishing Company, 2007), 8.

10 Membership in the Association of Professional Genealogists (APG) is open to anyone who affirms its code of ethics, which emphasizes a "truthful" and honest approach to sources and resources. See "Code of Ethics," *Association of Profes-*

sional Genealogists, 2012, www.apgen.org. For the decline of the amateur historian, see Bonnie G. Smith, *The Gender of History: Men, Women, and Historical Practice* (Cambridge, Massachusetts: Harvard University Press, 2000).

11 Hepps, email.

12 Courtney Bender, *The New Metaphysicals: Spirituality and the American Religious Imagination* (Chicago: University of Chicago Press, 2010). Leigh Eric Schmidt, *Restless Souls: The Making of American Spirituality* (San Francisco: HarperSanFrancisco, 2005).

13 Emily Sigalow, *American JuBu: Jews, Buddhists, and Religious Change* (Princeton, New Jersey: Princeton University Press, 2019).

14 Dan Rottenberg, *Finding Our Fathers: A Guidebook to Jewish Genealogy* (New York: Random House, 1977), 9.

15 Kurzweil, *Generation to Generation*, 81.

16 Jo David, *How to Trace Your Jewish Roots: Discovering Your Unique History* (New York: Kensington Publishing Corp., 2000), 22–23.

17 For the function of genealogies in Genesis, see David Noel Freedman, ed., *The Anchor Yale Bible Dictionary* (New Haven: Yale University Press, 2009 [1992]), vol. 2, s.v. "Genealogy, Genealogies."

18 See Noami Seidman, *The Marriage Plot: Or, How Jews Fell in Love with Love, and with Literature* (Stanford, California: Stanford University Press, 2016).

19 Arthur Kurzweil and Steven W. Siegel, "A Letter to Our Readers," *Toledot* 1, no. 1 (1977): 2–3. Rebecca DeHovitz, "Jewish Genealogy: The Search for Connection," *Avotaynu* 27, no. 2 (Summer 2011): 27–32. Hadassah Lipsius, an Orthodox Jew who is a member of the Executive Committee of the Jewish Genealogical Society of New York, told me that she saw her genealogical work in line with traditions of yikhus and shares her research with those who research rabbinic lineages, but others I spoke with at the JGS of New York did not. Hadassah Lipsius, interview by author, May 20, 2012.

20 Kurzweil, *Generation to Generation*, xxvi.

21 Arthur Kurzweil, "Foreword: Genealogy as a Spiritual Pilgrimage," in *Avotaynu Guide to Jewish Genealogy*, eds. Gary Mokotoff and Sallyann Amdur Sack (Bergenfeld, New Jersey: Avotaynu, 2004), ix–xii.

22 Leonard R. Kofkin, "Compiling the Family Tree: Hobby, Commitment or Mitzvah?" *Avotaynu* 21, no. 4 (Winter 2005): 30.

23 Lipsius. Roni Seibel Leibowitz, interview by author, May 20, 2012.

24 Wade Clark Roof, *Spiritual Marketplace: Baby Boomers and the Remaking of American Religion* (Princeton, New Jersey: Princeton University Press 2001), 83.

25 "Shul" is Yiddish for synagogue. Ben-Zion Saydman, "Genealogy: A Spiritual Journey," *Avotaynu* 20, no. 1 (Spring 2004): 59.

26 Saydman, 59.

27 Roof, 82.

28 Paul Cowan, *An Orphan in History: Retrieving a Jewish Legacy* (Garden City, New York: Doubleday & Company, Inc., 1982), ix.

29 For Jews and the frontier, both geographical and metaphorical, see Shari Rabin, *Jews on the Frontier: Religion and Mobility in Nineteenth-Century America* (New York: New York University Press, 2017).

30 François Weil, *Family Trees: A History of Genealogy in America* (Cambridge, Massachusetts: Harvard University Press, 2013).

31 In the Church of Jesus Christ of Latter-day Saints, rites performed for the salvation of the dead can only be performed when adequate information about an individual is known, including the person's name, birth date, and parents' names. The storage facility of the Family History Library in Salt Lake City contains over a million rolls of microfilm, which can be shipped to Family History Centers to be accessed by genealogists of any religion around the world. Samuel M. Otterstrom, "Genealogy as Religious Ritual: The Doctrine and Practice of Family History in the Church of Jesus Christ of Latter-day Saints," in *Geography and Genealogy: Locating Personal Pasts*, eds. Dallen J. Timothy and Jeanne Kay Guelke (Burlington, Vermont: Ashgate Publishing Company, 2007): 149. Rachel E. Fisher, "A Place in History: Genealogy, Jewish Identity, Modernity" (Ph.D. diss., University of California, Santa Barbara, 1999), 40.

32 James B. Allen, Jessie L. Emobry, and Kahlile B. Mehr, *Hearts Turned to the Fathers: A History of the Genealogical Society of Utah: 1894–1994* (Provo, Utah: BYU Studies, Brigham Young University, 1995).

33 Warren Blatt directs Jewish genealogists to Latter-day Saints' Family History Centers, assuring them that while "the Mormons' interest in genealogy stems from their religious beliefs . . . patrons at their library facilities are not objects of proselytizing efforts." Warren Blatt, *FAQ: Frequently Asked Questions about Jewish Genealogy* (Teaneck, New Jersey: Avotaynu, 1996), 23. Jewish genealogist Gary Mokotoff has influenced the Church's policy on baptizing Holocaust victims. Brady McCombs, "Mormon Baptisms of Holocaust Victims Draw Ire," *Associated Press*, December 21, 2017, www.apnews.com.

34 Hepps, email.

35 Fisher, 36. For the development of American Jewish heritage and popular history, see Beth Wenger, *History Lessons: The Creation of American Jewish Heritage* (Princeton: Princeton University Press, 2010).

36 Malcolm H. Stern, *Americans of Jewish Descent: A Compendium of Genealogy* (New York: American Jewish Archives, 1960).

37 When pressed about historical inaccuracies in his work, Haley defended his work as the "symbolic history of a people." As Haley recognized, the significance of *Roots* was not in its details but in its ability to inspire Americans' to create personal connections to ethnic pasts. Alison Landsberg, *Prosthetic Memory: The Transformation of American Remembrance in the Age of Mass Culture* (New York: Columbia University Press, 2004), 105.

38 Landsberg, 105.

39 Sallyann Amdur Sack, "Susan King Steps Down as JewishGen Director: Warren Blatt Assumes Leadership," *Avotaynu* 24, no. 1 (Spring 2008): 20.

40 Matthew Frye Jacobson, *Roots Too: White Ethnic Revival in Post-Civil Rights America* (Cambridge, Massachusetts: Harvard University Press, 2006), 2. Marc Dollinger, *Black Power, Jewish Politics: Reinventing the Alliance in the 1960s* (Waltham, Massachusetts: Brandeis University Press, 2018). Rachel Kranson, *Ambivalent Embrace: Jewish Upward Mobility in Postwar America* (Chapel Hill: University of North Carolina Press, 2017).

41 Jeffrey Shandler, *While America Watches: Televising the Holocaust* (New York: Oxford University Press, 1999), 160.

42 Rachel Leah Jablon, "Virtual Legacies: Genealogy, the Internet, and Jewish Identity" (Ph.D. diss., University of Maryland College Park, 2012), 30.

43 Rottenberg, 40.

44 Neil Rosenstein, "Founding of Jewish Genealogical Society, Inc.," *Avotaynu* 13, no. 1 (Spring 1997): 3. "Guide to the Papers of Steven Siegel, 1938–2008," Center for Jewish History, http://findingaids.cjh.org.

45 Fisher, 67.

46 Sallyann Amdur Sack, interview by author, April 28, 2012.

47 Barbara Krasner-Khait, "Innovators: Susan E. King: Founder of JewishGen," *Genealogical Computing* (October–December 2004): 23–25.

48 Susan King, interview by author, May 2, 2012.

49 Sack, "Susan King," 19.

50 Sack, interview.

51 Krasner-Khait, 23.

52 The Talmud interprets the biblical covenant between the Israelites and God at Mt. Sinai as including all subsequent generations of those born Jewish and all converts in the future. b. Shevuot 39a.

53 Jennifer Fulkerson, "Climbing the Family Tree," *American Demographics* 17, no. 12 (December 1995): 44.

54 For Jewish heritage travel in Europe, see Ruth Ellen Gruber, *Virtually Jewish: Reinventing Jewish Culture in Europe* (Berkeley: University of California Press, 2002).

55 Susan King, "The Future of JewishGen: JewishGen's Perspective," *Avotaynu* 19, no. 1 (Spring 2003): 3. Sack, "Susan King," 19. On Ellis Island, see Barbara Kirshenblatt-Gimblett, *Destination Culture: Tourism, Museums, and Heritage* (Berkeley: University of California Press, 2009). For Jews and the Statue of Liberty, see Rachel B. Gross, "Is the Statue of Liberty a Jewish Woman?" *J. The Jewish News of Northern California*, July 3, 2017, www.jweekly.com.

56 David G. Marwell, "About the JewishGen and Ancestry.com Alliance," *Avotaynu* 14, no. 2 (Summer 2008): 3.

57 Today, Ancestry, the largest for-profit genealogy company in the world, has three million paying subscribers across its family history websites. "Company Overview," *Ancestry*, www.ancestry.com. Dan Ruby, "JewishGen–Ancestry Deal Called an Alignment of Interests," *Ruby Family History Project*, August 20, 2008, http://rubyfamily.blogspot.com. Though it has undergone numerous mergers, Ancestry.

com has its roots in companies founded by Latter-day Saints. After a brief period as a public company, in October 2012, Ancestry.com was acquired by a private equity group. Tom Dickinson, "Ancestry.com Acquired by Private Equity Group for $1.6 Billion," *TechFruit*, October 22, 2012, http://techfruit.com.

58 Marwell.

59 Sallyann Amdur Sack, "As I See It," *Avotaynu* 24, no. 2 (Summer 2008): 53.

60 Eviatar Zerubavel, *Ancestors and Relatives: Genealogy, Identity, and Community* (New York: Oxford University Press, 2012), 64–65.

61 Bender, 62.

62 Roof, 40.

63 Kathryn Lofton, *Consuming Religion* (Chicago: University of Chicago Press, 2017), especially Chapter 7, "Religion and the Authority in American Parenting," 141–153.

64 Rottenberg, ix–x.

65 David, xviii.

66 Zerubavel, 64–65.

67 David, xiv.

68 Jonathan D. Sarna, "Into the Past," review of *From Generation to Generation: How to Trace Your Jewish Genealogy and Personal History*, by Arthur Kurzweil, *Commentary* 70, no. 2 (August 1980): 69–71.

69 Sarna, "Into the Past," 70.

70 Jonathan D. Sarna, letter to the editor, *Commentary* 70, no. 6 (December 1980): 22.

71 Robert N. Bellah et al., *Habits of the Heart: Individualism and Commitment in American Life* (Berkeley: University of California Press, 2008 [1985]), 63. For a reassessment of Sheilaism, see Leigh Eric Schmidt, *Restless Souls: The Making of American Spirituality* (San Francisco: HarperSanFransico, 2005).

72 Jonathan D. Sarna, conversation with author, November 5, 2012.

73 Linda Cantor, interview by author, May 20, 2012.

74 Hepps, email.

75 Tammy Hepps, "Statement of Purpose," *Homestead Hebrews*, http://homesteadhebrews.com.

76 Fisher. Elizabeth Shown Mills, "Genealogy in the 'Information Age': History's New Frontier?" *National Genealogical Society Quarterly* 91 (December 2003): 263.

77 For academics' resistance to sentimentality, see Eve Kosofsky Sedgwick, *Epistemology of the Closet* (Berkeley: University of California Press, 1990), 154, and Landsberg, 130–131.

78 "Mission: Aims," *International Institute for Jewish Genealogy*, accessed August 9, 2012, www.iijg.org.

79 "Family History/Genealogy," Brigham Young University Department of History, https://history.byu.edu.

80 Eileen Polakoff, "Building a Family History Website," *Avotaynu* 21, no. 2 (Summer 2005): 24, 26.

81 Avrum Geller, "JGS Program Reports: Write Your Family History NOW!" *Dorot: The Journal of the Jewish Genealogical Society* 29, no. 2 (Winter 2007–2008): 10.

82 "Mike Karsen: Professional Speaker," www.mikekarsen.com.

83 Polakoff, 26. Emphasis added.

84 Steven Lasky, interview by author, May 16, 2012.

85 Tammy Hepps, "About," *Treelines*, accessed September 25, 2012, www.treelines. com. Tammy Hepps, interview by author, July 10, 2012. For more on Hepps's work, see Diana Nelson Jones, "Former New York Tech Administrator Finds Passion in Uncovering Homestead's Jewish History," *Pittsburgh Post-Gazette*, May 23, 2015, www.post-gazette.com.

86 "Praise," *Treelines*, accessed May 26, 2014, www.treelines.com.

87 Tammy Hepps, "Lin-Manuel Miranda's Questions and Answers," *Treelines Blog*, May 11, 2016, http://b.treelines.com.

88 Samantha Katz Seal, interview by author, May 22, 2012.

89 *The Women's Haggadah*, included in E. M. Broner, *The Telling: The Story of a Group of Jewish Women Who Journey to Spirituality Through Community and Ceremony* (San Francisco: HarperSan Francisco, 1993), 197. See Vanessa L. Ochs, *Inventing Jewish Ritual* (Philadelphia: Jewish Publication Society, 2007), 12, and Vanessa L. Ochs, *The Passover Haggadah: A Biography* (Princeton, New Jersey: Princeton University Press, 2020), 151.

90 Marla Raucher Osborn, interview by author, August 24, 2012. For more on the work of Marla Raucher Osborn and Jay Osborn, see Benjamin E. Cohen, "American Couple Aims to Preserve Remnants of a Ukrainian Shtetl," *Tablet*, April 13, 2017, www.tabletmag.com.

91 Ann Goodsell, "Sooner or Later You're History," *Avotaynu* 22, no. 4 (Winter 2006): 52.

92 Goodsell, 52.

93 While studies of the material culture of American Holocaust memorials abound, few scholars have placed the work of Jewish genealogists within this analysis. For material culture analysis of Holocaust memorials, among many other works, see James E. Young, *The Texture of Memory: Holocaust Memorials and Meaning* (New Haven: Yale University Press, 1994).

94 Gary Mokotoff and Warren Blatt, *Getting Started in Jewish Genealogy* (Bergenfield, New Jersey: Avotaynu, Inc., 2000).

95 Kurzweil, *Generation to Generation*, 17.

96 As American studies scholar Erika Doss writes, American memorials "are archives of public affect, 'repositories of feeling and emotions' that are embodied in their material form and narrative content." Erika Doss, *Memorial Mania: Public Feeling in America* (Chicago: University of Chicago Press, 2010), 13. On public feeling, see also Ann Cvetkovich, *Depression: A Public Feeling* (Durham, North Carolina: Duke University Press, 2012).

97 Helen Epstein, *Where She Came From: A Daughter's Search for Her Mother's History* (Boston: Little, Brown and Company, 1997), 18.

98 Seal. "Hall of Names," *Yad Vashem*, www.yadvashem.org. Shoah, literally meaning "catastrophe," is the Hebrew word for the Holocaust.

99 Norberg Weinberg, "Megillat Ester: The Story of Irene Weinberg," *Museum of Jewish Family History*, www.museumoffamilyhistory.com.

100 Norbert Weinberg, post on the Museum of Family History Facebook page, July 19, 2012, www.facebook.com.

101 David Mink, interview by author, June 3, 2015. David Mink, haggadah, unpublished document shared with author. For the development of the homemade haggadah, see Ochs, *Inventing Jewish Ritual*, 12, and Ochs, *The Passover Haggadah*.

102 Mink, haggadah.

103 McCombs.

104 Gary Mokotoff, "Mormons Baptize Holocaust Victims," *Avotaynu* 10, no. 1 (Spring 1994): 11. Presumably Mokotoff means that Jews particularly object to baptisms in which the baptized have little or no choice in the matter, not to the practice in general.

105 Fisher, 42.

106 Church of Jesus Christ of Latter-day Saints, *Member's Guide to Temple and Family History Work* (Salt Lake City: Church of Jesus Christ of Latter-day Saints, 2009).

107 Gary Mokotoff, "Mormon/Jewish Controversy: The Problem That Won't Go Away," *Nu? What's New? News About Jewish Genealogy from Avotaynu* 7, no. 13 (February 12, 2012), www.avotaynu.com.

108 Associated Press, "Utah: Mormons Apologize for Baptism," *New York Times*, February 14, 2012.

109 Dan Gilgoff, "After Anne Frank Baptism, Mormons Vow to Discipline Members," *CNN Belief Blog*, February 22, 2012, http://religion.blogs.cnn.com.

110 McCombs.

111 Jeff Jacoby, "Mormon Ritual Is No Threat to Jews," *Boston Globe*, February 29, 2012.

112 Michael Levenson, "Romney Asked to Denounce Baptisms; Elie Wiesel Criticizes Mormon Tradition for Deceased Jews," *Boston Globe*, February 18, 2012. Wiesel passed away in 2016.

113 Kurzweil, "Genealogy as a Spiritual Pilgrimage," x.

114 On the concept of truth and dominant Jewish narratives, see Aaron J. Hahn Tapper, *Judaisms: A Twenty-First-Century Introduction to Jews and Jewish Identities* (Oakland, California: University of California Press, 2016), Chapter 1, "Narratives," 12–27.

115 See, for example, Manny Hillman, "Beware of Both Documented and Oral Histories," *Avotaynu* 20, no. 2 (Summer 2004): 24–25.

116 Harold Rhode, "The Importance of Jewish Religion, Culture, and History," in *Avotaynu Guide to Jewish Genealogy*, eds. Gary Mokotoff and Sallyann Amdur Sack (Bergenfeld, New Jersey: Avotaynu, 2004), 43.

117 Sallyann Amdur Sack, "Grandpa Didn't Tell the Truth," *Every Family Has a Story: Tales from the Pages of Avotaynu*, ed. Gary Mokotoff (Bergenfeld, New Jersey: Avotaynu, 2008), 45–46. First published in *Avotaynu* (Winter 2002).

118 Hillman, 24–25.

119 Elie Wiesel, remarks at "The Legacy of Holocaust Survivors" Conference, Yad Vashem, April 2002, on *Yad Vashem*, www.yadvashem.org.

120 Kurzweil, *Generation to Generation*, 46, 49.

121 Kurzweil, *Generation to Generation*, 46, 49.

122 Sarah Imhoff and Hillary Kaell, "Lineage Matters: DNA, Race, and Gene Talk in Judaism and Messianic Judaism," *Religion and American Culture: A Journal of Interpretation* 27, no. 1 (2017): 116.

123 See also Sarah Imhoff, "Traces of Race: Defining Jewishness in America," in *Who Is a Jew?* ed. Leonard Greenspoon (West Lafayette, Indiana: Purdue University Press, 2014), 15.

124 Family Tree DNA, "Family Tree DNA Reaches a Historic Milestone: Over 500,000 DNA Tests," *Family Tree DNA*, www.familytreedna.com.

125 Bennett Greenspan, interview by author, May 2, 2012.

126 Karl Skorecki et al., "Y Chromosomes of Jewish Priests," *Nature* 385 (January 2, 1997): 32.

127 Greenspan, interview.

128 Among other partnerships, Family Tree DNA partnered with literary critic Henry Louis Gates, Jr. to create AfricanDNA, the first company dedicated to offering both genetic testing and genealogical tracing services for African Americans. "Harvard Professor Henry Louis Gates, Jr. Joins Forces with Family Tree DNA to Launch AfricanDNA.com," *AfricanDNA*, November 15, 2007, www.africandna.com.

129 Autosomal DNA, inherited from both parents, controls physical characteristics. Autosomal DNA testing scans all of an individual's chromosomes without gender restrictions and can establish family relationships back to the generation of a person's great-great-great-great-grandparents. Sallyann Amdur Sack-Pikus, "Family Tree DNA Develops Cross-Gender Test to Find Cousins," *Avotaynu* 26, no. 1 (Spring 2010): 12–13.

130 Sack-Pikus, "Family Tree DNA."

131 Gary Mokotoff and Sallyann Amdur Sack, "It Is Time for a Consolidated Jewish DNA Database," *Avotaynu* 23, no. 2 (Summer 2007): 3.

132 Mokotoff and Sack.

133 Barbara Pash, "Taking a Swipe at Genealogy," *Baltimore Jewish Times* 293, no. 6 (December 8, 2006): 56–59.

134 Pash.

135 "Jessica Biel," *Who Do You Think You Are?*, season 8, episode 5, April 2, 2017.

136 Lee Chottiner, "DNA Revolutionizing Today's Genealogy, Dardashti Says," *Jewish Chronicle* (Pittsburgh), December 12, 2013: 18.

137 Sallyann Amdur Sack, "Current State of Jewish Genealogical Societies," *Avotaynu* 22, no. 1 (Spring 2006): 36–40.

CHAPTER 3. GHOSTS IN THE GALLERY

1 Roberta Brandes Gratz, Foreword, "Flashlight into History," in Larry Bortniker, *Beyond the Façade: A Synagogue, a Restoration, a Legacy: The Museum at Eldridge Street* (London: Scala Books, 2011), 8.

2 Roberta Brandes Gratz, "History of the Eldridge Street Synagogue," *Museum at Eldridge Street*, www.eldridgestreet.org.

3 For the white ethnic heritage movement, see Matthew Frye Jacobson, *Roots Too: White Ethnic Revival in Post-Civil Rights America* (Cambridge, Massachusetts: Harvard University Press, 2006).

4 For theorization of heritage sites, see Barbara Kirshenblatt-Gimblett, *Destination Culture: Tourism, Museums, and Heritage* (Berkeley: University of California Press, 1998).

5 "Shul" is the Yiddish term for synagogue. The name "Vilna Shul" indicates that the founding congregants came from Vilna, now Vilnius, Lithuania.

6 Riv-Ellen Prell, "'How Do You Know That I Am a Jew?': Authority, Cultural Identity, and the Shaping of Postwar Judaism," in *Jewish Studies at the Crossroads of Anthropology and History: Authority, Diaspora, Tradition*, eds. Ra'anan S. Boustan, Oren Kosansky, and Marina Rustow (Philadelphia: University of Pennsylvania Press, 2011), 33.

7 Giovanni Galli, "Nostalgia, Architecture, Ruins, and Their Preservation," *Change Over Time* 3, no. 1 (Spring 2013): 18. Rebecca J. Erickson, "The Importance of Authenticity for Self and Society," *Symbolic Interaction* 18, no. 2 (Summer 1995): 121–144.

8 Stephen E. Weil, "From Being about Something to Being for Somebody: The Ongoing Transformation of the American Museum," *Daedalus* 128, no. 3, America's Museums (Summer 1999): 242.

9 Erika Doss, *Memorial Mania: Public Feeling in America* (Chicago: University of Chicago Press, 2010), 13.

10 Jenna Weissman Joselit, "Best-in-Show: American Jews, Museum Exhibitions, and the Search for Community," in *Imagining the American Jewish Community*, ed. Jack Wertheimer (Waltham, Massachusetts: Brandeis University Press, 2007), 141–142.

11 David Chidester and Edward T. Linenthal, "Introduction," in *American Sacred Space*, eds. David Chidester and Edward T. Linenthal (Bloomington: Indiana University Press, 1995), 17.

12 Peter Clecak, *America's Quest for the Ideal Self: Dissent and Fulfillment in the 60s and 70s* (New York: Oxford University Press, 1983).

13 Celeste Olalquiaga, *The Artificial Kingdom: A Treasury of the Kitsch Experience* (New York: Pantheon Books, 1998), 122–123.

14 While there were few efforts to preserve and maintain sites of former Jewish communities in the decades immediately following World War II, as Michael Meng has traced, by the late 1970s, Germans and Poles began to restore the historic traces of Jewish life. Michael Meng, *Shattered Spaces: Encountering Jewish Ruins in Postwar Germany and Poland* (Cambridge, Massachusetts: Harvard University Press, 2011).

15 Ruth Ellen Gruber, *Virtually Jewish: Reinventing Jewish Culture in Europe* (Berkeley: University of California Press, 2002), 165.

16 Lila Corwin Berman, "Jewish Urban Politics in the City and Beyond," *The Journal of American History* 99, no. 2 (September 2012): 492–493.

17 Andres Viglucci, "The 100-Year Story of Miami Beach," *Miami Herald*, March 25, 2015, www.miamiherald.com.

18 "Historic Buildings," *Jewish Museum of Florida*, http://jmof.fiu.edu. Accessed November 1, 2013. (The museum's website has changed since its merger with Florida International University.)

19 "Historic Buildings."

20 Alan Lupo, "The Saving of a Shul," *Boston Globe*, December 16, 1989, 27.

21 Ethan Bronner, "Beacon Hill; Proposed Sale of Vilna Synagogue Assailed; Official Cites a Lack of Support While Opponents Say They Want to Preserve Jewish Heritage," *Boston Globe*, February 3, 1986, 18.

22 Constance L. Hays, "Deserted Synagogue of 1919 Sets Off Boston Tug-of-War," *New York Times*, December 21, 1989.

23 Peter J. Howe, "Synagogue Preservation Issue Has Stirred Passionate Debate," *Boston Globe*, January 22, 1990, 13.

24 Kevin Cullen, "Police Arrest Complaining Landlord on Drug Charges," *Boston Globe*, December 10, 1988, 25.

25 Peter J. Howe, "A Step to Save Landmark Synagogue," *Boston Globe*, September 27, 1990, 31.

26 Havurah on the Hill follows the trend of proliferating lay-led *minyanim* (prayer groups) that draw together young adults, particularly singles, who are uninterested in paying membership dues to join synagogue congregations dominated by their parents' generation and geared toward families. Kristin Erekson, "Havurah Hits Spirituality's Sweet Spot," *Jewish Advocate*, October 6, 2006, 8.

27 Jeff Adler, "Going Back to Shul," *Boston Globe*, November 3, 2002, 3.

28 Wade Clark Roof, *Spiritual Marketplace: Baby Boomers and the Remaking of American Religion* (Princeton, New Jersey: Princeton University Press 2001), 83.

29 Katie Zezima, "A Start-Up Congregation Revives an Old Synagogue," *New York Times*, December 11, 2004.

30 Barry Shrage, interview by author, June 28, 2012. Doug Most, "Boston's Jewish Renaissance," *Boston Globe*, November 6, 2005.

31 See, for example, Gary Rosenblatt, "Jewish Giving Strong, But Concerns Loom, New Study Finds," *New York Jewish Week*, September 4, 2013, www.thejewishweek.com.

32 Adler.

33 Svetlana Boym, *The Future of Nostalgia* (New York: Basic Books, 2001), 79.

34 The philosopher Theodor Adorno believed that museum exhibits display "objects to which the observer no longer has a vital relationship and which are in the process of dying. They owe their preservation more to historical respect than to the needs of the present." Quoted in Oren Baruch Stier, *Committed to Memory: Cultural Mediations of the Holocaust* (Boston: University of Massachusetts Press, 2003), 114. Carol S. Jeffers, "Museum as Process," *Journal of Aesthetic Education* 37, no. 1 (Spring 2003): 107–119. Carol Duncan, *Civilizing Rituals: Inside Public Art Museums* (New York: Routledge, 1995). Stephen E. Weil, *Making Museums Matter* (Washington, D.C.: Smithsonian Institution Press, 2002), 195–196.

35 Duncan, 8–9.

36 Jessica Antoline, interview by author, June 26, 2012.

37 Mary Jo Valdez, interview by author, August 15, 2012.

38 Touro Synagogue was built by enslaved men, including men enslaved by members of the congregation. Enslaved men who built the synagogue included Zingo Stevens, Malbo Samford, and George Brown. "Notes on Newport Synagogue," *American Hebrew* 61, May 21, 1897, 101.

39 Theodore Lewis, "History of Touro Synagogue," *Bulletin of the Newport Historical Society* 48, no. 159 (Summer 1975): 317–318.

40 Morris Aaron Gutstein, *The Story of the Jews of Newport: Two and a Half Centuries of Judaism* (New York: Bloch Publishing Co., 1936).

41 Congregation Jeshuat Israel, *Touro Synagogue*, www.tourosynagogue.org.

42 Anthony Weiss, "Touro Struggles with Its Historic Legacy," *Forward*, May 27, 2009, 1, 10.

43 Valdez.

44 Louis M. Solomon, "Profaning History at Touro Synagogue," *New York Jewish Week*, June 30, 2016, https://jewishweek.timesofisrael.com.

45 Katie Mulvaney, "Appeals Court Upholds NY Congregation as Owners of Newport's Touro Synagogue," *Providence Journal*, www.providencejournal.com.

46 Julie Salamon, "From the Brink of Death to Life Overflowing," *New York Times*, March 30, 2005, G4.

47 Salamon.

48 Jenna Weissman Joselit, "Museum Woe," *Forward*, January 2, 2008, https://forward.com. A member of the Eldridge Street congregation commented on Joselit's online article with a reminder that the congregation benefited from restoration, which enabled it to use the restored main sanctuary for Saturday morning services.

49 Bonnie Dimun, interview by author, July 10, 2012.

50 A cantor (hazzan in Hebrew) is a clergyperson who sings liturgical music and leads prayer in a synagogue. Hershtik performed liturgy from the "golden age" of American Jewish cantors of the 1920s and 1930s, when cantors regularly gave acclaimed musical performances for Jewish and non-Jewish audiences, as well as more recent cantorial pieces. Cynthia R. Fagen, "Cantorial Classics on Lower East Side," *New York Post*, December 2, 2012: 23.

51 George Robinson, "Netanel Hershtik's 'Mission,'" *The New York Jewish Week*, November 27, 2012, www.thejewishweek.com.

52 There is a long history of American cantorial performance confusing the categories of music for worship and for entertainment. Jeffrey Shandler, *Jews, God, and Videotape: Religion and Media in America* (New York: New York University Press, 2009).

53 "Museum Membership," *Jewish Museum of Florida*, www.jewishmuseum.com. Accessed November 1, 2013. Emphasis in original.

54 Galli, 18.

55 Jack Swartz, "Please Spread the Word," *Vilna Scribe* 16, no. 2 (Fall 2010): 1.

56 The idea that Jewish feelings create Jewish objects and spaces dates back to Talmudic times. Barbara Mann reads Rabban Gamliel's interpretation of the statue of Aphrodite in the bathhouse—"I did not enter her territory; she entered mine" (M. Avodah Zarah 3:4)—as "scripting a Jewish space that in effect overlaps with that of the pagan environs." Barbara Mann, *Space and Place in Jewish Studies* (New Brunswick, New Jersey: Rutgers University Press, 2012), 92–93. Jason von Ehrenkrook, "A Jewish Aphrodite?" *Frankel Institute Annual* (2010): 9–11.

57 Valdez.

58 Duncan, 10. For visitors' behavior at museums, see John H. Falk and Lynn D. Dierking, *The Museum Experience Revisited* (Walnut Creek, California: Left Coast Press, 2013).

59 Orthodox men are required to pray during three specific time periods, and it is ideal to pray with a minyan (prayer quorum) of ten men. In Orthodox services, women do not count toward a minyan, and, traditionally, women are only required to pray once a day.

60 For conflicts between visitors' expectations and museum staff members' plans, see Falk and Dierking. On staff members' and visitors' shared authority, see Bill Adair, Benjamin Filene, and Laura Koloski, eds., *Letting Go? Sharing Historical Authority in a User-Generated World* (Philadelphia: The Pew Center for Arts & Heritage, 2011).

61 Sara Lowenburg, interview by author, June 11, 2014.

62 Bonnie Dimun, quoted in "A New East Window on Eldridge Street," *New York Times*, October 18, 2010.

63 Amy Stein Milford, quoted in "A New East Window on Eldridge Street," *New York Times*, October 18, 2010.

64 Dimun, interview.

65 Pia Catton, "Downtown, a New Window on the World," *Wall Street Journal*, October 6, 2010, A.29.

66 Marjorie Ingall, "A Very New Window in a Very Old Shul: The Museum at Eldridge Street's Welcome Makeover," *Tablet*, October 19, 2010, www.tabletmag.com.

67 Amy Waterman, "In the Spirit: Values, Authenticity and Interpretation," in *Jewish Space and Jewish Stories: American Jewish Museums Interpret the Synagogue*, eds. Avi Y. Decter and Kathi Lieb (New York: Council of American Jewish Museums, National Foundation for Jewish Culture, 1993), 24.

68 Amy Waterman, "Public Programming for Jewish Sites: Lessons from Two Historic Synagogues: The Eldridge Street Project, New York," *Jewish Heritage Report* 1, no. 2 (Summer 1997), www.isjm.org.

69 "Women's Chandelier," *Museum at Eldridge Street*, www.eldridgestreet.org.

70 Annie Polland recounts this story in *Landmark of the Spirit: The Eldridge Street Synagogue* (New Haven: Yale University Press, 2009), 64–66. See also Paula Hyman, "Immigrant Women and Consumer Protest: The New York City Kosher

Meat Boycott of 1902," *American Jewish History* 70, no. 1 (September 1, 1980): 91–105.

71 "The Real Housewives of Eldridge Street," advertisement for event on May 12, 2013, *Museum at Eldridge Street*, www.eldridgestreet.org.

72 While this is a story of consumer activism, the progressive political activism of Jews on the Lower East Side and other urban Jewish neighborhoods is more often remembered through stories of labor activism, and the Eldridge Street Synagogue story should be interpreted in that context. Immigrant Jewish labor activism is often remembered as a feminist story, as the history of the Triangle Shirtwaist Factory fire of 1911, which helped spur the growth of the International Ladies' Garment Workers' Union, making it appropriate for docents and staff members to allude to this progressive history through a story in the women's balcony of synagogue. For the history of immigrant Jewish women and labor activism in the early twentieth century, see Susan A. Glenn, *Daughters of the Shtetl: Life and Labor in the Immigrant Generation* (Ithaca, New York: Cornell University Press, 1990).

73 Jo Ann Arnowitz, interview by author, July 24, 2012.

74 Carol Hamoy, interview by author, January 8, 2013. Stephanie Crawford and Fernanda Perrone, "Guide to the Carol Hamoy Papers, ca. 1970–2016," Special Collections and University Archives, Rutgers University Libraries (October 2016), www2.scc.rutgers.edu/ead/manuscripts/Hamoyb.html. Gloria Orenstein, "Vision and Visibility: Contemporary Jewish Women Artists Visualize the Invisible," *Femspec* 4, vol. 2 (June 2003): 46–82.

75 Carol Hamoy, "Welcome to America/Eldridge Street Synagogue," unpublished document shared with author. Hamoy, interview.

76 Orenstein.

77 Miriam Seidel, "Hana Iverson at Eldridge Street Synagogue," *Art in America* (January 2001). C. Carr, "World of Our Mothers: An Artist Returns to Her Ancestral Synagogue," *Village Voice*, September 12, 2000, www.villagevoice.com. Billie Cohen, "Immigrant Song," *Time Out New York*, May 2000. Stanley Mieses, "Returning to the Fold on Their Own Terms: The Art of 'Secular Spirituality,'" *Forward*, 24 November 2000, 11.

78 Hana Iverson, interview by author, January 8, 2013.

79 Nathan Glazer and Daniel Patrick Moynihan, *Beyond the Melting Pot: The Negroes, Puerto Ricans, Jews, Italians, and Irish of New York City* (Cambridge, Massachusetts: MIT Press, 1970), xcvii. Jacobson, 178.

80 Gerard R. Wolfe, *The Synagogues of New York's Lower East Side: A Retrospective and Contemporary View* (New York: Fordham University Press, 2013), 33.

81 Jacobson, 319–320.

82 In 2015, Silver was convicted on federal corruption charges, and he resigned as Speaker of the Assembly. His first conviction was overturned; he was convicted again in a retrial in 2018, and in 2020 a federal appeals court partially overturned the 2018 conviction but allowed much of it to stand. At the time of this book's

publication, Silver is awaiting sentencing. Benjamin Weiser, "Sheldon Silver's Corruption Conviction Is Partly Overturned," *New York Times*, January 21, 2020.

83 "Charter is Granted to Touro Society," *New York Times*, February 27, 1948, 3.

84 Mary Korr, "Ginsburg Shares in American Jewry's 350th Celebration," *Jewish Alliance of Greater Rhode Island*, September 10, 2004, www.jfri.org.

85 Steve Ahlquist and Chuck Flippo, "Jessica Ahlquist Honored at Touro Synagogue," *RI Future*, August 21, 2012, www.rifuture.org. Elisabeth Harrison, "R.I. Student Draws Ire Over School Prayer Challenge," *NPR*, February 7, 2012, www.npr.org.

86 "The 16th Annual Egg Rolls, Egg Creams and Empanadas Festival is Sunday," *The Lo-Down*, June 17, 2016, www.thelodownny.com.

87 An egg cream is a beverage composed of milk, seltzer, and chocolate syrup. While some claim that the egg cream was invented on the Lower East Side, it is particularly associated with Jews in Brooklyn and the Bronx in the early twentieth century. Jennifer Berg, "From the Big Bagel to the Big Roti? The Evolution of New York City's Jewish Food Icons," in *Gastropolis: Food and New York City*, ed. Annie Hauck-Lawson and Jonathan Deutsch (New York: Columbia University Press, 2009), 252–273.

88 The Chinese game of mahjong became popular in the 1920s and 1930s among American Jewish women, who developed a standard American version of the game that differs from the Chinese version. Christi Cavallaro and Anita Luu, *Mah-jongg: From Shanghai to Miami Beach* (San Francisco: Chronicle Books, 2005).

89 Hanna Griff-Sleven, interview by author, February 8, 2013.

90 Julia Gerasimenko, "Egg Rolls and Egg Creams Festival '11," *Museum at Eldridge Street Blog*, June 14, 2011, www.eldridgestreet.org.

91 Salamon.

92 Griff-Sleven.

93 Hasia Diner describes the same phenomenon among Jewish visitors to the Tenement Museum, located a few blocks from the Museum at Eldridge Street, where visitors can view restored apartments and listen the stories of former occupants. While Tenement Museum staff members explicitly work to depict families of multiple faiths and national origins, Jewish visitors insist on seeing the building as a Jewish site. Hasia R. Diner, *Lower East Side Memories: A Jewish Place in America* (Princeton, New Jersey: Princeton University Press, 2002), 188.

94 *Breed Street Shul Project*, http://breedstreetshul.org.

95 Julie Gruenbaum Fax, "On Road to Renewal, Shul Gets Multipurpose Life," *Jewish Journal of Greater Los Angeles*, July 13, 2011, http://jewishjournal.com.

96 Judy Greenspan and Miriam Bader, *Shining Again: The Story of the Eldridge Street Synagogue and Museum* (New York: Modern Publishing, 2011), n.p.

CHAPTER 4. TRUE STORIES

1 Although the terms "picture books" and "illustrated books" are often used interchangeably, picture books are specifically designed to communicate through a com-

bination of words and images. Images interact with and extend the text to a greater extent in picture books than in illustrated books. Carole Scott, "Dual Audiences in Picture Books," in *Transcending Boundaries: Writing for a Dual Audience of Children and Adults*, ed. Sandra L. Beckett (New York: Garland, 1999), 101.

2 Svetlana Boym, *The Future of Nostalgia* (New York: Basic Books, 2001).

3 Jodi Eichler-Levine, *Suffer the Little Children: Uses of the Past in Jewish and African-American Children's Literature* (New York: New York University Press, 2013), 74.

4 Robert A. Orsi, "Printed Presence: Twentieth-Century Catholic Print Culture for Youngsters in the United States," in *Education and the Culture of Print in Modern America*, eds. Adam R. Nelson and John L. Rudolph (Madison, Wisconsin: University of Wisconsin Press, 2010), 82.

5 Jana Pohl, *Looking Forward, Looking Back: Images of Eastern European Jewish Migration to America in Contemporary American Children's Literature* (New York: Rodopi, 2011), 19.

6 Eichler-Levine, xv.

7 Eichler-Levine, xix.

8 Melissa R. Klapper, *Jewish Girls Coming of Age in America, 1860–1920* (New York: New York University Press, 2005).

9 Robin Bernstein, *Racial Innocence: Performing American Childhood from Slavery to Civil Rights* (New York: New York University Press, 2011), 23. Catherine Robson, *Men in Wonderland: The Lost Girlhood of the Victorian Gentleman* (Princeton, New Jersey: Princeton University Press, 2003).

10 Mary Antin, *The Promised Land* (Boston: Houghton Mifflin Company, 1912), 364. For changing attitudes toward *The Promised Land*, see Michael P. Kramer, "Assimilation in *The Promised Land*: Mary Antin and the Jewish Origins of the American Self," *Prooftexts* 18, no. 2 (1998): 121–122.

11 Antin, xi.

12 Lily Kong and Lily Tay, "Exalting the Past: Nostalgia and the Construction of Heritage in Children's Literature," *Area* 30, no. 2 (June 1998): 136.

13 Rachel Gross, "'Draydel Salad': The Serious Business of Jewish Food and Fun in the 1950s," in *Religion, Food, and Eating in North America*, eds. Benjamin Zeller et al. (New York: Columbia University Press, 2014), 91–113.

14 K. Healan Gaston, *Imagining Judeo-Christian America: Religion, Secularism, and the Redefinition of Democracy* (Chicago: University of Chicago Press, 2019).

15 Rachel Kranson, *Ambivalent Embrace: Jewish Upward Mobility in Postwar America* (Chapel Hill: University of North Carolina Press, 2018), 4.

16 Elaine Tyler May, *Homeward Bound: American Families in the Cold War Era* (New York: Basic Books, 1988), 29.

17 For the changes in formal Jewish education, see Jenna Weissman Joselit, *New York's Jewish Jews: The Orthodox Community in the Interwar Years* (Bloomington: Indiana University Press, 1990).

18 Charles A. Madison, *Jewish Publishing in America: The Impact of Jewish Writing on American Culture* (New York: Sanhedrin Press, 1976), 88–89.

19 Jacob S. Golub, "American Jewish Juvenile Literature, 1949–1950," *Jewish Book Annual* 9 (1950–51): 27–29.

20 Sydney Taylor, *All-of-a-Kind Family* (New York: Follett, 1951), 34.

21 Pohl, 243.

22 Hasia Diner, *Lower East Side Memories: A Jewish Place in America* (Princeton, New Jersey: Princeton University Press, 2000), 61.

23 Such depictions of Jewish family life have political ramifications. As Matthew Frye Jacobson explains, since at least the mid-twentieth century, stories of white immigrant families, not least including Jews, provided the normative version of the American family, against which the "pathologies" of black families were contrasted. Matthew Frye Jacobson, *Roots Too: White Ethnic Revival in Post-Civil Rights America* (Cambridge, Massachusetts: Harvard University Press, 2006), 204.

24 Marcia W. Posner, "Fifty Years of Jewish Children's Books in the *Jewish Book Annual*," *Jewish Book Annual* 50 (1992–1993): 81–98.

25 Jonathan Sarna, *JPS: The Americanization of Jewish Culture* (New York: Jewish Publication Society, 1989), 289.

26 Eichler-Levine, 43. Barbara Cohen, *Molly's Pilgrim* (New York: HarperTrophy, 1983). *Molly's Pilgrim*, directed by Jeffrey D. Brown, written by Jeffrey D. Brown, Barbara Cohen, and Chris Pelzer (Phoenix Films, 1985), 24 minutes.

27 Kate Rosenblatt, Lila Corwin Berman, and Ronit Stahl, "How Jewish Academia Created A #MeToo Disaster," *Forward*, July 19, 2018, https://forward.com. For interfaith Jewish-Christian families, see Samira K. Mehta, *Beyond Chrismukkah: The Christian-Jewish Interfaith Family in the United States* (Chapel Hill: University of North Carolina Press, 2018).

28 Jacob Berkman, "Reaching Out with Book Giveaway," *Jewish Telegraphic Agency*, November 20, 2007.

29 PJ Library has expanded from the United States and Canada into Mexico and Australia. A version of the program called Sifriyat Pijama (Hebrew for "Pajama Library") distributes books to preschools in Israel, in partnership with the Israeli Ministry of Education.

30 Meredith Lewis, telephone interview by the author, March 1, 2016.

31 Rachel B. Gross, "People of the Picture Book: PJ Library and American Jewish Religion," in *Religion and Popular Culture in America*, third edition, eds. Bruce David Forbes and Jeffrey H. Mahan (Oakland, California: University of California Press, 2017), 177–194.

32 Dianne Hess, interview by author, December 2, 2013. Dianne Hess, email to author, June 25, 2014

33 Jeffrey Shandler, *Shtetl: A Vernacular Intellectual History* (New Brunswick, New Jersey: Rutgers University Press, 2014).

34 Amy Hest, *When Jessie Came Across the Sea* (Cambridge, Massachusetts: Candlewick Press, 1997), n.p.

35 Amy Hest, interview by author, January 6, 2014.

36 Hest, interview.

37 Hest, *Jessie*, back flap of PJ Library edition. Chris Barash, director of the PJ Library Book Selection Committee, writes the PJ Library reading guides, though her authorship is not noted on the books. "PJ Library Staff," *PJ Library*, www.pjlibary.org, accessed May 30, 2014.

38 Hest, *Jessie*, front flap of PJ Library edition.

39 Eric A. Kimmel, *When Mindy Saved Hanukkah* (New York: Scholastic Press, 1998). Elsa Okon Rael, *When Zaydeh Danced on Eldridge Street* (New York: Simon and Schuster Books for Young Readers, 1997). Zaydeh is the Yiddish word for grandfather. *When Zaydeh Danced* is not a PJ Library book, but another book by Rael, *What Zeesie Saw on Delancey Street*, featuring the same young protagonist and also located on the Lower East Side, was a PJ Library book in 2012. Elsa Okon Rael, *What Zeesie Saw on Delancey Street* (New York: Simon and Schuster Books for Young Readers, 1996).

40 Dianne Ashton, *Hanukkah in America: A History* (New York: New York University Press, 2013).

41 Kimmel, *Mindy*, back flap.

42 "When Mindy Saved Hanukkah and the Eldridge Street Synagogue," *Museum at Eldridge Street*, December 8, 2014, www.eldridgestreet.org. "Preservation Detectives: When Mindy Saved Hanukkah," *Time Out New York*, November 24, 2015, www.timeout.com.

43 Barbara McClintock, interview by author, November 27, 2013.

44 McClintock. Eric Kimmel and Dianne Hess also recalled that the Eldridge Street Project used McClintock's illustration for their funding and renovation efforts, though current staff members at the Museum at Eldridge Street were not able to corroborate this story. Eric Kimmel, interview by author, November 14, 2013. Hess, interview. Nancy Johnson, email to author, March 7, 2014.

45 "When Zaydeh Danced on Eldridge Street," *Publishers Weekly*, September 1, 1997, http://reviews.publishersweekly.com.

46 Rael, *Zaydeh*, n.p.

47 Wade Clark Roof, *Spiritual Marketplace: Baby Boomers and the Remaking of American Religion* (Princeton, New Jersey: Princeton University Press 2001).

48 Sheldon Oberman, *The Always Prayer Shawl* (Pennsylvania: Boyd Mills Press, 1994), n.p.

49 Oberman, *Prayer Shawl*, n.p.

50 Association of Jewish Librarians awarded Oberman the Sydney Taylor Award in 1994 for the *The Always Prayer Shawl*. The book won the 1994 National Jewish Book Award in the children's picture book category, and it received the American Bookseller's "Pick of the List Award," *A Child's Magazine*'s "Best Book of the Year," the National Council of Social Studies's "Notable Book in the field of Social Studies," and Canada's "Choice List," awarded by the Canadian Children's Book Centre. Winnipeg Jewish Theatre, "Sheldon Oberman Wins Award for 'The Always Prayer Shawl,'" March 1, 1995, press release. Retrieved at Sheldon Oberman

Collection, Archives and Special Collections, University of Manitoba, Canada (hereafter SOC), MSS328, Box 3, Folder 1.

51 Karen R. Long, "The Fabric of History: Tale of Shawl Universal Saga," *Plain Dealer* (Cleveland, Ohio), April 27, 1994, 1F.

52 "Draw Close and Remember," *Winnipeg Free Press*, March 5, 1995, SOC MSS 328, Box 6, Folder 3. Sheldon Oberman, "Playwright's Note," *The Always Prayer Shawl* (1995), bound script. Retrieved at SOC, MSS 328, Box 6, Folder 3. "'Always Prayer Shawl' a Hit at Toronto Jewish Festival," *Winnipeg Sun*, July 26, 1995. Retrieved at SOC, MSS 328, Box 6, Folder 3. The Katz JCC Eleventh Annual Festival of Arts, Books & Culture, "The Always Prayer Shawl," (Cherry Hill, New Jersey, December 3, 1995), playbill. Retrieved at SOC, MSS 328, Box 3, Folder 1.

53 Zaida, like zaydeh, is a transliteration of the Yiddish word for grandfather.

54 Sheldon Oberman, "The Gift of the Prayer Shawl," *Women's League Outlook* 66, no. 4 (June 30, 1996): 8. Long, 1F.

55 Oberman, "The Gift," 9.

56 Oberman, "The Gift," 9. The end of Oberman's life, like his most well-known story, was also marked by a ritually innovative bar mitzvah. Oberman died of esophageal cancer in March 1994 at the age of 54. When he and his second wife, Lisa Dveris, learned that his cancer was terminal, they accelerated plans for their twelve-year-old son Jesse's bar mitzvah. The bar mitzvah was held in a hospital chapel so that Oberman could attend. "Jesse had his bar mitzvah, with his dad there, and it was everything we needed it to be," said Dveris. Brian Brennan, "Writer Performed His Stories," *Globe and Mail*, May 25, 2004, R5.

57 Elspeth Probyn, *Outside Belongings* (New York: Routledge, 1996), 112.

58 In Foucault's words, this form of history provides "a suprahistorical perspective." Michel Foucault, "Nietzsche, Genealogy, History," *Language, Counter-Memory, Practice: Selected Essays and Interviews*, trans. Donald F. Bouchard and Sherry Simon (Ithaca, New York: Cornell University Press, 1977), 152.

59 Dallas Hansen, "Old Prayer Shawl Inspires Book," *Winnipeg Free Press* [?], n.d., SOC, MSS 328, Box 3, Folder 1.

60 Long, 1F.

61 Long, 1F.

62 While Sephardi Jews name children after living relatives, Ashkenazi Jews avoid doing so because of a folk belief that when the Angel of Death came for the older relative, he would mistakenly take the younger one instead.

63 "Meet the Illustrator: Ted Lewin," *The Bridge* (Boyd Mills Press), SOC, MSS 328, Box 3, Folder 1. Sheldon Oberman, "Family, Tradition, and 'The Story of the Story,'" *The Bridge* (Boyd Mills Press), SOC, MSS 328, Box 3, Folder 1.

64 Larry Rosler, interview by author, March 2, 2014.

65 Brennan.

66 Rosler.

67 Brennan.

68 Linda Heller, *The Castle on Hester Street* (Philadelphia: Jewish Publication Society of America, 1982).

69 Jonathan Sarna, *JPS: The Americanization of Jewish Culture* (New York: Jewish Publication Society, 1989), 289.

70 Heller, *Castle*, n.p.

71 Heller, *Castle*, n.p.

72 Arthur Kurzweil, *From Generation to Generation: How to Trace Your Jewish Genealogy and Family History* (San Francisco: Jossey-Bass, a Wiley Imprint, 2004), 46.

73 A Customer, "A clever way to introduce the immigrant experience," Amazon user review of *The Castle on Hester Street*, May 19, 1999, www.amazon.com/Castle-Hester-Street-Linda-Heller/dp/0689874340.

74 JPS also received the prestigious Philadelphia Book Clinic award for the design, printing, and binding of *The Castle on Hester Street* at the 38th Philadelphia Book Show. Muriel M. Berman, "From the Annual Report of JPS President Muriel M. Berman," *American Jewish Year Book* (Jewish Publication Society of America, 1984), 7.

75 Merrie Lou Cohen, review of *The Castle on Hester Street* by Linda Heller, *School Library Journal* (February 1983): 66.

76 Linda Heller, *The Castle on Hester Street* (New York: Simon & Schuster Books for Young Readers, 2007).

77 "The Castle on Hester Street," *Booklist*, December 15, 2007, 48–49.

78 "The Castle on Hester Street," *Kirkus Reviews* 75, no. 19 (October 1, 2007): 1048. Linda Heller, telephone interview by author, January 7, 2014.

79 Heller, *Castle*, n.p. PJ Library, back flap, *Castle*. For more on PJ Library and religion, see Gross, "People of the Picture Book."

80 "Lindsey Bergman," *American Girl Wiki*, http://americangirl.wikia.com.

81 Allen Salkin, "American Girl's Journey to the Lower East Side," *New York Times*, May 22, 2009; Julie Gruenbaum Fax, "American Girl Introduces First Jewish Doll," *Jewish Journal of Greater Los Angeles*, May 27, 2009.

82 PapaRosenbaum, "Mazel Tov AG," product review of Rebecca Doll, Book & Accessories, June 6, 2009; NanaFL, "Beautiful Doll," product review of Rebecca Doll, Book & Accessories, August 12, 2011, *American Girl*, http://store.americangirl.com.

83 The price of a doll and one book has since increased to $115, and American Girl has discontinued some of the Rebecca items and sets.

84 Kathryn Lofton, *Consuming Religion* (Chicago: University of Chicago Press, 2017), 9.

85 The company was called Pleasant Company until 2004, when it officially changed the name of the company to match the name of its product line, American Girl.

86 Pleasant T. Rowland, Pleasant Company website, 1998, quoted in Carolina Acosta-Alzuru and Peggy J. Kreshel, "'I'm an American Girl . . . Whatever That Means': Girls Consuming Pleasant Company's American Girl Identity," *Journal of Communication* 52, no. 1 (March 2002): 139.

87 In May 2014, consumers responded with anger and frustration to American Girl's announcement of the impending "retirement" of Ivy, the only Asian American historical character. "I am disappointed to know that Asian American Girls will no longer have a doll. #AmericanGirlDiversityMatters," wrote one Facebook commenter. Katie Kindelan, "American Girl Rebuts Critics After Dropping Minority Dolls," *ABC News*, May 28, 2014, http://abcnews.go.com.

88 Bernstein, 152.

89 American Girl advertises Rebecca's school set by suggesting that consumers "Help her succeed in the classroom with this set." Online reviewers of all ages report their approval that the tiny pencil included in the set can really write in the miniature notebook and that girls can "sing along" with Rebecca by following in the miniature sheet music for "You're a Grand Old Flag," Rebecca's patriotic song of choice. "Rebecca's School Set," *American Girl*, http://store.americangirl.com.

90 Before her American Girl series, Greene had published two chapter books about Portuguese Sephardi Jewish sisters in the seventeenth century. As Greene told me, she came to write her first book about Sephardi history as she tried to learn more about her own heritage. Greene's father is Ashkenazi and her mother Sephardi; her maternal grandmother is from Smyrna, Greece, now Izmir, Turkey. She grew up surrounded by Ladino-speaking family members and her family observed Sephardi customs. Jacqueline Dembar Greene, *Out of Many Waters* (New York: Walker, 1988). Jacqueline Dembar Greene, *One Foot Ashore* (New York: Walker, 1994). Greene's third book on Sephardi history, *The Secret Shofar of Barcelona* was published the same year as the Rebecca series. *The Secret Shofar* is a PJ Library book. Jacqueline Dembar Greene, *The Secret Shofar of Barcelona* (Minneapolis, Minnesota: Kar-Ben Publishing, 2009). Jacqueline Dembar Greene, interview by author, November 19, 2013.

91 Greene, interview.

92 Jacqueline Dembar Greene, *Meet Rebecca* (Middleton, Wisconsin: American Girl Publishing, 2009), 22.

93 Unlike the fictional Rebecca Rubin, an Ashkenazi Jew of Russian descent, the Tenement Museum's Victoria Confino is based on a former resident of the museum's building whose Sephardi Jewish family emigrated from the Ottoman city of Kastoria, in what is now northern Greece. While Tenement Museum staff strive to demonstrate the diversity of Jewish and non-Jewish populations of the historic Lower East Side, many Jewish tourists persist in viewing the building's history in line with the predominant narratives of Eastern European nostalgia. Jack Kugelmass, "Turfing the Slum: New York City's Tenement Museum and the Politics of Heritage," in *Remembering the Lower East Side*, eds. Hasia R. Diner, Jeffrey Shandler, Beth S. Wenger (Bloomington: Indiana University Press, 2000), 179–211.

94 See Chapter 5 for a discussion of kosher-style cuisine, which engages Ashkenazi culinary traditions while jettisoning traditional Jewish dietary requirements in whole or in part. "An American Girl," *Tenement Museum Blog*, May

26, 2009, http://tenement-museum.blogspot.com. Cathy Lynn Grossman, "American Girl Dolls Up Jewish History: Kaya, Meet Rebecca," *USA Today*, http://content.usatoday.com.

95 Ashton.

96 Jacqueline Dembar Greene, *Candlelight for Rebecca* (Middleton, Wisconsin: American Girl Publishing, 2009).

97 Greene, *Candlelight for Rebecca*, 67.

98 Greene, interview. For the history of the relationship between Hanukkah and Christmas in the United States, see Ashton.

99 Mehta, 160.

100 Bernstein, 78.

101 Joellyn Wallen Zollman, "The Gifts of the Jews: Ideology and Material Culture in the American Synagogue Gift Shop," *American Jewish Archives Journal* 58, no. 1 (2006): 51–77.

102 Anthropologist A. F. Robertson argues that collectible dolls should not be con-sidered in the same category as children's playthings. Nevertheless, I find that Ellis Island dolls function both as collectors' items and as children's playthings, as American Jews purchase them both for adults and for children. American Girl dolls are much more expensive than Ellis Island dolls, but they have a vinyl "skin" and damage to them can be repaired—for a fee—by the American Girl doll "hospital." Ellis Island dolls, though less expensive, have fragile porcelain heads and limbs, making them less suitable as toys for young children. How-ever, this does not stop some consumers from buying them for children. A.F. Roberston, *Life Like Dolls: The Collector Doll Phenomenon and the Lives of the Women Who Love Them* (London: Routledge, 2004).

103 Simone Ellin, "All Dolled Up," *Baltimore Jewish Times*, August 14, 2009: S8–S10.

104 "Ellis Island Dolls," *Copa Judaica*, www.copajudaica.com.

105 Barbara Kirshenblatt-Gimblett, *Destination Culture: Tourism, Museums, and Heritage* (Berkeley: University of California Press, 1998).

106 "Leah Lili," *Copa Judaica*, www.copajudaica.com.

107 "Ellis Island Doll—Ruth," *Jewish Bazaar*, www.jewishbazaar.com.

108 Blue, "Final Farewell from Gali Girls," *A Doll's Day*, November 7, 2013, https://adollsday.wordpress.com. "FAQ," *Gali Girls*, www.galigirls.com, May 24, 2006. Accessed via the Internet Archive. "Gali Girls, Inc.—Gali Girls," *Just Magic*, www.justmagicdolls.com. Sally Kalson, "Gali Girls Line of Dolls Celebrates Jewish His-tory, Values," *Pittsburgh Post-Gazette*, March 6, 2007, C1, C3.

109 Sharon Schlegel, "Books, Dolls, Illuminate Jewish Girls' Stories," *Chicago Tribune*, January 11, 2006, http://articles.chicagotribune.com.

110 B. Memolo, "Beautiful and educational," Amazon customer review of *Miriam's Journey: Discovering a New World (The Gali Girls Jewish History Series)*, February 3, 2006.

111 Robin K. Levinson, *Miriam's Journey: Discovering a New World* (Teaneck, New Jersey: Gali Girls, 2006), 1.

112 Rebecca Kobrin, "Rewriting the Diaspora: Images of Eastern Europe in the Bialys-
    tok Landsmanshaft Press, 1921–45," *Jewish Social Studies* 12, no. 3 (Spring–Summer
    2006): 1–38. Jacqueline Dembar Greene, *Rebecca and Ana* (Middleton, Wisconsin:
    American Girl Publishing, Inc., 2009).

113 Lisa Marcus, "Dolling Up History: Fictions of American Jewish Girlhood," *Girl-
    hood Studies* 5, no. 1 (Summer 2012): 33.

114 Greene, *Rebecca and Ana.*

115 Jacqueline Dembar Greene, *Changes for Rebecca* (Middleton, Wisconsin: Ameri-
    can Girl Publishing, 2009).

116 Greene, *Changes for Rebecca*, 77.

117 Heather, *Goodreads* review of *Changes for Rebecca*, February 3, 2017, www.
    goodreads.com.

118 Mom2JPB, "We Love Rebecca!" user review of Rebecca Doll, Book & Accessories,
    American Girl, March 6, 2014, http://store.americangirl.com.

119 kate1441, "Five Year Old Love [*sic*] It!" user review of Rebecca Doll, Book & Ac-
    cessories, *American Girl*, March 6, 2014, http://store.americangirl.com.

120 Kimmel, interview.

121 "Sheldon Oberman Wins Award for 'The Always Prayer Shawl,'" *Winnipeg Sun*,
    March 15, 1995. Retrieved at SOC, MSS 328, Box 3, Folder 1.

122 Riva Harrison, "Generation Wrap," *Winnipeg Sun*, March 9, 1995. Retrieved at
    SOC, MSS 328, Box 6, Folder 3. Oberman, *Always Prayer Shawl*, bound script.

123 Long, 3F. Linda Rosborough, "Kids' Story Fits Every Family Circle," *Winnipeg Free
    Press*, March 6, 1995, SOC, MSS 328, Box 6, Folder 3.

124 Janet Dirks, interview by Terry MacLeod, review of *The Always Prayer Shawl*,
    CBC Radio Morning Show, transcript, SOC, MSS 328, Box 6, Folder 3.

125 Harrison.

126 Greene, interview.

127 Greene, interview. As part of his "mitzvah campaigns" encouraging non-
    observant Jews to engage in traditional Jewish rituals, Menachem Mendel
    Schneerson, the last Chabad rebbe, began a campaign in the 1970s to encourage
    Jewish women to light Shabbat candles. As a related move, he encouraged par-
    ents to have all girls over age three light their own Shabbat candles. Schneerson's
    campaign had a dramatic influence on American Jews, though family practices
    still vary.

128 Greene, interview.

129 Greene, interview.

130 Lofton, 5.

CHAPTER 5. REFERENDUM ON THE JEWISH DELI MENU

  1 *Referendum on the Jewish Deli Menu*, video recording of panel at the Jewish
    Community Center of the East Bay, February 9, 2010, http://fora.tv. Tracey Taylor,
    "Organic or Authentic? The Saul's Deli Debate," *New York Times*, Bay Area blog,
    February 4, 2010, http://bayarea.blogs.nytimes.com.

2 *Referendum.*

3 See discussion of popular conceptions of museums as containers of dead objects in Chapter 3.

4 Glatt means "smooth" in Yiddish and refers to a lack of blemish on the internal organs of a slaughtered animal. In the case of a scab or lesion on a cow's lungs, most Ashkenazi Jews have traditionally held that the animal is kosher if the patch can be removed and the lungs are still airtight, while Sephardi Jews and Hasidim have held that any sort of blemish on the lungs would render the animal not kosher. Glatt kosher meat, which is held to the more stringent requirements, was produced in extremely limited quantities until the mid-twentieth century. Interest in glatt meat rose in the 1960s and 1970s, as Hasidim influenced kosher certification in the United States. The Orthodox Union (OU), the world's largest kosher certifying agency, adopted a policy of requiring exclusively glatt meat in the late 1970s. Glatt is now the dominant standard of kosher meat in America. Gil Marks, *Encyclopedia of Jewish Food* (Hoboken, New Jersey: John Wiley & Sons, Inc., 2010), 225–227. Sue Fishkoff, *Kosher Nation: Why More and More of America's Food Answers to a Higher Authority* (New York: Schocken Books, 2010).

5 Mary L. Zamore, "Ethical Eating: The New Jewish Food Movement," in *Chosen Food: Cuisine, Culture, and American Jewish Identity*, eds. Avi Y. Decter and Juliana Ochs Dweck (Baltimore, Maryland: The Jewish Museum of Maryland, 2011), 85–86. Nathanial Popper, "In Iowa Meat Plant, Kosher 'Jungle' Breeds Fear, Injury, Short Pay," *Forward*, May 26, 2006, http://forward.com. For more on Agriprocessors and the Postville raid, see Aaron S. Gross, *The Question of the Animal and Religion: Theoretical Stakes, Practical Implications* (New York: Columbia University Press, 2015). Fishkoff, *Kosher Nation.*

6 Zamore.

7 Gefilte fish is a ball or oval-shaped cake of finely chopped fish, usually whitefish, pike, or carp, mixed with crumbs, eggs, and seasonings, cooked in a broth, and usually served chilled. Kvass is a fermented beverage made from black or rye bread that is popular in Eastern Europe.

8 Jeffrey Yoskowitz, interview by author, June 21, 2013.

9 Both Gefilte Talk and Let's Brisket were organized by culinary curator Naama Shefi. Gefilte Talk was held at the Center for Jewish History (CJH) in New York on September 6, 2012. Let's Brisket was held at the CJH on December 18, 2012. Brisket is a cut of meat from the breast or lower chest of beef or veal. In Ashkenazi Jewish cooking, brisket is often braised as a pot roast. The cut became popular because it was one of the cheaper kosher cuts of meat.

10 Deli Summit: The Renaissance was organized by Saul's Deli and held at the Jewish Community Center of the East Bay in Berkeley, California, on May 19, 2011. At that event, Levitt and Adelman continued the conversation of their Referendum with several of their colleagues in the Jewish deli business. The Future of Jewish Food, organized by Noah and Rae Bernamoff of Mile End Deli in Brooklyn, was held in New York on October 13, 2012.

11 Mitchell Davis, interview by author, August 15, 2013. Davis holds a Ph.D. from New York University in Food Studies, a program he helped to create by serving on its advisory board.

12 "About the Festival," *The Great Big Jewish Food Fest*, www.jewishfoodfest.com.

13 Ted Merwin, *Pastrami on Rye: An Overstuffed History of the Jewish Deli* (New York: New York University Press, 2015), 66, 146

14 Susan Sontag, "Notes on Camp," *The Partisan Review* (December 1964): 515–530. Eve Kosofsky Sedgwick, *Epistemology of the Closet* (Berkeley: University of California Press, 1990).

15 Ligaya Mishan, "Mile End," *New York Times*, February 8, 2011, www.nytimes.com. Pletzl is a flatbread with toppings, similar to focaccia.

16 Merwin, 9.

17 David C. Kraemer, *Jewish Eating and Identity Through the Ages* (New York: Routledge, 2007), 48–49.

18 Jessamyn Neuhaus, *Manly Meals and Mom's Home Cooking: Cookbooks and Gender in Modern America* (Baltimore: Johns Hopkins University Press, 2003), 192–193.

19 Merwin, 122.

20 The term "hipster" has its cultural and etymological roots in the term "hep cats," which referred to Harlem musicians and performers as well as other African American innovators of the 1930s. Norman Mailer's "The White Negro" (1957) reframed hipster discourse to be more relevant to the lifestyles available to white middle-class men. It was particularly associated with Beat Generation writers at mid-century. Beginning in the 1960s, the word "hippie" was applied to predominantly white, countercultural youth. In the 1990s and early 2000s, the term "hipster" was revived, first in reference to indie music culture and then, more broadly, in reference to other forms of demeanor, tastes, and fashion sensibilities, particularly those of young white men. Zeynep Arsel and Craig J. Thompson, "Demythologizing Consumption Practices: How Consumers Protect Their Field-Dependent Identity Investments from Devaluing Marketplace Myths," *Journal of Consumer Research* 37, no. 5 (February 2011): 791–806.

21 Christy Wampole, "How to Live Without Irony," *New York Times*, November 17, 2012, http://opinionator.blogs.nytimes.com.

22 Arsel and Thompson.

23 Wampole.

24 William G. McLoughlin, *Revivals, Awakenings, and Reform: An Essay on Religion and Social Change in America, 1607–1977* (Chicago: University of Chicago Press, 1978), vii, 2.

25 Mitchell Davis, *The Mensch Chef: Or Why Delicious Jewish Food Isn't an Oxymoron* (New York: Clarkson Potter, 2002), ix. The Borscht Belt is a colloquial term for the mostly defunct summer resorts of the Catskill Mountains in upstate New York that were a popular vacation spot for New York City Jews from the 1920s to the 1970s. Many comedians began their careers by performing at Borscht Belt resorts. "Bubbe" is the Yiddish word for grandmother.

26 Josh Ozersky, "The Kugel Conundrum," *Time*, April 28, 2011, http://content.time. com. Lokshen kugel is a traditional Ashkenazi dish of noodle pudding.

27 Neuhaus, 18–22, 177–178.

28 David Sax, *Save the Deli: In Search of Perfect Pastrami, Crusty Rye, and the Heart of Jewish Delicatessen* (Boston: Houghton Mifflin Harcourt, 2009), 33. For the Jewish history of Crisco, see Rachel B. Gross, "A Slippery Slope: Jews, Schmaltz, and Crisco in the Age of Industrial Food," in *Feasting and Fasting: The History and Ethics of Jewish Food*, eds. Aaron S. Gross, Jody Meyers, and Jordan D. Rosenblum (New York: New York University Press, 2020), 189–211.

29 Merwin, 24–25.

30 Merwin, 23. See Glenn Dynner, *Yankel's Tavern: Jews, Liquor, and Life in the Kingdom of Poland* (New York: Oxford University Press, 2013).

31 Merwin. Marks, 156–158.

32 David Sax, interview by author, July 23, 2013.

33 Frank Bruni, "Cooking Up a Big Idea in Little Italy," *New York Times Magazine*, April 27, 2011, www.nytimes.com. "Torrisi Italian Specialties," *New York Magazine*, http://nymag.com.

34 Lynne Rossetto Kasper, "How Momofuku's David Chang Learned to Embrace the Word 'Fusion,'" *The Splendid Table*, www.splendidtable.org.

35 Ozersky.

36 Nick Zukin and Michael C. Zusman, *The Artisan Jewish Deli at Home* (Kansas City: Andrews McMeel Publishing, LLC, 2013), xvi–xvii.

37 Davis, interview. A knish is a turnover consisting of a filling, often mashed potato, covered with dough and baked, grilled, or deep-fried.

38 Adeena Sussman, "Haimish to Haute in New York: All Over Town, Transformation of Jewish Cuisine Takes Hold," *Forward*, March 28, 2012, http://forward.com. Ben Sales, "The Gentrification of the Gefilte," *Jewish Week* (New York), April 10, 2012, www.thejewishweek.com. Devra Ferst, "The Great American Deli Rescue: Bringing Jewish Eateries Back from Oblivion," *Forward*, November 15, 2012, http://forward.com. Haimish is Yiddish for homey or folksy. Julia Moskin, "Everything New Is Old Again: The New Golden Age of Jewish-American Deli Food," *New York Times*, May 27, 2014, www.nytimes.com.

39 Rae Bernamoff, Preface to *The Mile End Cookbook: Redefining Jewish Comfort Food from Hash to Hamantaschen*, Noah Bernamoff and Rae Bernamoff (New York: Clarkson Potter/Publishers, 2012), 10. The Bernamoffs ended their involvement with Mile End in 2018. Serena Dai, "Big Changes Are Happening for Popular Deli Mile End," *Eater NY*, August 23, 2018, https://ny.eater.com.

40 Hasia Diner, *Hungering for America: Italian, Irish, and Jewish Foodways in the Age of Migration* (Cambridge, Massachusetts: Harvard University Press, 2001), xvi.

41 Noah Bernamoff, Introduction to *The Mile End Cookbook*, 14.

42 Giovanni Galli, "Nostalgia, Architecture, Ruins, and Their Preservation," *Change Over Time* 3.1 (Spring 2013): 18.

43 Noah Bernamoff, interview by author, June 27, 2013.

44 Noah Bernamoff at Let's Brisket, Center for Jewish History, New York, December 18, 2012. "Let's Brisket," Past Programs, *Center for Jewish History*, www.cjh.org.

45 Rebecca Meiser, "Challah Food Truck Hits the Road in Columbus," *Tablet*, July 8, 2013, www.tabletmag.com.

46 Meiser.

47 "Holler for Challah!" *Dykes on Mikes* podcast, hosted by Brooke Cartus and Lori Gum, June 28, 2013.

48 Meiser.

49 "Holler for Challah!"

50 Sax, interview. For nostalgic images of Jewish families in marketing packaged foods, see Elliot Weiss, "Packaging Jewishness: Novelty and Tradition in Kosher Food Packaging," *Design Issues* 20, no. 1 (2004): 48–61.

51 Sax, interview.

52 Noah Arenstein, interview by author, June 18, 2013.

53 Chris E. Crowley, "Anatomy of a Smorgasburg Pop Up: Introducing Scharf & Zoyer," *Serious Eats*, April 8, 2013, http://newyork.seriouseats.com.

54 Scharf & Zoyer Facebook page, accessed June 19, 2014, www.facebook.com.

55 Molly Yeh, "New York's Newest Jewish Food Artisan—Scharf & Zoyer," *Forward*, April 9, 2013, http://blogs.forward.com.

56 Arenstein.

57 The spelling of Hungerford's food truck has appeared as both "Shhmaltz" and "Schmaltz."

58 Sontag.

59 Melanie Haupt, "Schmaltz," *Austin Chronicle*, March 22, 2013, www.austin-chronicle.com.

60 Amy Kritzer, "Schmaltz Food Truck Offers Vegetarian Twist on Classic Deli Fare," *Jewish Outlook* (Austin), March 1, 2013, www.thejewishoutlook.com.

61 Beth Lebwohl, "New Trailer Schmaltz Puts a Veggie Spin on Classic Jewish Deli Fare," *CultureMap: Austin*, June 2, 2012, http://austin.culturemap.com. Kvell is a Yiddish term for feeling pride, particularly a demonstratively enthusiastic pride in one's progeny.

62 Ken Gordon, email to author, July 18, 2013.

63 Catherine Cole, "Interview: Chef Ken Gordon," *Portland Food and Drink*, September 26, 2008, http://portlandfoodanddrink.com.

64 Zach Kutsher, interview by author, July 9, 2013. Veria Lifestyle Inc. purchased Kutsher's Hotel and Resort in the Town of Thompson, New York, in 2013 with the intention of turning the location into a health and wellness resort. Demolition of the resort began in the summer of 2014. Nathan Brown, "Kutsher's Transformation Will Begin in a Week or Two," *Times Herald-Record* (Middletown, New York), May 15, 2014, www.recordonline.com.

65 Gordon, email.

66 Moskin.

67 "The Gefilteria Are Picklers-in-Residence on Myrtle Avenue," *Myrtle Avenue Brooklyn*, February 18, 2014, https://myrtleavenue.org.

68 Rose Surnow, "Gefilte Fish, Bringing Sexy Back," *Haaretz*, August 1, 2012, www.haaretz.com.

69 Shmuel Ben Eliezer, comment on A. Sussman.

70 Lance J. Sussman, "The Myth of the Trefa Banquet: American Culinary Culture and the Radicalization of Food Policy in American Reform Judaism," *American Jewish Archives Journal* 57, no. 1–2 (2005): 35.

71 Jenna Weissman Joselit, *The Wonders of America: Reinventing Jewish Culture, 1880–1950* (New York: Henry Holt and Company, 1994), 172.

72 Gaye Tuchman and Harry Gene Levine, "New York Jews and Chinese Food: The Social Construction of an Ethnic Pattern," *Journal of Contemporary Ethnography* 22 (April 1993): 382–406.

73 Joselit, 173.

74 Jennifer Berg, "From Pushcart Peddlers to Gourmet Take-Out: New York City's Iconic Foods of Jewish Origin, 1920 to 2005" (Ph.D. diss., New York University, 2006), 73.

75 Marks, 111.

76 Sarah Davidson, "Kenny & Zuke's Gave Portland What It Wanted," *Jewish Review*, September 23, 2009, www.jewishreview.org.

77 Gordon, email.

78 Florence Fabricant, "Gefilteria: Upscale Fish Without the Fuss," *New York Times*, Diner's Journal, March 29, 2012, http://dinersjournal.blogs.nytimes.com.

79 Julia Hungerford, quoted in Lebwohl.

80 N. Bernamoff, interview.

81 Gordon, email.

82 Kutsher.

83 Alan Wilzig, June 14, 2011, comment on "Kutsher's Tribeca: The Menu," *Tribeca Citizen*, May 11, 2011, http://tribecacitizen.com. Glatt kosher meat is held to stringent kosher standards. Wilzig employs the term as a shorthand reference to people who only eat glatt kosher meat.

84 "Matzo Balls Meet Bacon at Top Chef's Restaurant," *NPR*, March 12, 2011, www.npr.org.

85 N. Bernamoff, interview.

86 Ligaya Mishan, "Traif," *New York Times*, August 10, 2010. Hasidic Judaism (practiced by Hasidim, plural of Hasid) is a branch of Orthodox Judaism that emphasizes mysticism and spiritual fervor. Each of the many Hasidic dynasties follows its own principles and spiritual leaders.

87 See, for example, Tara Bahrampour, "A 'Plague of Artists' Is a Battle Cry for Brooklyn Hasidim," *New York Times*, February 17, 2004, and Michael Idov, "Clash of the Bearded Ones: Hipsters, Hasids, and the Williamsburg Street," *New York Magazine*, April 11, 2010, http://nymag.com. *Hasid or Hipster*, http://hasido-

rhipster.tumblr.com. For Hasidim as representations of Jewishness, see Shaina Hammerman, *Silver Screen, Hasidic Jews: The Story of an Image* (Bloomington, Indiana: Indiana University Press, 2018).

88 *Traif*, http://traifny.com.

89 Mishan.

90 See Jonathan Brumberg-Kraus, *Gastronomic Judaism as Culinary Midrash* (Lanham, Maryland: Lexington Books, 2019).

91 Sedgwick, 156.

92 *Bad Jew BBQ*, http://badjewbbq.com.

93 S. Brent Plate, *Blasphemy: The Art that Offends* (London: Black Dog, 2006).

94 Caryn Aviv and David Shneer, *New Jews: The End of the Jewish Diaspora* (New York: New York University Press, 2005), 137.

95 Aviv and Shneer, 7.

96 Sax, 5.

97 Berg, 198.

98 Recording of Gefilte Talk panel, "September 6, 2012: Gefilte Talk," Past Programs, *Center for Jewish History*, www.cjh.org.

99 Boichik Bagels, https://boichikbagels.com.

100 Alix Wall, "Boichik Bagels 'Taste Like Home'—and Maybe Like H&H," *J. The Jewish News of Northern California*, December 1, 2017, www.jweekly.com.

101 Wendy S., review on Yelp.com, December 7, 2011.

102 Gordon, email. Ellipses in original.

103 "About," *Saul's Restaurant and Delicatessen*, http://saulsdeli.com.

104 "About," *Saul's*. Andy Altman-Ohr, "Saul's Owners Seeking Buyer to Keep Jewish Deli Tradition Alive in Berkeley," *J. The Jewish News of Northern California*, March 11, 2016, www.jweekly.com.

105 *Referendum*.

106 Sue Fishkoff, "A New Generation of Jewish Delis Embraces Sustainability," *Jewish Telegraphic Agency*, May 20, 2011, www.jta.org.

107 Karen Adelman, interview by author, August 1, 2013. Fox's U-Bet chocolate syrup is considered by many to be an essential ingredient in a classic egg cream. Saul's Deli makes its own chocolate syrup for use in egg creams within the restaurant, but customers may buy Fox's syrup to take home. Adelman, interview.

108 Adelman, interview.

109 N. Bernamoff, Introduction, 13.

110 N. Bernamoff, interview.

111 Augie's Montreal Deli, which opened in Berkeley in 2018, also presents Montreal-style smoked meat as a Jewish food. Alix Wall, "Smoke Meat, a Jewish Montreal Culinary Icon, Lands in Berkeley," *J. The Jewish News of Northern California*, February 15, 2018, www.jweekly.com.

112 A. Pontius, "Potatobird," *Tables for One*, July 10, 2013, www.tablesforone.com.

113 Berg, 55.

114 Sally Schneider, "Table for One's Fab Imaginary Restaurant Reviews," *The Improvised Life*, April 5, 2013, www.improvisedlife.com.

115 Florence Fabricant, "Brews and Bites Off the Usual Track," *New York Times*, May 29, 2012, www.nytimes.com. Moskin.

116 Jennifer Strom, "Knishery NYC: A Modern Twist on an Ancient Street Food," *The Lo Down*, October 13, 2011, www.thelodownny.com.

117 Strom.

CONCLUSION

1 For the sake of clarity, I refer to the couple as the Byrneheims but refer to them individually by the names they had before marriage.

2 Courtney Byrne-Mitchell, interview by author, August 17, 2018.

3 Matthew Frye Jacobson, *Roots Too: White Ethnic Revival in Post-Civil Rights America* (Cambridge, Massachusetts: Harvard University Press, 2006).

4 Alisa Solomon, *Wonder of Wonders: A Cultural History of Fiddler on the Roof* (New York: Picador, 2013). Jeffrey Shandler, *Adventures in Yiddishland: Postvernacular Language and Culture* (Berkeley: University of California Press, 2008). Magdalena Waligórska, *Klezmer's Afterlife: An Ethnography of the Jewish Music Revival in Poland and Germany* (New York: Oxford University Press, 2013). Joshua B. Friedman, "Yiddish Returns: Language, Intergenerational Gifts, and Jewish Devotion" (Ph.D. diss., University of Michigan, 2015).

5 Sarah Imhoff and Hillary Kaell, "Lineage Matters: DNA, Race, and Gene Talk in Judaism and Messianic Judaism," *Religion and American Culture* 27, no. 1 (Winter 2017): 95–127.

6 Cynthia M. Baker, *Jew* (New Brunswick, New Jersey: Rutgers University Press, 2017).

7 Statistics on "people of Jewish background" and "people with a Jewish affinity" were collected by Pew Research Center's *Portrait of Jewish Americans*, but these categories were not categorized as Jewish in the report precisely because they identify with another religion in addition to or instead of Judaism. Pew Research Center. Pew Research Center, *A Portrait of Jewish Americans: Findings from a Pew Research Center Survey of U.S. Jews*, October 1, 2013.

8 Jewish Museum of Florida–FIU, https://jmof.fiu.edu.

9 Judy Bolton-Fasman, "Vilna Shul to Break Ground on Renovations in October," *JewishBoston*, July 9, 2018, www.jewishboston.com.

10 For representation of American Jewish history in American civic life, see Jacobson and Beth Wenger, *History Lessons: The Creation of American Jewish Heritage* (Princeton: Princeton University Press, 2010).

11 Pac Pobric, "Kiki Smith: *Below the Horizon*," *Brooklyn Rail*, June 5, 2018, https://brooklynrail.org. Talya Zax, "At Historic Synagogue, A Hopeful Meditation On Loss Takes Flight," *Forward*, June 14, 2019, https://forward.com. Allison Meier, "Kiki Smith Takes Over the Eldridge Street Synagogue with 50 Artworks," *Hyperallergic*, June 5, 2018, https://hyperallergic.com.

12 "PJ Library Impact Evaluation," June 2017, https://pjlibrary.org.

13 Lesléa Newman, *Gittel's Journey: An Ellis Island Story* (New York: Abrams Books for Young Readers, 2018). JBC Staff, "2019 National Jewish Book Award Winners," *Jewish Book Council*, January 15, 2020, www.jewishbookcouncil.org.

14 Joanne Oppenheim, *The Knish War on Rivington Street* (Chicago: Albert Whitman & Company, 2017).

15 Tony Cantu, "Houndstooth Coffee Gets Into the Spirit of the Season in Austin," *Patch*, October 15, 2018, https://patch.com.

16 Zach Kutsher, interview by author, July 9, 2013.

17 Joel Rose, "'The Gefilte Manifesto': A Loved, And Loathed, Jewish Staple Gets Updated," *NPR*, September 13, 2016, www.npr.org.

18 Matthew Singer, "Portland Pastrami Staple Kenny & Zuke's Is Filing For Bankruptcy," *Williamette Week*, September 18, 2019, www.wweek.com. Brooke Jackson-Glidden, "Quintessential Jewish Deli Kenny & Zuke's Will Close Its Bagel Shop This Month," *Eater Portland, OR*, October 10, 2019, https://pdx.eater.com.

19 Serena Dai, "Big Changes Are Happening for Popular Deli Mile End," *Eater NY*, August 23, 2018, https://ny.eater.com. Serena Dai, "Smoked Meats Shop Mile End Shutters Noho Outpost," *Eater NY*, October 15, 2018, https://ny.eater.com.

20 Wise Sons, http://wisesonsdeli.com.

21 Alix Wall, "At 'Oy Bay BBQ,' Jewish Chefs Who Say Food Is More Than a Business," *J. The Jewish News of Northern California*, January 24, 2018, www.jweekly.com.

22 On sexism in the restaurant industry, see, for instance, Jen Agg, "A Harvey Weinstein Moment for the Restaurant Industry?" *New Yorker*, October 26, 2017, www.newyorker.com. Tracie McMillan, "When the Kitchen Isn't Safe for Women," *New York Times*, October 30, 2017, www.nytimes.com.

23 Kathryn Lofton, *Consuming Religion* (Chicago: University of Chicago Press, 2018), 285.

24 Jonathan Boyarin, *Jewish Families* (New Brunswick, New Jersey: Rutgers University Press, 2013), 3.

25 Kafrissen lists "linguistic continuity, musical continuity, artistic continuity, folkways continuity, foodways continuity, nusakh continuity, tikhl continuity, kayver oves continuity, continuity continuity . . ." (@RokhlK, Twitter, July 20, 2018), https://twitter.com/RokhlK/status/1020330688510332928. Nusakh is a Jewish liturgical style or melody. A tikhl is a headscarf worn by many married Orthodox Jewish women. Kayver oves is the practice of visiting the graves of ancestors.

INDEX

Rachel B. Gross is John and Marcia Goldman Chair in American Jewish Studies in the Department of Jewish Studies at San Francisco State University. She is a religious studies scholar whose work focuses on twentieth- and twenty-first-century American Jews.

Lightning Source UK Ltd.
Milton Keynes UK
UKHW012204220922
409287UK00002B/189